LIBRARY OF NEW TESTAMENT STUDIES

449

formerly the Journal for the Study of the New Testament Supplement series

Editor

Mark Goodacre

DECISIVE MEALS

Table Politics in Biblical Literature

Edited by
Nathan MacDonald,
Luzia Sutter Rehmann and
Kathy Ehrensperger

t&t clark

Published by T&T Clark International
A Continuum imprint
The Tower Building, 11 York Road, London SE1 7NX
80 Maiden Lane, Suite 704, New York, NY 10038

www.continuumbooks.com

British Library Cataloguing-in-Publication Data
A catalogue record for this book is available from the British Library

ISBN: HB: 978-0-567-52601-4

Typeset by Free Range Book Design & Production Limited
Printed and bound in Great Britain

CONTENTS

List of Contributors

Soham Al-Suadi, PhD University of Basel, 2010, is Assistant at *Bergische Universität Wuppertal*, teaching New Testament and Ancient Church History. Her dissertation has been published as *Essen als Christusgläubige* (Tubingen, Basel: Francke).

Peter Altmann completed his doctorate in biblical studies, Old Testament, at Princeton Theological Seminary in 2010 with a dissertation on Deuteronomy's festive meals. He is currently working as a postdoctoral researcher and assistant in Old Testament at the University of Zurich.

Kathy Ehrensperger is Reader in New Testament Studies at the University of Wales, Trinity Saint David, UK. Among her publications are *That We May Be Mutually Encouraged: Feminism and the New Perspective in Pauline Studies*, and *Paul and the Dynamics of Power: Communication and Interaction in the Early Christ-Movement*. She is the chair of the SBL group Romans Through History and Cultures, and a member of the steering committee of the SNTS Seminar 'Reading Paul in Context: Theological and Social-Scientific Approaches'.

Esther Kobel is Assistant at the Chair of New Testament of the Theological Faculty of the University of Basel. Her publications include *Dining with John. Communal Meals and Identity Formation in the Fourth Gospel and its Historical and Cultural Context* (Leiden: Brill, 2011).

Nathan MacDonald is Leader of the Sofja-Kovalevskaja Research Team at the Georg-August-Universität Göttingen and Reader in Old Testament, University of St Andrews. Educated in Cambridge and Durham, he has published three books and numerous articles on the Pentateuch, theological interpretation and eating and drinking in the Old Testament.

Susanne Plietzsch is Professor for Jewish Studies at the Center for Jewish Cultural History at the University of Salzburg. Her fields of research are Rabbinic literature, Jewish and Christian Bible hermeneutics, and gender topics in this realm. Her publications include *Kontexte der Freiheit: Konzepte der Befreiung bei Paulus und im rabbinischen Judentum.*

Ursula Rapp is working at the chair of Old Testament Exegesis at the University of Lucerne (Switzerland) and Private Dozent at the University of Bamberg (Germany). A forthcoming publication is *Weisheitsbeziehung als Geschlechterbeziehung. Texte über Frauen und Ehe im Buch Jesus Sirach.*

Angela Standhartinger is Professor for New Testament at the Philipps University at Marburg, where she teaches New Testament Studies. She received her PhD from the University of Frankfurt. She has written on the image of women in the ancient Jewish novel, *Joseph and Aseneth*, and Jewish women in the Second Temple period, and is a member of the SBL seminar on Meals in the Greco-Roman World.

Luzia Sutter Rehmann is Professor of New Testament at the Theological Faculty of the University of Basel. From 2008 to 2011 she was research director of the Swiss National Science Foundation project 'Meal communities in the period of Second Temple Judaism until Early Christianity: Places forming religious practice and identity'. She is the author of several books and translated the Gospel of Luke for the gender sensitive Bible translation, Gütersloh 2006, revised 2011.

Hal Taussig is Visiting Professor of New Testament at Union Theological Seminary in New York and Professor of Early Christianity at the Reconstructionist Rabbinical College in Wyncote, PA, USA. He is author or co-author of ten books on early Christianity, including the recent *In the Beginning Was the Meal: Social Experimentation and Early Christian identity.*

INTRODUCTION

What happens when biblical studies scholars get together and present their research on shared meals? Does it make sense at all to bring together texts of diverse epochs and cultures, that is Old and New Testament texts, and into conversation with one another? Has not everything been said that there is to say about Hellenistic banquets and the common patterns of the symposia so that in the end discussions focus on this or that detail in utterly disparate texts?

The essays presented in this volume were originally presented at the Biblical Studies Symposium 'Decisive Meals – Was sich beim Essen entscheidet' held at the conference centre of the University of Basel, the Landgut Castelen, Augst, BL in Switzerland on the 18–19 February 2011. The symposium focused on the broad perspective on meal traditions, albeit not at the expense of detailed analysis. As the concluding event of a larger research project, 'Tischgemeinschaften. Orte religiöser Praxis und Identität im Judentum zur Zeit des Zweiten Tempels und im frühen Christentum', funded by the Swiss National Funding Council, it brought together an international group of scholars from different disciplines related to, but not confined to, biblical studies to discuss meal traditions in biblical literature. The symposium presented a forum for focusing on decisive aspects of meal narratives and traditions in a wide range of biblical literature and their interpretation from different perspectives. The diverse ways in which biblical texts present meal scenes and traditions as events of stilling hunger, social interaction, boundary negotiation and political decision were explored and discussed, identifying loci of decision at a range of levels and of multi-layered significance.

This collection of essays thus seeks to come to a deeper understanding of common or shared meals in biblical texts that have been assessed in diverse ways in biblical scholarship. Hermeneutical and theoretical approaches vary in biblical studies in relation to the sources (Old Testament, New Testament, Rabbinical writings, extra-biblical writings), as do the underlying perceptions of the cultural sciences concerning the diverse cultural interactions in the Ancient Near East and the Mediterranean (Graeco-Roman meals, the refusal of table hospitality shared by Jews and non-Jews, the order of gender at symposia, distancing oneself or embracing one's environment). Hence these contributions are exploring what their communities at the time might have considered to be 'decisive' in their common meals.

In biblical texts, meals are often occasions of decisive actions, a pivotal point in the narrative, the centre of communities, climaxes or low points, places where fate is determined. Who 'we' are, 'to whom' we belong, with whom we make 'common cause' is decided at the table. Here, identity not only manifests itself, but can also be transformed as the meal goes on. How we eat, with whom we eat, what becomes significant during the meal, can turn out to be decisive for those gathered at the table. In the end, eating or non-eating decides about life and death.

The contributions gathered in this volume discuss where, how and when taking part in a meal becomes important. How is this expressed concretely in the texts? What does eating together do to the hungry, to those who eat together, to the gathered company? By addressing concrete texts, a diversity of different approaches is applied and the texts themselves are presented in such a way that what is decided at the table is made visible.

In '"The Eyes of All Look to You": The Generosity of the Divine King', Nathan MacDonald examines the way that the traditional Israelite image of YHWH as king was transformed through encounter with Mesopotamian ideologies of royal feasting. In the petty states of the Levant, affirmations of YHWH's kingship meant declaring his rule over the gods for the sake of his people. With the experience of empire, the imagery of kingship changed and YHWH is envisaged as a monarch with a universal kingdom. This kingdom enjoys the generous beneficence of YHWH who supplies for his subjects on a vast scale. The psalmists extend Mesopotamian hyperbole about royal generosity and declare it to be reality: YHWH does provide for all his creatures, animals and humans.

In Peter Altmann's contribution, 'Everyday Meals for Extraordinary People: Eating and Assimilation in the Book of Ruth', issues of identity and belonging are the focus of the analysis. They are found near the centre of the book of Ruth as seen in the constant refrain of 'Ruth the Moabite'. Gifts of food, shared meals and festive events play central roles in the plot's development of these identity questions with regard to the inclusion of the outsider Ruth and the reintegration of her mother-in-law Naomi in Ruth 2 and 3. Ruth 2 deals with the dynamics of food production and consumption, the means through which Boaz signals Ruth's inclusion within the community's boundaries: providing a common source for food (2.9) and hosting a common (non-ritual) meal (2.14). Furthermore, Ruth in turn shares this meal with Naomi as a further extension of common identity confirmation (2.18). Altmann's interpretation of these verses is enriched by the appearance of similar events in the story of Rebecca (Genesis 24) and the counter-example of Moabites in Deuteronomy 23. Feasting, sexuality and blessing – the elements found in the narrative of idol worship and God's judgement in Numbers 25 – reappear but are reversed in Ruth 3. Thus the meal dynamics in Ruth are not only important in their own right, but also make for a dynamic conversation within the biblical canon.

The essay of Susanne Plietzsch, 'Eating and Living: The Banquets in the Esther Narratives', deals with the utterly basic connection between 'eating' and 'living' that characterizes the Esther narrative and its reception among Jews. The numerous banquets that structure this narrative depict diverse aspects of this linkage right up to the anti-banquet which culminates in an execution or to the fasting which paradoxically is supposed to serve life. The story's humour occasionally threatens to turn into its opposite so that the actual perspective of the narrative, namely that after all everything turned out well in the end, is not always to be taken for granted. This vacillation between humour and seriousness is characteristic especially for the Feast of Purim.

Ursula Rapp reflects on the table politics of Jesus ben Sirach ('You Are How You Eat: How Eating and Drinking Behaviour Identifies the Wise According to Jesus Ben Sirach'). The text about behaviour at a symposium in Ben Sira 31.12–32.1,13 is mainly understood as a guideline for proper manners at the table of a rich man. Her contribution starts with the view of symposia as reflections and constructions of social identity of a group or an ancient club. '*Writing* about "eating" means to render conventions explicit; it can also be an indication that what had been taken for granted about eating meals has been upset.' Ben Sirach's word selection and the structure of the text show that what he has in mind is the expression of wise identity through the manner of eating, the selection of food and the relation to other participants at the meal. Ben Sira's words do not teach young men how to behave politely but they teach wise behaviour und wise relation to opulent food. Looked at in this way lets the texts fit well into their context, especially into 29.24-28; 30.16-25; 31.1-11. The texts are more about group identity, which is constructed through a group meal, than about individual behaviour.

Angela Standhartinger ('"And All Ate and Were Filled" (Mark 6.42 par.): The Feeding Narratives in the Context of Hellenistic-Roman Banquet Cultures') points out that the gospel's feeding narratives would have been heard in antiquity in relation to other narratives about public banquets. For most hearers and readers of the gospels, feeding large groups and those representing them was part of their experience, at least by hearsay. Hence this paper analyzes what is unique in the feeding narratives of the gospels, what is emphasized and what is missing in comparison to other feedings. Ancient authors rarely tell of four to five thousand people reclining at table in the aristocratic position without any social differentiation. The feeding narratives present a milieu that was excluded from most other feedings and corn-distributions elsewhere. When the wine, which is elsewhere regularly part of the public banquet, is missing, it becomes clear that those people who told this story are more used to food distributions than taking part in a symposium. Also missing is the emphasis on the donor's generosity and how adequately the distribution was at the appropriate location in honour of a worthy cause. Instead, what is emphasized is the necessity to feed the hungry who were in danger of starving. The narratives take up the political-religious praxis and ideals of public and civic banquets and mass-feedings. From here they developed the underlying expectation and hope that the common meal of all turns out to become really the (u)topia where indeed all will be truly 'filled'.

Esther Kobel in her multi-perspective reading, 'The Various Tastes of Johannine Bread and Blood', finds that John 6 plays a decisive role with regard to the accounts of communal meals. The passage 6.51-58 in particular with Jesus' exhortation to his audience to chew his flesh and drink his blood is among the most disputed in the entire gospel. It invites the audience to hear allusions of various kinds. Taking seriously the hybrid environment from which the gospel evolved, this article exposes John 6.51-58 against a number of backgrounds and thereby explores a range of themes to which the passage may possibly allude. First, it identifies allusions to Eucharistic traditions, then it singles out echoes of motifs from Dionysian traditions and finally it demonstrates that striking correspondences emerge from sources about enclaves bonding around the consumption of human flesh and blood. The multi-faceted character of the Fourth Gospel with regard to its manifold intertextual relationships, demonstrated with reference to John 6.51-58, suggests that the gospel has the ability to address people from very diverse backgrounds. In other words, the Fourth Gospel has the capacity to bring out a number of flavours, thereby attracting and satisfying a wide range of people with possibly very different tastes.

Luzia Sutter Rehmann places her contribution of the account of Peter in Joppa and Caesarea ('What Happened in Caesarea? *Symphagein* as Bonding Experience (Acts 10–11.18)') in the context of scarcity. Eating together is a necessity of life and gives foundation to a community that without common meals would break apart. In Acts 10–12 the small community of Joppa unites itself with the household of the Roman centurion and Peter interprets this bonding experience as an incident of God's good creation shining forth. But the decisive aspect of the common meal in Caesarea is the context of famine; its shadow rests over the whole narrative. Therefore Sutter Rehmann calls attention to various social historical material, which informs readers about scarcity and how communities tried to deal with it. A hermeneutics of hunger also has to be developed so that the shadow of hunger may become perceptible. Well-satiated people are in danger of reading from a perspective of an abundance of food, overlooking the signals the text sends out to the hungry. Text markers lead the readers of Acts 10–11.16 to Ezek. 4.14-17 and the announcement of an extreme food shortage – which horrifies Ezekiel as much as it does Peter. The analysis of the vision in Joppa also reveals connections to Genesis 1.24, 30 and the divine provision of food.

Kathy Ehrensperger's 'To Eat or Not To Eat: Is this the Question? Table Disputes in Corinth' analyses why table disputes in Corinth may have arisen in the first place. The disputes are seen as part of inner-Jewish negotiations of boundaries between social interaction and actual idolatry in the context of the Diaspora where the demarcations were often not absolutely clear. Ehrensperger argues that Paul develops two lines of argument. One focuses on the concern for a brother/sister who might accidentally commit idolatry by following the example of the 'knowledgeable' and participate in a public temple meal. The behaviour of the knowledgeable which potentially could hurt a brother/sister is seen as constituting a decisive threat to the holiness of the community, which is one of Paul's key concerns in this passage. In addition, Paul maintains that the decisive aspect of the meals discussed in these Corinthian passages is not the food eaten but the fellowship at the table. The food is only relevant in relation to the table fellowship which is established through the context in which it is eaten. The identity of the *koinonia* at the table is decisively defined by the host, the exclusivist claim of worshipping only the one God of Israel is interpreted as being established at the table of the Lord Jesus Christ. This rules out any other *koinonia* at any table which is related to worshipping (even if it is only the worshipping of demons). To be deprived of participation at 'free' temple meals could have caused real problems for Christ-followers living at or below subsistence level. This context renders the Lord's Table as a replacement for the tables of other deities (although not the altar in Jerusalem), and as a table where an actual meal is shared of decisive significance in the early Christ-movement.

Soham Al-Suadi ('The Power of an Invitation: Early Christian Meals in their Cultural Context') finds common agreement among scholars that communal meal gatherings are contexts for highly developed social skills. They allow a person's religious, social or cultural transformation. The sociological background for the communal performance is largely described as Hellenistic. This paper elaborates the necessity to contextualize the Hellenistic influences on the meal practice and argues for a differentiated approach regarding cultural interdependencies. It exemplifies this need with the discussion of an underestimated part of the meal – the meal invitation. Invitations are examined in relevant sources, including the New Testament, to explore the importance of the invitation for the whole meal practice. To verify the contextual differences regarding the incorporation of Hellenistic meal features, invitations of the cult of Sarapis are compared to the Pauline argumentation. This paper argues for similar Hellenistic religious identification that emerged differently.

Hal Taussig reads Revelation from the perspective of ritual theory in 'Meals as Acts of Resistance and Experimentation: The Case of the Revelation to John'. This reading of the Revelation to John places itself in the meals of early Christ movements in western Asia Minor as a way of thinking about those movements' elaboration of social identities and their enacting a range of resistance modalities to Roman imperial rule. Based within both the new typology of the Graeco-Roman meal established by Matthias Klinghardt and Dennis Smith and ritual analysis of that same meal typology, the reading destabilizes essentialist meanings of the text and advances a performative understanding of the Revelation to John, the meals of early Christ movements, and larger emergent identities within the first 150 years of these movements. The performance of identity in this case is a subtle combination of the expression of anger within the safety of the meal setting, the healing and deflection of drawing humorous pictures of Rome's downfall, the development of irony as a way of safeguarding hope and realism, and group appropriation of sarcasm. Through performance of the text, social experimentation at the meal generates a complex, resistant and somewhat free identity, which needs further performance of the same and other texts in order to continue the complex construction of Christian identity under pressure.

It emerges from the diversity of approaches and perspectives represented in these essays that a number of issues highlighted remain controversial and a matter for further debate, whereas on the other hand there is significant convergence on a number of issues despite the 'broad perspective' in terms of time, space and literary genre.

The central focus of the papers is 'decisive meals'. But *which* meals, *for whom*, and *in what ways* are they decisive? The contributions presented here demonstrate that the biblical texts are literary products of the highest complexity, and so are the meal dynamics described in these texts. A number of the essays show that identity itself is determined at the table, and thus even the questions of which, for whom and in what ways are transformed in the process of eating. And so it is the exegetes who decide what they learn from the 'table' and to what they relate their insights, for the complexity of the 'table' seems boundless.

Over the last 30 years, biblical studies have been characterized by considerable methodological ferment, and the essays collected here are no exception. Interdisciplinary stimulus for the examination of food issues within biblical texts has come particularly from anthropological and social historical studies, and this influence is reflected in many of the contributions. Nevertheless, various other methodological tools are utilized, including narrative analysis (Altmann, Plietzsch), intertextuality (Kobel), and liberation hermeneutics (Sutter Rehmann). In his contribution, Taussig seeks to introduce ritual theory as an important perspective for examining identity formation during meals. What methodological approaches will prove particularly serviceable for which text, and how to prioritize their application, remain matters of disagreement.

The examination of meals within New Testament studies has been stimulated by the thesis that Hellenistic meals provided an important model for understanding Jewish texts from the Hellenistic period, including the New Testament. This was true whether these meals were described as Jewish or non-Jewish. Since this thesis is now widely accepted, it can be asked whether or not meal descriptions from Jewish writers are reducible to the Hellenistic model. At this point the symposium showed considerable divergence, particularly as to the extent to which Old Testament sources are also to be drawn upon for understanding New Testament meal texts. The essays by MacDonald and Altmann show not only that there was a food consciousness in Judaism prior to the impact of Hellenism, but that this was part of a wider Near Eastern consciousness. A question for future reflection is whether the Hellenistic meal model is an important instance of a wider pattern of meals across the wider cultural area of the Mediterranean and Near East, or whether we can speak of different meal cultures in various forms of interaction.

Some of the contributors wanted to press that not only eating but also not-eating should be considered as a decisive context for an examination. Eating is decisive for life and death; this is true especially for hungry people. Consequently, the dimension of common meals in times of scarcity requires more attention or, at least, should also be looked at from the perspective of the poor. The question is how to develop a hermeneutics of hunger. A strong case for the more conscious incorporation of hunger, the shadow side of eating, and its potential contribution is made by Sutter Rehmann.

A number of shared ideas and overlapping themes became apparent in the various contributions.

For biblical texts it is foundational that YHWH is the host of common meals. As divine king, YHWH provides food for all his creatures – animals and humans. This becomes apparent in Nathan MacDonald's comparison of the Psalms; but also in Luzia Sutter Rehmann's reading of Peter's vision in Joppa (Acts 10.11-12; 11.5-6). YHWH appears as the provider of food for all living creatures, particularly if Genesis 1.24-30 should inform our understanding of Peter's experience at Joppa as Luzia Sutter Rehmann proposes. That such conversation between New and Old Testament texts is necessary is apparent as well in discussions on idolatry in 1 Corinthians concerning participation at pagan tables, for it is decisive also in Corinth whether YHWH is the host of a table fellowship or not. Kathy Ehrensperger views the disputes in Corinth as part of inner-Jewish negotiations of boundaries between social interaction and actual idolatry in the context of the Diaspora where the demarcations were often not absolutely clear.

In this sense, decisive boundaries that would have been drawn through a common meal were less of an issue in the essays of this volume than might have been anticipated. Instead, the transformative power of meals became increasingly evident – whether in the experimental praxis of Revelation or in the manner of inviting people to a meal. In relation to the meals in the Book of Revelation, Hal Taussig shows how, through the performance of the text, social experimentation at the meal generates a complex, resistant and somewhat free identity. Experimentation was permitted at the table, allowing for the emergence of a free space where a potential counter-publicity could try itself out. This may also be seen as a way for the Christian communities of Asia Minor to keep their boundaries open, to express anger, mock or treat someone or something ironically, play theatre – all in order to discover a new common disposition. Through this experimental character, the meal performance becomes a transformative power that takes hold of everyone at the table and lets them participate in a new reality. But even just the invitation to a common meal can also set much in motion (Soham Al-Suadi).

In Peter Altmann's reading of the Book of Ruth, the transformative power of meals is shown in the way a foreign woman is integrated into the community. He presents that book as a narrative that puts questions of identity-formation at the centre in its concentration on grain and meals. These meals structure the book and show how eating can affect integration and, as the Book of Ruth portrays them, open the community boundaries to foreigners.

Two other late writings speak of the transformative power of meals. In the fortress of Susa, meals are places of royal table politics. The boundaries drawn there are between the royal court and the populace which is affected by the court conspiracies but is not permitted to join in the meals and have a say. But the intrigue against the Jews renders these boundaries porous: on account of Queen Esther, the needs of the Jews reach the court. The transformative power of fasting confronts the royal binges and the king's table politics.

Jesus Ben Sirach tries to counteract the excessiveness, greed and inhumanity that we have seen at the court of Susa with his proposal of a wise table-community. 'The decisive issue is not whether one behaves "well" but whether one does or does not belong to this group of wise people' (Ursula Rapp). Sirach's writing sketches out an egalitarian utopia where Wisdom lays the table and where everyone participating in the meal can belong to the community of the wise.

In connection with the gospels' feeding narratives, Angela Standhartinger points out their embeddedness in the widely-known mass feedings by kings and the rich in antiquity. And yet, the underlying characteristic in the gospels' stories is also a utopia, for everyone's hunger is to be stilled; in comparison to other contemporary material, this feature is unique to the feeding narratives of the gospels.

The mass feedings reveal the table politics of kings and the wealthy elites in a context of scarcity. But it is precisely in that very context that the common meals are not to be an utopia – a non-place – any more but are to have their place in the gospel communities who provide bread for the poor and hungry.

The context of hunger pervades the Book of Ruth, and the feeding narratives of the gospels; in Acts 10–11, however, hunger escalates into a threatening famine. While most exegetes are concerned with the categorization of the Christian meal-practice set free from the law and the concepts of 'clean' and 'unclean', Sutter Rehmann reads the narrative of Peter in Caesarea in light of an impending famine. The inclusion of the context of hunger unveils the community's plan of actions in the face of famine. Boundaries open up instead of being drawn. Seeing how this happens is facilitated by the inclusion of Old Testament writings which present God as provider of all creatures, including Roman soldiers and hungry Jews.

What Esther Kobel emphasizes in relation to John 6 also applies to all common meal narratives, namely that allusions of various kinds give form to the descriptions of meals: eating does not take place in some 'neutral environment' but in the maelstrom of everyday life where boundaries are porous, in the context of multiple influences and discussions – be they Old Testament texts and traditions, accounts known at the time of mass feedings in antiquity or, as the author points out in relation to John 6, Dionysian traditions, as the form-giving force. The hybrid environment permeates the accounts of John 6. The focal issues of the day cast their shadow on other eating narratives, as Kathy Ehrensperger shows in connection with the eating praxis in 1 Corinthians. There is a Eucharistic tradition for various tastes in John and in Corinth: the Corinthian context renders the Lord's Table a replacement for the tables of other deities (although not the altar in Jerusalem), and a table where an actual meal is shared of decisive significance in the early Christ-movement.

It emerges from the contributions in this volume that meals were of decisive significance in the communities represented in these biblical texts spanning a wide period of time and space. However, rather than being loci of clear boundaries, of inclusion and exclusion (especially between Jews and Christ-followers), meals are seen as loci of identity formation and transformation, the stilling of hunger and the overcoming of injustice. The table politics in biblical literature (at least in the texts analysed in the essays of this volume) point towards the key role of the host of the table, a host who is seen to be the provider for all.

Kathy Ehrensperger
Nathan MacDonald
Luzia Sutter Rehmann
Lampeter, Göttingen, Basel, September 2011

Chapter 1

'THE EYES OF ALL LOOK TO YOU':
THE GENEROSITY OF THE DIVINE KING*

Nathan MacDonald

The pithy clauses of the Lord's Prayer express effortlessly the universal sovereignty of Jesus' father and the dependence of human beings on him. The disciples, as subjects of the divine kingdom, look to their king and father for their most basic needs and for pardon of their misdemeanours. The liturgical familiarity of these words can easily lead us to forget that this is not the only, or perhaps even the most obvious, way to describe God and his kingdom. In this essay we will examine the Old Testament roots of this portrayal giving particular attention to Psalms 145–147. Through a comparison to the earlier 'YHWH is king' psalms (Pss. 29, 47, 93, 95–99), we will see how the later psalms connect YHWH's rule to his provision in a manner quite absent in earlier psalms. The relation of these different presentations of YHWH's kingship to Israel's shifting experience of monarchy as the result of its own loss of independence will be explored. In particular, we will see how Jewish writers appropriated and transformed the ancient Near Eastern propaganda of the royal table as a microcosm.

1.1. *YHWH's Beneficent Provision in Psalms 145–147*

In words reminiscent of the Lord's Prayer, the composer of Psalm 145, identified by the superscription as David, describes the way in which YHWH is loving to all he has made (vv. 13, 17).[1]

*   The research for this essay was undertaken as part of the Sofja-Kovalevskaja project on early Jewish monotheisms supported by the Alexander von Humboldt Stiftung and the German Federal Ministry of Education and Research.
1.   Verse 13b, the *nun*-bicolon, is absent from MT. It is found in LXX and 11QPs^a. It is difficult to be certain whether the psalm originally lacked the bicolon or whether it dropped out accidentally.

The eyes of all look to you,
and you give them their food in due season.
You open your hand,
satisfying the desire of every living thing. (Ps. 145.15-16)[2]

This divine generosity in providing food for all is part of the evidence that YHWH is a good and glorious king, the main theme of this acrostic psalm. Those to whom the psalms are familiar will recognize in these verses an allusion to an earlier psalm:

These all look to you,
to give them their food in due season;
when you give to them, they gather it up;
when you open your hand, they are filled with good things. (Ps. 104.27-28)

Psalm 104 is a magnificent hymn of praise in which the psalmist celebrates not only YHWH's formation of the world (*creatio prima*), but his continued presence as creator God (*creatio continua*). All God's creation – animals and humans – look to him for daily nourishment. The appropriation of these verses in Psalm 145 maintains the creational context, but sees creation as an expression of YHWH's royal sovereignty.

Recent research on the Psalms has emphasized the pivotal role of Psalm 145 in the Masoretic tradition, for it not only concludes a collection of Davidic psalms (Psalms 138–145), but also introduces the small collection of Hallel-psalms in Psalms 146–150.[3] The Hallel-psalms appear to draw inspiration from Psalm 145 and echo many of its themes,[4] including YHWH's creation of all, his power, the dependence of the poor upon YHWH, and the praiseworthiness of YHWH.[5] Amongst those themes of Psalm 145

---

2.   All biblical quotations unless otherwise indicated are taken from NRSV.

3.   See Reinhard Gregor Kratz, 'Das Schema' des Psalters: Die Botschaft vom Reich Gottes nach Psalm 145', in *Gott und Mensch im Dialog* (Festschrift Otto Kaiser; BZAW, 345/II; Berlin: Walter de Gruyter, 2004), pp. 623–38 (628–9). In particular, the Hallel-psalms have been seen as a response to 145.21: 'My mouth will speak the praise of the LORD, and all flesh will bless his holy name for ever and ever.' Psalm 146 begins with the individual psalmist rousing himself to praise YHWH and Psalm 150 ends with the exhortation to every creature to praise YHWH (v. 6). Taken together, the Hallel-psalms are an extended doxology which rounds off the whole Psalter (Gerald Henry Wilson, *The Editing of the Hebrew Psalter* (SBLDS, 76; Chico, CA: Scholars Press, 1985), pp. 189–90, 193–4, 226–8).

4.   This can be seen in the way that individual verses express similar or identical ideas with similar or identical words: Psalm 146: vv. 8 (145.14), 9 (145.20); Psalm 147: vv. 5 (145.3), 11 (145.16, 19); Psalm 148: vv. 5 (145.21), 14 (145.10); Psalm 149: vv. 1, 5, 9 (145.10); Psalm 150: v. 2 (145.3).

5.   In the Hallel-psalms, however, the central position of Zion and Israel within the LORD's creating and saving acts is emphasized, whilst this is at most implicit in Psalm 145. In this sense the Hallel-psalms can be seen as an interpretation of the last Davidic psalm parsing its universal perspective. Frank-Lothar Hossfeld and Erich Zenger, *Psalmen 101–150* (HTKAT; Freiburg im Breisgau: Herder, 2008), p. 808.

that find their echo in the Hallel-psalms are YHWH's kingdom and the generous provision of food as a characteristic feature of that kingdom. This is particularly clear in Psalm 146. 'Who gives food to the hungry' (v. 7) is part of a catalogue of actions that YHWH makes on behalf of the oppressed. Again, those to whom the psalms are familiar may well wonder whether we have an allusion to Psalm 107, where YHWH's provision of the hungry is mentioned in a psalm which also celebrates YHWH's freeing of prisoners and those in darkness. The various activities described – freeing prisoners, upholding the cause of the oppressed, and so on – are often identified elsewhere in the Old Testament as royal prerogatives (esp. Deut. 10.17-18).[6] In Psalm 107 no explicit mention is made of these as royal activities, but the situation is quite different in Psalm 146. This is clear not only from the concluding verse, which states 'the LORD will reign for ever' (v. 10), but also from the exhortation in v. 3 not to trust in princes. In this psalm the divine monarch has no human monarch acting as regent on earth; instead the divine monarch stands in contrast to human monarchs.

In Psalm 147, YHWH is celebrated as the one who brings the rain and causes plants to grow (v. 8), he provides food for cattle and ravens (v. 9), and satisfies Israel with wheat (v. 14). The description of the rain, the growth of the grass and the feeding of the cattle appears to be a reworking of Ps. 104.13-15, and the reference to the ravens probably draws upon Job 38.41. Finally, Ps. 81.16 describes Israel's satisfaction with wheat in almost identical terms. Whilst none of these texts refer to YHWH's kingdom, the same is also true of Ps. 147. Nevertheless, we are probably right to see it as implicit in Psalm 147's references to YHWH's commands and laws (vv. 15-20), his lack of trust in horses and men (v. 10; cf. 33.16-17) and his granting of peace to Zion's borders (vv. 12-14).

Thus, in each of the three psalms that we have examined, Psalms 145–147, existing biblical texts about YHWH's beneficent provision for his creatures have been appropriated and reused. The original contexts in which these texts are found have themes in common with Psalms 145–147: creation theology or an emphasis on YHWH's power or sovereignty. What is novel in their reuse is their placement within a context that foregrounds YHWH's kingship.

---

6.   See Norbert Lohfink, *Lobgesänge der Armen: Studien zum Magnifikat, den Hodajot von Qumran und einigen späten Psalmen* (SBS, 143; Stuttgart: Katholisches Bibelwerk, 1990), 110.

1.2. *'YHWH is King' Psalms and Psalms 145–150*

The focus on YHWH's kingship in Psalms 145–150 naturally raises the question of how these psalms compare to the famous 'YHWH is king' psalms (Pss. 29, 47, 93, 95–99), that have occupied such a central place in modern critical study of the Psalter. The essential features of the 'YHWH is king' psalms have been extensively explored and can be described in brief compass. First, the kingship of YHWH is seen in his exaltation above the gods. YHWH is 'a great king above all gods' (95.3; cf. 29.1; 96.4; 97.9). Whilst the other gods are idols (96.5; 97.7), YHWH is revealed in splendour and majesty (93.1; 95.6; 97.1-6). Second, the kingship of YHWH is expressed in creation and throughout the world. YHWH has established the world and it obeys his rule (93.1-2; 95.3-5; 96.10). The subjugation of the world is seen not only in the natural sphere, but also in the political. The nations are under the rule and justice of YHWH (47.3; 96.10). Third, YHWH is king in Israel. YHWH's reign is from Zion and for the sake of his people (97.8-9; 98.3; 99.1-2).

The importance of these 'YHWH is king' psalms for scholarly research has lain particularly in the apparent closeness of their ideas to those found in the Ugaritic texts. They illustrate the indebtedness of Israelite thinking about YHWH to a broader Levantine religious context. From this perspective, Psalms 145–150 reflect a quite different set of theological influences. Their composition appears to be a conscious attempt to conclude the book of Psalms and draws upon numerous other biblical texts through various intertextual links.[7] We might say that, if the 'YHWH is king' psalms reflect a consciousness of 'Canaanite' religious culture, Psalms 145–150 reflect a consciousness of a developing canon of Jewish Scriptures.

In light of these influences, it is not surprising that scholars have often dated these psalms at different ends of the history of the Old Testament's composition. The 'YHWH is king' psalms were frequently viewed as pre-exilic compositions; Mowinckel famously saw them as central elements of a pre-exilic enthronement festival.[8] Some of these psalms have been dated very early in Israelite history, most especially Psalm 29 which, it has even been suggested, was originally a Canaanite paean to Baal. For Psalms 145–150 various factors suggest dating them to the late Persian period, or even later. First, their placement in the book of Psalms suggests they number amongst some of the latest compositions in the book. Second, they exhibit a high degree of inner-biblical allusion and citation.[9] Third, various features of late biblical Hebrew can be found in these psalms.

---

7.   See especially Reinhard Gregor Kratz, 'Die Gnade des täglichen Brots: Späte Psalmen auf dem Weg zum Vaterunser,' *ZTK* 89 (1992), pp. 1–40.

8.   Sigmund Mowinckel, *The Psalms in Israel's Worship* (2 vols; Oxford: Blackwell, 1962).

9.   See Hossfeld and Zenger, *Psalmen 101–150*, pp. 814–15, 827–8, 861, 876.

In light of this apparent chronological distance, it is hardly surprising that, as Kratz observes, 'zwischen dem Hymnus auf den in der Götterversammlung thronenden Wettergott und dem Gebet zum Schöpfer aller Dinge, "meinem Gott und König', liegen Welten"'.[10] One of the most striking differences is the absence of reference to other gods in Psalms 145–150. YHWH is not presented as king of the gods, and his royal rule relates only to the world that he has created and to Israel. The closest we come to this idea is in Ps. 148.2, where the angels and the heavenly hosts are charged with worshipping YHWH. Yet despite differences, the presentation of kingship in the two collections also has many similarities. First, in both collections YHWH's kingship is closely related to his creation of the world. In Psalms 145–150, however, the creation serves the divine bidding, waits dependently on YHWH or joins in his praise. In the 'YHWH is king' psalms the creation joins in the praise of YHWH, but there is also evidence of the waters seeking to resist YHWH, but being forced into submission (Psalms 29, 93).

Second, the kingship of YHWH is universally acknowledged. Both collections affirm YHWH's kingship over the entire earth, and not just Israel. Neither collection affirms an undifferentiated universalism; rather, Israel is a particular beneficiary of YHWH's actions (e.g., Ps. 147.19-20). The prospect for other nations seems more positive in Psalms 145–150 than in the 'YHWH is king' psalms. In the 'YHWH is king' psalms the nations are fearful, put to shame, or subdued under Israel. One royal function that receives particular attention is YHWH's role as righteous judge (96.10-13; 98.9; 99.4). Since the Psalmist expects the people to be fearful and ashamed, we should probably imagine a sentence of judgement to be passed upon the nations. Israel, on the other hand, rejoices because of the anticipated vindication. In Psalms 145–150, on the other hand, there is only a single reference to vengeance upon the nations (149.6-9), although Israel and Zion are named as the recipients of divine salvation (147.2-3, 12-14, 19-20; 148.14; 149.2-5). On many other occasions the salvation of YHWH is spoken of in ways that appear less nation-specific. YHWH upholds the cause of the oppressed, he feeds the hungry and gives sight to the blind (146.7-8). These psalms speak not so much of YHWH opposing the nations, but the wicked (145.20; 146.9; 147.6). Whilst we may imagine that for the psalmists there was often considerable overlap between the nations and the wicked, many post-exilic texts see Israel as an admixture of the good and the wicked. Despite the concern with the wicked, there is a persistent emphasis on YHWH's goodness to *all* his creatures. YHWH's provision of food to his creatures is one of the paramount expressions of this goodness, and an idea nowhere to be found in the 'YHWH is king' psalms.

10.   Kratz, 'Das Schema' des Psalters: Die Botschaft vom Reich Gottes nach Psalm 145', p. 634.

1.3. *The Metaphor of God as King*

In recent decades the relationship between theology and metaphor has received close attention. Human speech about God is an activity that trades on metaphor. Metaphors gain their meaning from the contexts in which they apply. We may continue to employ the same metaphor, but as the context changes so does the metaphor. No starker illustration of this exists in modern times than feminist discussion of 'father' language, which has not only highlighted how 'God is a father' can mean quite different things to different people, but has also itself drastically altered our perception of this metaphor. What is true of contemporary discourse about God is no less true of Israel's attempts to witness to YHWH's character. This should be especially apparent with political metaphors like 'king' and 'kingdom'. It is, consequently, helpful to set each collection of psalms within the context of the different ideas of kingship known in the late Iron Age, on the one hand, and the Persian and early Hellenistic periods, on the other.

The 'YHWH is king' psalms can be interpreted with some insight in the late Iron Age. During the Iron Age the Levant was a complex patchwork of competing kingdoms with waxing and waning fortunes. Towards the end of the Iron Age, the Mesopotamian empires of Assyria and Babylon increasingly make their presence felt, in the first instance probably not with a decisive change to the perception of monarchy. Assyria and Babylon are of the same species, only larger and more sophisticated monarchies. This political reality had its own reflection in the divine sphere. In the 'YHWH is king' psalms Israel has its god, YHWH, and the nations have theirs. YHWH numbers amongst the gods of the nations, even though he is also conceived to be superior (Ps. 95.3). He is their king, his rule earned through decisive action at creation, but also repeated in the defeat of enemy nations in the present (47.2). The idea of competing nations and competing deities is evident, but so too is the idea of YHWH's universal power. Israel is aware of the world beyond its borders and claims that YHWH too has mastery here. Israel was probably no different to other nations in this respect: the mastery that nations sought to exert over others in their military campaigns, they claimed also for their gods. Kingdoms are defined by their boundaries, and characterized by their claims to have none.

Psalms 145–150, on the other hand, originate from a time when Jews had become used to life within a global empire. From the late Iron Age onwards, the Israelites and Judeans began to experience life at the edge of the expanding Mesopotamian empires, and finally an existence within the imperial domain. From the eighth century BCE onwards, Israel and Judah lost their sway over neighbouring states and finally their own independence as Assyrian, Babylonian, Persian and then Greek empires successively dominated the Near East. As with the 'YHWH is king' psalms, the kingdom described in Psalms 145–150 is universal. But YHWH's universal kingdom looks quite different in these psalms. There are no rival kingdoms; instead, the enemies are internal. They are described as the wicked, but YHWH will destroy them. This kingdom has a definite centre in Israel and Zion. The other kings are not divine. Nor are they serious rivals, but instead find themselves corralled for acts of praise (148.11-14).

This contrast between the petty kingdoms of Iron Age Levant and the global polity of the Near Eastern empires appears to make some sense of some of the differences between the 'YHWH is king' psalms and Psalms 145–150. If this is the case, there may be some advantage to comparing the provision of all creation within what we know of imperial ideology about the king's provision.

1.4. *The Royal Table as the World's Table*

In the great empires of the ancient Near East the royal table was an important expression of the king's political power and royal ideology. Historically our impressions of this institution have been formed most especially by Greek and Jewish accounts of the feasting activities of the Persian monarchs. These accounts exhibit both fascination with and revulsion for the perceived excesses of the Persian table. Distorted though these accounts are, they provided for many centuries the only access to this venerable institution.

Since the rediscovery of the long lost Mesopotamian civilizations in the nineteenth century, however, it has become apparent that feasting on a grand scale was not unique to the Persians, but that they were heirs to imperial practices and ideologies that stretched back millennia. The earliest evidence for large royal feasting goes back to the third millennium BCE. An inscription of Sargon of Akkad records that '5,400 men daily eat in the presence of Sargon, king of the world, the king to whom the god Enlil gave no rival.'[11] If the numbers appear excessive, they are by no means unparalleled – indeed, they are often exceeded – in accounts of feasting under later Mesopotamian monarchs.[12] Even allowing for a degree of exaggeration, it is clear that daily provision of such a host was a public display of Sargon's power and capabilities as a ruler. If later parallels provide appropriate insight into this early period, it is probably not necessary to take 'in the presence of Sargon'

11. Douglas Frayne, *Sargonic and Gutian Periods (2334–2113 BC)* (The Royal Inscriptions of Mesopotamia, 2; Toronto: University of Toronto Press, 1993), p. 31, cf. p. 29.

12. In their own way and despite their expressions of revulsion for Persian excess, the Greeks and Romans were heirs to this practice. See Angela Standhartinger's contribution in this volume.

literally. The king ate with a small number of highly placed officials and aristocrats; the larger number represents the total number of persons who were supplied from the king's table.[13] In the Mesopotamian empires like Sargon's the royal table was a central institution for the redistribution of economic resources which were traded for loyalty and prestige. The king was the central figure in this redistributive economy. He claimed tribute, taxation and spoils which were then redistributed through the king's table to nobles and servants. The royal table confirmed the king's power and prestige. The king's differentiated generosity created hierarchical positions, earning the loyalty of courtiers as well as providing a context for them to attain success and status. The long duration and wide distribution of the institution points to its success in buttressing royal authority. Extant cuneiform texts refer to large-scale royal feasts at second millennium Mari and first millennium Assyria. Myths such as *Enuma Elish* represent even the gods feasting as they decide the fates of all mortals.

It was only when Greeks encountered the Persian empire that this basic imperial tool began to be critiqued. The abundance of the feasts excited the imagination of writers like Herodotus, Polyaenus, Athenaeus and Xenophon. The spectacle of the feasts, their size and the variety of their fare receive extended attention in these writers who contrast the 'barbarian' excess with the modesty of Greek appetite and fare. Many of these clichés are taken up in later Jewish writings such as Esther, Judith and Daniel. There they serve to underscore an alternative national ethic of moderation, which could already be found in somewhat different form in the prophetic and wisdom literature.[14]

There are many features of these grand feasts that merit comment, but I want to focus on just one of these: the cosmic nature of the feasts. There is considerable evidence that the feast was understood as an expression of the king's universal domain. Pierre Briant draws attention to the fact that the royal table was 'symbolic of the territorial and material power of the Great King'.[15] In particular, Briant quotes Athenaeus: 'They used to set on the king's table all the delicacies produced by the country over which the king ruled, the choice first-fruits of each. For Xerxes did not think that the princes should use any foreign food or drink; this is why a custom forbidding such use arose later' (*Deipnosophists* XIV.652b-c). Similarly in *Agesilaus* §9.3, Xenophon writes, 'The Persian king has vintners scouring every land to find some drinks that will tickle his palate; an army of cooks contrives dishes for

---

13.   Pierre Briant, *From Cyrus to Alexander: A History of the Persian Empire* (Winona Lake, IN: Eisenbrauns, 2002), p. 315.

14.   Nathan MacDonald, *Not Bread Alone: The Uses of Food in the Old Testament* (Oxford: Oxford University Press, 2008), pp. 196–218.

15.   Briant, *From Cyrus to Alexander*, p. 314.

his delight.'[16] Just as the diversity of the army mirrored the vast extent of the Persian domain, so did the rich variety of the king's table.

The symbolism of the royal table was not a Persian novelty; it too had a venerable history. It is, perhaps, suggested by the description of Sargon as 'king of the world', but is certainly explicit in a couple of monumental inscriptions from Sargon's reign. In one, Sargon describes how he celebrated his taking up residence in his new palace. 'With the princes of (all countries), the governors of my land, scribes and superintendents [justices], nobles, officials and elders of Assyria, I took up my abode in that palace and instituted a feast of music.'[17] The participants at another feast are described in more detail: 'From the princes of the four regions [of the world], who had submitted to the yoke of my rule, whose lives I had spared, together with the governors of my land, the scribes and superintendents, the nobles, officials and elders [?], I received their rich gifts as tribute. I caused them to sit down at a banquet and instituted a feast of music.'[18] The presence of these other princes at Sargon's feast points to their subservience and dependence upon him.

In the neo-Assyrian empire, the feast remained a conscious expression of the extent of the king's rule. Esarhaddon describes how, 'the nobles and the people of my land, all of them, I made to sit down therein, at feasts with banquets of choice dishes, and gratify their appetites'.[19] Even more explicit is the account of Ashurnasirpal II's feast. The king describes how he added lands and populations to the Assyrian empire. In the context of this territorial expansion he describes his building of a palace at Calah. At the palace's inauguration he celebrates an enormous feast, which is described in considerable detail. To this feast the gods are invited as well as many human participants. 'When I consecrated the palace of Calah, 47,074 men [and] women who were invited from every part of my land, 5,000 dignitaries [and] envoys of the people of the lands Suḫu, Ḫindāna, Patinu, Ḫatti, Tyre, Sidon, Gurguma, Malidu, Ḫubušku, Gilzānu, Kummu [and] Muṣaṣiru, 16,000 people of Calah, [and] 1,500 zarīqū of my palace, all of them – altogether 69,574 [including] those summoned from all lands and the people of Calah – for ten days I gave them food, I gave them drink, I had them bathed, I had them anointed. [Thus] did I honour them (and) send them back to their lands in peace and joy.'[20] The envoys from other lands are not representatives

16.   Briant, *From Cyrus to Alexander*, p. 200.

17.   Daniel David Luckenbill, *Ancient Records of Assyria and Babylonia* (Chicago, IL: The University of Chicago Press, 1926), II, p. 38.

18.   Luckenbill, *Ancient Records*, pp. 50–1.

19.   Luckenbill, *Ancient Records*, pp. 269–70.

20.   Albert Kirk Grayson, *Assyrian Rulers of the Early First Millennium BC I (1114–859 BC)* (The Royal Inscriptions of Mesopotamia, 2; Toronto: University of Toronto Press, 1991), p. 293.

of nations outside Assyria's sphere of influence, who stand on an equal footing with Assyria, but nations that had been defeated in Ashurnasirpal II's campaigns. Whatever honour Ashurnasirpal II claimed to bestow upon them, he received much more in return.

In the Mesopotamian ideology of the royal feast, then, the king's table is a political microcosm. Its foods and participants represent the rich diversity of the Mesopotamian empires, that is, the known world. The king's feasts are a mirror of the feasts of the gods, where the deities of all lands meet and feast together.

1.5. *Biblical Reflections on the Royal Table as the World's Table*

The microcosmic symbolism of the table was not lost on Israelite and Jewish writers and we find it occurring on a number of occasions in biblical texts. The most obvious is the feasting of Xerxes in Esther 1.

> This happened in the days of Ahasuerus, the same Ahasuerus who ruled over one hundred and twenty-seven provinces from India to Ethiopia. In those days when King Ahasuerus sat on his royal throne in the citadel of Susa, in the third year of his reign, he gave a banquet for all his officials and ministers. The army of Persia and Media and the nobles and governors of the provinces were present, while he displayed the great wealth of his kingdom and the splendour and pomp of his majesty for many days, one hundred and eighty days in all. (1.1-4)

The author emphasizes the global extent of Xerxes' kingdom and the explicit purpose of the banquet is to celebrate the splendour of the kingdom, which is ultimately the splendour of the king himself. Michael Fox rightly draws attention to the baroque style of the book which finds expression in this convoluted opening sentence.[21] It hardly needs to be said that the presentation is literary rather than historical, for the absence of the provincial officials for half a year is not realistic.[22]

Greek writers suggest that the Persian satraps and other nobles held their own feasts which mirrored the feasts of the Great King, but on a much reduced scale. In Yehud, Nehemiah, too, held feasts as governor of the province. He recounts that 'there were at my table one hundred and fifty people, Jews and officials, besides those who came to us from the nations around us. Now that which was prepared for one day was one ox and six choice sheep; also fowls were prepared for me, and every ten days skins of wine in abundance' (Neh. 5.17-18). A striking feature of this portrayal is the presence of representatives

---

21.   Michael V. Fox, *Character and Ideology in the Book of Esther* (2nd edn; Grand Rapids, MI: Eerdmans, 2001), p. 14.

22.   For the literary dimensions of feasting in Esther, see Susanne Plietzsch's contribution in this volume.

from the surrounding nations. Williamson is typical of most commentators in his remarks: 'the meals provided for the 150 Jewish officials were no doubt part of their salary, and to these had to be added a steady stream of foreign diplomatic visitors such as characterize all government activity down to the present day'.[23] The feast was, of course, an important context for entertaining foreign visitors and securing support and alliances with neighbours, but comparative evidence suggests that we must not overlook the symbolic significance of the feast's international participants. This is something of a literary topos, even if Nehemiah's visitors were not dependent upon him as those at the Great King's table were dependent on their Persian overlord.

The royal table as symbol of the world is probably to be found in the perplexing conclusion of 2 Kings. In the midst of the Babylonian exile, Jehoiachin, former king of Judah, is released from prison and given a place at the royal table.

> In the thirty-seventh year of the exile of King Jehoiachin of Judah, in the twelfth month, on the twenty-seventh day of the month, King Evil-Merodach of Babylon, in the year that he began to reign, released King Jehoiachin of Judah from prison; he spoke kindly to him, and gave him a seat above the other seats of the kings who were with him in Babylon. So Jehoiachin put aside his prison clothes. Every day of his life he dined regularly in the king's presence. For his allowance, a regular allowance was given him by the king, a portion every day, as long as he lived. (2 Kgs 25.27-30)

It would appear that the vassal kings were supplied from the royal table. Again it may not be that they were literally in his presence, but the idiom of them eating in the king's presence emphasizes the microcosmic nature of the Babylonian king's royal table and the dependence of the vassal kings upon his generosity.[24]

A narrative with similar symbolic resonances is the description of the royal table of Adoni-bezeq in Judges 1. After being captured and having his thumbs and big toes cut off, Adoni-bezeq confesses the justice of his fate. 'Seventy kings with their thumbs and big toes cut off used to pick up scraps under my table; as I have done, so God has paid me back.' The image is macabre; the maimed kings scrabble under the table for food. The black humour of the scene is further enhanced if the name Adoni-bezeq is a deliberate misspelling

---

23. H. G. M. Williamson, *Ezra, Nehemiah* (WBC, 16; Waco, TX: Word Books, 1985), p. 245.

24. Only at a later period would worries emerge about Jews eating with gentiles. The shift is apparent in the differences between the Hebrew and Greek versions of Esther. The Esther of the Masoretic Text has no qualms about receiving portions of food in the palace of the Persian king (2.9) or participating in the many celebratory banquets. Greek Esther, however, refuses to participate in the royal feasts or drink the king's wine (14.16; cf. Jdt. 10.5; 12.1-3). The strictures of the biblical dietary laws were later read back into the Jewish experience of the Babylonian exile in Daniel 1.

of Adoni-zedek intended to make a pun on *bzq*, 'pebble' or 'fragment', as some commentators have suggested.[25] Is Adoni-bezeq lord of the crumbs under the table or the lost digits of his defeated foes? For our purposes it is important to observe the symbolic significance of 70. This number is the traditional membership of the council with its concomitant feast – whether human or divine – in ancient Near Eastern or biblical texts.[26] Seventy thus represents the entirety of the cosmos (see Genesis 10; Deut. 32.8).[27] The 70 kings who eat like dogs under Adoni-bezeq's table suggest a pretension on his part to worldwide rule.

1.6. *The Generosity of the Divine King*

In Psalms 145–147 the divine provision of food to all is seen as an act of the one who is both the Creator of all and the Ruler of all. As we have seen, the expressions used to describe this divine generosity are drawn from other psalms and biblical texts. In those original contexts the focus is on YHWH as creator of all. There is little, if any, emphasis on YHWH's kingship. The provision of food for all is an undertaking of the creator. This is apparent in other biblical texts such as Genesis 1 and 2. In Genesis 1, God does not only create men and animals, but assigns them food (vv. 29-30). Similarly, in Genesis 2 the first words of YHWH God to the man concerns the trees from which he is permitted to eat (vv. 16-17). The close relationship between creation and provision is apparent especially in texts from Egypt. The Great Hymn to the Aten, which has close thematic parallels to Psalm 104, associates the sun disk with the provision of life and food to humans:

> You made the earth as you wished, you alone,
> All peoples, herds and flocks;
> All upon the earth that walk on legs,
> All on high that fly on wings,
> The land of Khor and Kush,

25. For example, Philippe Guillaume, *Waiting for Josiah: The Judges* (JSOTSup, 385; London: T&T Clark International, 2004), p. 91 n. 66.

26. Baal prepares a feast for the 70 children of Athirat in the Ugaritic Baal cycle (*KTU* 1.4.VI.38–59) and 70 deities feast in the *zukru* festival at Emar (Emar 373: 39/37). For discussion of these texts, see Wayne T. Pitard and Mark S. Smith, *The Ugaritic Baal Cycle: Introduction with Text, Translation and Commentary of KTU/CAT 1.3–1.4* (VTSup, 114; Leiden: Brill, 2009); Daniel E. Fleming, *Time at Emar: The Cultic Calendar and the Rituals from the Diviner's Archive* (Mesopotamian Civilizations, 11; Winona Lake, IN: Eisenbrauns, 2000); P. Altmann, *Festive Meals in Ancient Israel: Deuteronomy's Identity Politics in Relation to Their Ancient Near Eastern Context* (BZAW; Berlin: de Gruyter, 2011).

27. Johannes Cornelis de Moor, 'Seventy!', in Manfried Dietrich and Ingo Kottsieper (eds), *'Und Mose schrieb dieses Lied auf': Studien zum Alten Testament und zum alten Orient* (AOAT, 250; Münster: Ugarit-Verlag, 1998), pp. 199–203.

The land of Egypt.
You set every man in his place,
You supply their needs;
Everyone has his food,
His lifetime is counted.[28]

In Psalms 145–147, earlier biblical texts about provision of food by the divine creator have been taken up and brought into a novel association with kingship.

It seems to me that a case could be made that the Israelite and Judean experience of Mesopotamia table ideology could have provided the catalyst for this new association of kingship with the provision of food. The biblical texts that employ the idea of the royal table as a microcosm originate no earlier than the neo-Babylonian period, and in many cases much later. This may well suggest that the utilization of this monarchic ideology by the biblical writers only took place in the neo-Babylonian or Persian period. This would agree with the absence of provision by the divine king in the 'YHWH is king' psalms and its conspicuous presence in Psalms 145–147.

The use of this imagery for the divine king is found on at least one other occasion in the Old Testament. This is the famous eschatological banquet of Isa. 25.6-8.

On this mountain the LORD of hosts will make for all peoples
a feast of rich food,
a feast of well-matured wines,
of rich food filled with marrow,
of well-matured wines strained clear.
And he will destroy on this mountain
the shroud that is cast over all peoples,
the sheet that is spread over all nations;
he will swallow up death for ever._

The context for this meal is provided in 24.21-23 where YHWH deposes the heavenly and earthly potentates and takes up the reins of power with Mount Zion as his royal seat. The similarities between the banquet on Mount Zion and the Persian repasts are clear, most especially in the striking emphasis on the abundance of the meal.

The appropriation of this royal ideology in the description of Israel's God moves far beyond that envisaged in the Mesopotamian portrayals or even in Nehemiah 5. However grand or generous those feasts were, they were always an elite occasion. The whole world might be present at the meals of the Great King, but it was only the kings, rulers and other notables who took their seat

---

28.   COS I: 46. For additional texts, see Claus Westermann, *Genesis 1–11: A Commentary* (Minneapolis: Augsburg, 1984), pp. 163–4.

and enjoyed the fare. Such feasts were more than political occasions, but they were not less than that. As such, only the political classes benefitted from their generosity. The former inhabitants of Judah were perhaps meant to take some comfort from Jehoiachin's treatment by Evil-Merodach, but it was not something that they would experience. Even the almost boundless literary imagination of the writer of the book of Esther was constrained at this point. The nobles and officials enjoyed six months of feasting; the entire city of Susa, only seven days. In the psalms we have examined, however, YHWH, the creator of all, does indeed provide food for all. Not only that, he is explicitly said to provide it for the poor and hungry (Pss. 145.14; 146.5-9). Near Eastern imperial claims are to become reality, but only through the negation of human kingship. In Psalm 146 and Isaiah 24–25 human pretensions to rule are repudiated; only YHWH reigns. The psalmist joyfully affirms that YHWH's kingdom does stretch across the whole cosmos, and *all* creatures – humans and animals – receive from his generous and open hand.

Chapter 2

EVERYDAY MEALS FOR EXTRAORDINARY PEOPLE:
EATING AND ASSIMILATION IN THE BOOK OF RUTH

Peter Altmann

When one thinks of the story of Ruth, what generally comes to mind is
the transformation of Ruth's identity from a foreign, unattached, childless
woman to an established great-grandmother of David.[1] This narrative
storyline intertwines the themes of loss and emptiness in Moab with fertility
and fullness in the land of Israel through the development of the identity of
the central character – Ruth the Moabitess.

Two studies that highlight this movement, one an older dissertation –
Green's 'A Study of Field and Seed Symbolism in the Biblical Story of Ruth'
from 1980 – and one a paper presented at SBL 2010 in Atlanta – Tim Stone's
'Six Measures of Barley: Seed Images and Inner-Textual Interpretation in
Ruth' – show that fertility and fullness, and their symbolic representation
in the motif of grain, structure the plot in Ruth.[2] These interpretations build
on the basic presupposition that, as Green states, 'The Hebrew story is most
beautifully told with numerous indications of carefully planned artistry – all

---

1.   K. Nielsen, *Ruth* (trans. E. Broadbridge; OTL; Louisville, KY: Westminster John
Knox, 1997), p. 1. K. D. Sakenfeld, *Ruth* (Interpretation; Louisville, KY: John Knox, 1999), p. 4:
'This commentary therefore takes as its starting point the primary alternative suggested by many
commentators from the rabbis onward: an emphasis on instruction concerning the community's
view of outsiders. David is foregrounded as the storyteller's means of legitimizing an inclusive
attitude towards foreigners, perhaps especially toward foreign women.' P. H. W. Lau's monograph,
Identity and Ethics in the Book of Ruth: a Social Identity Approach (BZAW, 416; Berlin: de
Gruyter, 2011), provides much detail on the construction and transformation of Ruth's identity;
however, very little discussion takes place of the meal (i.e., Lau, *Identity and Ethics*, pp. 60, 99).
2.   B. Green, 'A Study in Field and Seed Symbolism in the Biblical Story of Ruth'
(unpublished doctoral dissertation, Graduate Theological Union, 1980), spends a large portion of
her monograph on cross-cultural comparisons from ancient Greece and Rome, Ugarit, Sumer, and
the North American Iroquois. T. Stone, 'Six Measures of Barley: Seed Images and Inner-Textual
Interpretation in Ruth' (paper presented at the annual meeting of the SBL, Atlanta, 20 November
2010), shows how the plot closely interweaves Ruth's pregnancy with the land's fertility.

of which can help convey meaning.'[3] The content and form of the story are intentional and fraught with meaning rather than haphazard. Building on this foundation Green concludes that 'the story's main point is to relate the restoration of seed: food in the land, food for Naomi and Ruth, a husband for Ruth, a redeemer for Naomi, and an heir for the whole people'.[4] I would, however, supplement Green's 'main point' by noting that the story highlights exactly how this 'restoration' takes place through the character of Ruth the Moabitess.[5]

Within this overall appreciation of the themes of fertility and fullness, attention has generally focused on the *production* of fullness, rather than its *consumption*. In this paper I would like to read the text closely and in conjunction with other biblical texts, in this case to argue that meals (that is consumption) – explicitly named in 2.14 and 3.7, and also implied in 2.18 – provide both key settings for and also essential elements in the turning points bringing about Ruth's acceptance by the residents of Bethlehem. There are a number of factors, different in each of these scenes, which I believe make the meals *decisive* for the narrative as a whole.

2.1. *Setting the Table*

Before turning to the three specific texts I will lay out a few important background features that lay the foundation for my reading. First, as a Moabitess, the woman Ruth is firmly identified with Israel's enemies: for example, Deut. 23.3-6 forbids any Moabite from ever joining the Yahwistic congregation:

> No Ammonite or Moabite shall be admitted to the assembly of the LORD. Even to the tenth generation, none of their descendants shall be admitted to the assembly of the LORD, because they did not meet you with food and water on your journey out of Egypt, and because they hired against you Balaam son of Beor, from Pethor of Mesopotamia, to curse you. (Yet the LORD your God refused to heed Balaam; the LORD your God turned the

---

3.   Green, 'A Study in Field and Seed Symbolism', p. 3.
4.   Green, 'A Study in Field and Seed Symbolism', p. 76. I find it problematic that Green locates the particular symbol for Ruth as 'seed', given that there is a specific Hebrew word for 'seed' (זרע), but this word does not appear in Ruth. This does not mean that Green's observations are misplaced, but rather that the story of Ruth may instead bring together the food and offspring events differently. Green herself highlights 'death to life' as one possibility. Stone addresses the theme 'from empty to full', and notes, 'As tempting as it may be in our modern context to think of this pile of grain as representing semen, this is probably unlikely, because conceptually, seed was associated with offspring.'
5.   Green, 'A Study in Field and Seed Symbolism', pp. 161–2, notes this connection as well: 'In each story there is some emphasis on the relationship of the woman to the land. On the one hand she is foreign to it and her coming makes it fertile; on the other hand she is home with the land, so that she and it are the same; and her husband is the one who arrives.'

curse into a blessing for you, because the LORD your God loved you.) You shall never promote their welfare or their prosperity as long as you live. (NRSV)

This section specifically connects the provision of food and water (or lack thereof) and the attempt to call a curse down upon the Israelites with the prohibition against admitting these foreigners to the congregation. These concerns return in Ruth 2 as I will point out shortly.

Numbers 25 describes the same story with different highlights, telling how Moabite women led Israelite men astray through sex and feasts to serve the Moabite deities:

> While Israel was staying at Shittim, the people began to have sexual relations with the women of Moab. These invited the people to the sacrifices of their gods, and the people ate and bowed down to their gods. Thus Israel yoked itself to the Baal of Peor, and the Lord's anger was kindled against Israel. (Num. 25.1-3, NRSV)

The sexuality and serving foreign deities are tied together in the term לזנות ('to whore'), a term typically used either for a prostitute or for unacceptable cultic practice. The feasting connection is often overlooked, however. It is prominent in v. 2 both in the obvious 'the people ate', but perhaps just as strongly in the clause 'they invited the people to "sacrifice" to their deities'. The term 'sacrifice' (לזבחי) more precisely refers to a 'festive sacrificial meal'. Sexuality and feasting with a Moabitess serve as leitmotifs in the book of Ruth, yet here more specifically in chapter 3.

The foreign woman Ruth is termed 'the Moabitess' seven times in the four chapters of the book of Ruth, highlighting this connection. Almost every time her name is found *without* this designation it instead appears in a context where she is related intimately with her new Bethlehemite identity (i.e., as 'my daughter' by Boaz in 2.8).[6] Much of the book turns on this progression from one identity to the other, from 'other' to 'ours'.

Further determinations of Ruth's problematic origins are found in Ezra 9–10, which detail Ezra's disdain over the returned exiles' acquirement of foreign wives, including Moabites:

---

6.   A. Siquans, 'Foreignness and Poverty in the Book of Ruth: a Legal Way for a Poor Foreign Woman to be Integrated into Israel', *JBL* 128 (2009): 443–52 (447–9), lists a number of the important negative connotations related to the Moabites and the term נכריה, 'foreign woman', (2.10). E. James, 'A Portion of a Field: Agrarianism and the Book of Ruth' (paper presented in the Old Testament Seminar, Princeton Theological Seminary, 23 January 2010), shows how the book of Ruth depicts a distinctly 'agrarian' philosophy since its focus in not just on humans, but on human connection with the land: Ruth's identity is bound to particular agrarian communities. The interweaving of physical, social and religious identity appears in Ruth's classic statement (1.16-17): '… for where you go I will go [physical], and where you stay I will stay [physical], your people will be my people [social], and your deity will be my deity [religious]. Where you die I will die and there I will be buried [physical] …'

While Ezra prayed and made confession, weeping and throwing himself down before the house of God, a very great assembly of men, women, and children gathered to him out of Israel; the people also wept bitterly. Shecaniah son of Jehiel, of the descendants of Elam, addressed Ezra, saying, 'We have broken faith with our God and have married foreign women from the peoples of the land …' (Ezra 10.1-2a, NRSV)

Nehemiah 13.23-28 supports this view, noting that some of the exiles took women from Ashdod, Ammon and Moab to the effect that half of the children did not speak Judahite. Nehemiah responds by condemning them and even beating some, comparing the situation to that of Solomon, whom Neh. 13.26 declares was led into sin by marrying foreign women. Is this what threatens the man who marries Ruth? Perhaps the unnamed redeemer in Ruth 4.6 chooses loyalty to YHWH when he proclaims that he is unable to redeem the portion of the land Naomi is selling if it requires him to take on the responsibility of raising up children for Naomi's son Chilion through Ruth. One wonders if Ruth could ever overcome this stain.

If it is possible to look beyond Ruth's specific identification as a Moabitess, the motif of the 'liminal foreign woman' might open up to more positive connotations, or at least to the question: what kind of a foreign woman will she be? For the same items that describe a prostitute's attire and payment are those that accompany a bride-to-be.[7]

Of the many biblical stories that offer intertextual connections to Ruth, I find Genesis 24, the story of Abraham's servant meeting Rebekah at the well in Aram-naharaim, the most enlightening.[8] Like Ruth, Genesis 24 considers the acquisition of a bride from far away, though v. 3 specifically mentions 'not from the daughters of the Canaanites among whom [Abraham] is living', but from Abraham's relatives. Like Ruth, the bride must agree to travel to the land where Abraham lives, and Isaac must not return to her foreign residence. Like Ruth, significant action takes place around the drawing of water (vv. 11, 13, שאב). The concept of חסד (loyalty) – central to Ruth – appears: in Gen. 24.12, 14 Abraham's servant describes the provision of a wife as God's חסד to Abraham. The servant also inquires about what family she belongs to (24.23, 47), describing the family residence as בית אמה (her mother's house). There is only one other appearance of this

---

7. Green, 'A Study in Field and Seed Symbolism', p. 193, captures the ambiguous nature of the foreign woman well: 'Overlapping with this exile-return image are the allusions to the woman in the foreign land who is recognized, given gifts, betrothed, made part of a chosen people, brought into the community: she receives food, clothing, jewelry. But the same gifts mark clearly the disgrace of the woman: jewelry adorns the harlot, grain or a kid is the price of her hire.' The similar descriptions of the two women in Proverbs 8–9 immediately come to mind.

8. Significant overlap also exists with Gen. 29 (Rachel and Jacob), Gen. 38 (Tamar and Judah), Exod. 2 (Moses and Zipporah), among other biblical texts. See Nielsen, *Ruth*, pp. 12–17, and especially Green, 'A Study in Field and Seed Symbolism', pp. 159–90, for possible allusions and intertextuality.

phrase – Ruth 1.8. So is it possible that Ruth might be more like Rebekah the matriarch than the Moabite women of Israel's and Judah's nightmares? If so, how can this take place? The description of this process, often through shared food and drink, will be the main task of the rest of this paper.

2.2. *Lunch in the Field: Ruth 2.8-16*[9]

I begin with the main meal first. Boaz begins in 2.8 by speaking directly to Ruth by asking her – rhetorically – 'Have you not heard, my daughter? Do not go glean in another field ... but join here with my young women.' He opens with a term of close familial relationship, parallel to Naomi's address to Ruth in 2.2, but quite different than Ruth's usual description as the Moabitess, or her self-description in 2.10 as a foreigner. However, it also displays the power differential between the older, landowning, commanding male – the איש גבור חיל (literally, 'mighty man of power') – and the younger, dependant-on-handouts, widowed female.[10] By and large, I understand one of the messages here to be that Boaz asks Ruth to identify herself with him. The signs of his offer are 1) clinging to other young women reaping in vv. 8–9; 2) proclaiming protection from assault in v. 9; and finally, 3) drinking from their water jars in v. 9. This final sign is at the same time the first move towards commensality: it is a sharing of the same cup.

As I made reference to above, drawing of water is a significant literary *topos* in the narratives of the Old Testament. To start with the negative, the Gibeonites, who tricked Joshua into making a covenant with them in Joshua 9, are demoted to the duties of hewing wood and drawing water (שאב). In general, as Gen. 24.11 intimates with 'at the time when the women water drawers went out', it seems that it was women who went out to draw water from the well, so it is rather striking that Boaz offers Ruth water that the young *men* had drawn.[11]

---

9. M. C. A. Korpel, *The Structure of the Book of Ruth* (Pericope, 2; Assen: Van Gorcum, 2001), pp. 124–9, groups these verses together as a section with three subsections: vv. 8-10, 11-13, 14-16, which she delineates according to the early manuscript traditions.

10. I. Fischer, *Rut* (HThKAT; Freiburg i. B.: Herders, 2001), p. 172, comments with regard to 'my daughter': 'Sie ist gönnerhaft im Sinne eines «Liebespatriachalismus» und betont damit nicht nur die Großzügigkeit ungeschuldeter Zuwendung, sondern auch die Differenz im Sozialstatus. Der wohlhabende, inländische Mann steht im Kontrast zur armen, ausländischen Frau. Im Verhältnis der beiden spielen damit beinah alle Kriterien, nach denen die Hierarchie in einer patriarchalen Gesellschaft gegliedert wird, eine Rolle: Geschlecht, sozialer Stand, Alter, ethnische Zugehörigkeit – und Religion.'

11. Korpel, *The Structure of the Book of Ruth*, p. 125, notes 'She as a poor foreign woman taking advantage of her right to glean in his field should rather have drawn water for his men than the other way around. Boaz is turning the world upside down.' See also, Fischer, *Rut,* p. 174, and T. Linafelt, *Ruth* (Berit Olam; Collegeville, MN: Liturgical Press, 1999), p. 35.

Introducing the language of drawing water brings the theme of coupling and marriage to the forefront, especially given the intertextual relationship to Rebekah in Genesis 24 (see also Exod. 2.15-21). There is a change in social positioning even from Ruth 2.8, where Boaz perhaps speaks down to Ruth. At this point it is not Boaz himself who draws the water, however. Nonetheless, Ruth is invited to join the local women and men by partaking from the same water and by joining them in the field. The allusion to the motif of finding a marriage partner remains in the background for the time being. In fact, more potential suitors for Ruth are introduced.

In response to Boaz's offer, Ruth highlights the social differences between them: she makes herself physically small by bowing down. She then comments on his notice of her with a small wordplay on the Hebrew root 'to recognize' (נכר): 'Why have I found favour in your eyes that you recognize me (להכירני) an unrecognizable one' (נכריה), that is, a foreigner (v. 10). Boaz's next speech (v. 11) identifies her, however, not as a foreigner but as notable, on par with both the famous ancestress Rebekah and the *Urmensch* Adam. Boaz specifically mentions that she left behind her family and the land of her relatives to journey to a people unknown to her, which Rebekah had done. She mirrors Adam's action in Gen. 2.24 by abandoning father and mother. If one accepts that the narrator has in mind Boaz's statement recalling Ruth's commitment to Naomi in the oft-quoted verses of 1.16-17, then her clinging to her mother-in-law, like a man will with a woman in Gen. 2.24, further invigorates the narrative with marital implications. Their interchange continues for another two verses with yet more romantic or marital overtones, including Boaz's blessing in v. 12: 'May YHWH reward your deed, and may your payment be full from YHWH, God of Israel, under whose wing you have come to find refuge.'

So far my analysis follows many earlier interpretations, preparing the stage for the shared meal in 2.14, which takes place after an unstated elapse of time:

> Then Boaz said to her at mealtime, 'Come over here and eat some of the bread and dip your piece in the sour wine.'[12] So she sat beside the reapers. Then he took to her [or 'heaped up[13] for her'] parched grain. Then she ate, and she became full, and she had left over.

12.   M. Köhlmoos, *Rut* (ATD, 9, 3; Göttingen: Vandenhoek & Ruprecht, 2010), p. 44, argues '*Ḥomæṣ*, das "Säuerliche" (meist als "Essig" übersetzt) ist eine säuerliche, eventuell leicht alkoholische Flüssigkeit, die beim Gären von Getreide oder Trauben entsteht, dem Kwas oder Most vergleichbar.' If it truly is something more special than a mere vinegar this would strengthen the importance of the meal.

13.   For this Hebrew *hapax legomenon*, see HALOT: 997, 'pick up and offer to someone' bases its translation on the Akkadian meaning 'seize, grasp, take' and Ugaritic *mṣbṭm* 'tongs'; E. F. Campbell, *Ruth* (AB, 7; Garden City, NY: Doubleday, 1978), pp. 102–3, notes these connections but also notices that the verb used by LXX means 'to heap' and is also used in passages that deal with heaps in Gen. 41.35, 49. etc.

Let me stop and discuss this text in detail. First, the designation of the time as, literally, 'the time of eating', corresponds with anthropological theory with regard to ritual: there is a set time, hinting at a culture practice, or *habitus*, which accompanies what follows.[14] Having said that, our limited knowledge of ancient Israelite or Judaean culture does not allow too much in the way of grounded commentary on this particular 'time'.[15] However, before mentioning several 'ritualized features' in the text, I want to state very clearly that I am not arguing for a particular folk religion ritual practice or the like for this mundane meal. My intent is instead to highlight the structured nature of this meal, which overlaps with other more formal or more cultic meals.[16] As a time specified in the text – marked – it is somewhat ritualized. Second, Ruth is given a specific invitation to come to a specific place 'here': yet another marker of ritualized action. These mentions by the text of time and place emphasize the fact that an act of significant import is about to take place. To continue, she also joins in the eating of shared food: she is to take 'from the bread' (מִן־הַלֶּחֶם). It is not her bread, but all of theirs. This is also true of the dip: 'dip *your* morsel', בַּחֹמֶץ, 'in *the* vinegar/sour wine'. The very action of the meal exhibits and brings about Ruth's inclusion in the community. She – as the individual taking her portion – enters the community. Finally, she sits מִצַּד הַקּוֹצְרִים, 'beside of

14. Two helpful explanations of the concept of the *habitus* can be found in P. Bourdieu, *Outline of a Theory of Practice* (trans. R. Nice; Cambridge Studies in Social and Cultural Anthropology; Cambridge: Cambridge University Press, 1977; trans. of *Esquisse d'une théorie de la pratique, précédé de trois études d'ethnologie kabyle* (Travaux de droit d'économie, de sociologie et de sciences politiques 92, Geneva: Droz, 1972)), p. 80: 'The homogeneity of habitus is what – within the limits of the group of agents possessing the schemes (of production and interpretation) implied in their production – causes practices and words to be immediately intelligible and foreseeable, and hence taken for granted'; and Bourdieu, *Outline of a Theory of Practice*, p. 81: 'The habitus is precisely this immanent law, *lex insita*, laid down in each agent by his earliest upbringing, which is the precondition not only for the co-ordination of practices but also for the practices of co-ordination, since the corrections and adjustments the agents themselves consciously carry out presuppose their mastery of a common code and since undertakings of collective mobilization cannot succeed without a minimum of concordance between the habitus of the mobilizing agents (e.g. prophet, party leader, etc.) and the dispositions of those whose aspirations and world-view they express.'

15. It is, however, interesting to note that the rabbis appeared to designate the *time* of eating as a significant marker for communal identity according to D. Noy, 'The Sixth Hour is the Mealtime for Scholars: Jewish Meals in the Roman World', in I. Nielsen and H. S. Nielsen (eds), *Meals in a Social Context: Aspects of the Communal Meal in the Hellenistic and Roman World* (Aarhus studies in Mediterranean antiquity, 1; Aarhus: Aarhus University Press, 1998), pp. 134–44.

16. I am drawing here both on the foundational article by M. Douglas, 'Deciphering the Meal', in *Myth, Symbol and Culture* (ed. C. Geertz; New York: Norton, 1971), pp. 61–81; also on C. Bell, *Ritual Theory, Ritual Practice* (Oxford: Oxford University Press, 1992), p. 90. Note the helpful introduction to these theories in H. Taussig, *In the Beginning was the Meal: Social Experimentation & Early Christian Identity* (Minneapolis: Fortress, 2009), pp. 55–67.

the reapers'.[17] In this instance praxis brings the reality into being – at least partially.

As Sakenfeld notes, 'It is not a private tryst but a gesture of inclusion into the larger community.'[18] Given the general overloading of possible sexual tensions throughout the book, this comment is important. The meal brings the point of the story to the fore, and this is important to keep in mind for the next clause of this verse: 'and he heaped up for her roasted grain'. No doubt there is plenty that is sexually provocative in this remark – I think rightly so. However, the context remains a communal meal: she eats, she is satisfied, and she has left over. Ruth's eating to satisfaction may describe not only her physical state, but also her social acceptance and further social identification as she proclaimed in 1.16: 'your people will be my people'. The snapshot contains the proleptic fulfillment of the narrative as a whole, securing the decisive role of the communal meal.[19]

Furthermore, the connection between לחם ('bread') here and water in v. 9 is also found in Deut. 23.3-6, where the Moabites are denied access to the קהל יהוה ('congregation of the Lord') because they did not meet the Israelites with bread and water on their journey out of Egypt. In Ruth 2 the roles are reversed: the Israelite provides both – and at no cost, which contrasts with Deuteronomy 23 – to the Moabitess. Boaz even goes one step futher in countering the actions of the Moabites and Ammonites in Deuteronomy 23: he blesses Ruth, mimicking the role of God in Deut. 23.5, turning the curse into a blessing. When Balaam calls down a curse upon the Israelites at the request of the Moabites, God changes it into a blessing. The result, though not yet stated explicitly, is that this Moabitess, or at least her descendents, do join YHWH's assembly, most assuredly by the fourth generation, directly contradicting the command of Deuteronomy 23.[20]

---

17. The term מצד is difficult (literally 'from the side'), but comparison with 1 Sam. 20.25 and Ps. 91.7 highlight the notion of 'close proximity'. In 1 Sam. 20.25, Abner sits beside Saul, and in Ps. 91.7 'thousands fall at your side', though the Psalmist remains safe.

18. Sakenfeld, *Ruth*, p. 45; also Fischer, *Rut*, pp. 181, 182.

19. Linefeld, *Ruth*, p. 39: 'Sasson suggests that the gesture of presenting her with roasted grain may be "ceremonial, perhaps quasi-legal, in nature"; while there is no support for such a claim, it does capture the symbolism of Ruth's integration into Boaz's circle. One might also detect here a further conflation between Boaz's public concern for Ruth's relationship to God and his and/or the narrator's private concern for Ruth's relationship to Boaz, for as Hubbard points out, in twelve other occurrences of the phrase "to eat until satisfied" God is always the provider of the food. Boaz steps into that role here.'

20. See the discussion of Deut. 23 in N. MacDonald, *Not Bread Alone: The Uses of Food in the Old Testament* (Oxford: Oxford University Press, 2008), pp. 88–91.

2.3. *A Light Dinner at Home: Ruth 2.18-23*

The actions in the field, both the gleaning and the meal, spill over into Ruth's return to the village at the end of the day.

> So she gleaned in the field until evening, and she beat out what she had gleaned, and it was about an ephah of barley. So she carried and entered the city. Then her mother-in-law saw what she had gleaned and she brought out and gave to her what she had left over from [when] she was full. (2.17-18)

All inconsequential greetings are left aside when Ruth returns from the field. The first thing the mother-in-law sees (in v. 18) is what she gleaned – the ephah of barley (v. 17), likely around 30–40 litres.[21] The next reported action is Ruth's gift to her of what was left over from lunch. This is the extent of the reported meal: it is not the textual focus, merely a little evening snack. Yet the terminological connections back to 2.14 cast some light on the ongoing importance of communal eating for the plot. Three words: הותרה, 'she had left over'; משבעה, 'from her satisfaction'; and מכירך, 'one who recognized you' (v. 19) recall the interactions from earlier in the chapter. The first two terms specifically recall the meal in the field, showing the lingering effects of the meal in the concrete sharing of leftovers.

The significant result of this communing over food is the reconciliation between mother-in-law and daughter-in-law. First, Ruth's goods, or gifts, and then her story lead Naomi to speak to her daughter-in-law (as Ruth is designated in v. 20: a familial relation rather than Ruth's Moabite foreignness) and call for YHWH's blessing on the man because he did not forget the living – that is presumably Ruth and herself – and the dead – the husbands and sons (v. 20). With this statement Naomi puts Ruth and herself in the same category, and she goes on to cement this connection by commenting that Boaz is 'a relative of *ours*, the man himself is one of *our* redeemers'. Trible notes that this is the point when Naomi begins to speak with 'words of family inclusion'.[22] While Sakenfeld remarks, 'Thus chapter 2 ends in contrast to chapter 1; the two women are in harmony, Ruth no longer resisting the advice of her mother-in-law.'[23] Again the praxis of sharing food brings about social bonds.

The story must continue, however, as the lingering mention of 'Ruth the Moabitess' suggests in v. 21. She clings to Boaz's young women workers for the rest of the harvest season and dwells with her mother-in-law. But

---

21.   According to Sakenfeld, *Ruth*, p. 46, it was 42 quarts worth, enough for about 5–7 days for the two of them.

22.   P. Trible, *God and the Rhetoric of Sexuality* (OBT, 2; Philadelphia: Fortress, 1978), p. 179.

23.   Sakenfeld, *Ruth*, p. 50.

what will happen after the harvest? Inclusion through gleaning and a single satisfying meal is good, but it will not be enough to get the women through the winter. Integration and the reversal of the despised status of Moabite foreignness require multiple steps.

2.4. *After Dinner ...*

The role of the meal in ch. 3 remains much more in the background than in the two previous scenes. Nonetheless, celebratory feasting appears both in the preliminary conversation between Naomi and Ruth (3.3) and in the narration of events (3.7) as 'eating and drinking', complemented in 3.7 by 'his heart was pleased' (וייטב לבבו). The context is clearly one of feasting, which I would suggest recalls the previously mentioned narrative of feasting and sex in Numbers 25.

The chapter begins with Naomi, now revitalized by Boaz's concern as displayed through the provision of raw grain and of the 'take out' ready-to-eat meal that Ruth brings home at the end of ch. 2. It is not only provision but also inclusion that lead to her action. Naomi in turn now refers to Ruth solely in familial terms as 'my daughter' in v. 1. Similarly, Boaz is described as 'our relative' in v. 2.

Her advice to Ruth is to go down and remain unknown to the celebrants. Considered from the perspective of communal meals, I find it important to note that Ruth is not invited to nor does she take part in the feast. At this point Boaz's inclusion of her has only gone so far. As a result, this meal, rather than showing inclusion, actually points to Naomi's and Ruth's continued relegation to the fringe.

One might argue that only men would be present at the threshing floor,[24] and whether that is the case or not, the text is clear that Ruth is only to 'intrude' once the meal is over and the participants have bedded down for the night next to their prize: the grain for the year, grain in which Ruth and Naomi would also like to partake.

So, when Boaz startles in the middle of the night and asks about the identity of Ruth, who is lying next to him (vv. 8-9) – 'Now there was a woman lying at his feet! So he said, "Who are you?"' – the question is fraught with danger. In terms of the narrative, the question can easily be explained by the situation: Boaz is trying to pull himself together and assess the situation. Likely somewhat inebriated as well, the darkness of the night would make

---

24.   Trible, *God and the Rhetoric of Sexuality*, p. 182, writes, 'the threshing floor where the men are eating and drinking in celebration of the harvest', without commenting on the presence or absence of women.

determining someone's identity difficult. However, when considered in light of Numbers 25, the question is whether Ruth is a destructive foreigner or a life-giving insider.[25]

Given the preparation that has taken place through the communal meals and exchange of food, the answer is clear. Ruth no longer needs to identify herself as a Moabitess, designating herself instead in relation to Boaz as '*your* maidservant'. She has become 'one of ours'. Boaz notes (v. 11) that she is known 'by all in the gate' as a אשת חיל, 'woman of worth', paralleling his high position in the narrator's appraisal, and again calls forth a blessing upon her (v. 10). Sex, feasting and religion again intermingle.

While the *topos* of communal eating does not serve as the climactic point of Ruth's (and Naomi's) integration into Boaz's family and the Bethlehem community in chs 3–4, it nonetheless has been fundamental to the buildup and remains present in the heaps of grain surrounding Ruth and Boaz on the threshing floor. Furthermore, Boaz sends Ruth back to her mother-in-law with the promise of many more shared meals in the form of the six measures of barley (3.15-17). Naomi confirms the security of their shared future in the final verse of the chapter: 'For the man will not rest until he settles the matter today.'

2.5. *Conclusion*

In this paper I have argued that food and especially meals play a significant role in the progression of the plot of the Book of Ruth, a role that takes on even greater importance when read in light of the pentateuchal passages that concern Israelite–Moabite relations. If, as I have argued, the book details the passage of Ruth from an ambivalent boundary character – possibly a dangerous seductress because of her Moabite origins – into a praiseworthy ancestress of Israelite royalty, then the meals, with their interwoven sexual and religious implications, are decisive in Ruth's transformation.

The gifts of food, shared meals and festive events play central roles in the inclusion of the outsider and reintegration of her mother-in-law Naomi in Ruth 2 (and 3). Ruth 2 places the dynamics of food production and consumption centrally, and Boaz signals Ruth's inclusion within the community's boundaries by providing a common source for food (2.9) and through a common meal (2.14). Furthermore, Ruth in turn shares this meal with Naomi as a further extension of common identity confirmation (2.18). My interpretation of these verses was enriched by the appearance of similar

25. Lau, *Identity and Ethics in the Book of Ruth*, pp. 112–14, notes that Ruth's foreignness was never completely overcome in the book, since Boaz still refers to her as the Moabitess in the last chapter (twice; though the final two mentions of her are without this designation).

events in the story of Rebekah (Genesis 24) and the counter-examples of Moabites in Deuteronomy 23. Feasting, sexuality and blessing – the elements found in the downfall of Numbers 25 – return and are reversed in Ruth 3.

In terms of the theological tension found between the messages of Numbers 25, Deuteronomy 23, Ezra 9–10 and Nehemiah 13 on the one hand and Ruth on the other, I will only offer the following note: I am not sure that final resolution of the tension between these texts is either possible or desirable. Perhaps, however, it might help to frame the discussion in terms of 'eating, drinking, and blessing/cursing on whose terms, in which dialect, and inside whose communal boundaries'? The construct of Ruth 1.16-17 in contrast to Numbers 25 and Deuteronomy 23 may offer a way forward.

Chapter 3

EATING AND LIVING:
THE BANQUETS IN THE ESTHER NARRATIVES

Susanne Plietzsch

Which of the banquets in the story of Esther is the most 'decisive'? Is it her second one with Ahasuerus and Haman (Est. 7.1-9)? For it is there that the king decides to set aside Haman's plan to eradicate Esther's people and to have Israel's arch-enemy executed. But was the decision to keep the Jewish people alive in Ahasuerus' empire really made only at that moment? Looking back, does it not become obvious that this decision had already been made earlier when Ahasuerus ordered Haman to exalt Mordecai (6.6-11) after the first banquet where the same people were present (5.4-8)? Zeresh, Haman's spouse, understood the unmistakable signs and knew that her spouse could not prevail against Mordecai. She attributes this to Mordecai's Jewish origin: 'If Mordecai, before whom your downfall has begun, is of the Jewish people, you will not prevail against him, but will surely fall before him' (6.13). This allows us to place the time of the decisive reversal even further back: a victorious man had already entered the stage (2.15). *Now there was a Jew in the citadel of Susa whose name was Mordecai.* Or does the decision come in the narrative when Esther gets away alive from her encounter with the king that she had initiated? Or was it when she decided to venture such a risky encounter? If seen from this perspective, the banquet in Est. 7.1-9 is not so much an open-ended meeting as it is a narrative intensification of what has already taken place up to that event. Nothing that had not already been decided is being decided at that banquet.

This essay addresses the literary function of banquets and of eating in the Esther tradition. If the numerous banquets mentioned in this narrative, the *mishta'ot*, are not or not necessarily the places in the narrative where the cards are shuffled anew and decisions are being made – then what is their function? Why is there so much eating in the story of Esther but also so much fasting? Why does the action return again and again to eating and fasting? As I try to answer these questions, I shall begin with looking at the Masoretic text but also draw on the Septuagint and the rabbinic interpretation of Esther. This requires some words about matters of introduction and location, including what role the Book of Esther played in Jewish tradition and in connection with the Feast of Purim. The topic of eating is to be sketched out by way of the following aspects: 1) the correlation between eating and living; 2) the anti-banquet: perspectives on the condemnation of Vashti; and 3) the question of Esther and how she observed the dietary laws.

3.1. *The Different Versions of Esther: MT, LXX, A-Text*

The oldest extant narrative of Esther is the Masoretic Book of Esther (Esth MT), one of the youngest biblical writings. A number of interpreters now no longer date this text in the Persian but in the Hellenistic era, that is, in the third century BCE, but locate its place of origin in Persia.[1]

The Septuagint's version of Esther is not so much a word-for-word translation as a transcription. It dates from the first century CE, quite late in the process of the composition of the LXX.[2] The LXX version of Esther is known particularly for its so-called additions inserted into the flow of the Masoretic narration. They embellish the story and in some places change the characteristics of the narrative completely. This is because of the structural frame they impose on the narrative which is set out here.

A – before Est. (MT) 1	a) Mordecai's dream: the fight of the dragons b) Mordecai learns of the planned plot against Artaxerxes (Ahasuerus); this arouses Haman's hatred towards him
B – after Est. (MT) 3.13	Wording of the letter Haman caused to be written in the name of the king (cf. Est. 3.8 MT)
C – after Est. (MT) 4	a) Mordecai's prayer (11 verses) b) Esther's prayer (19 verses)
D – after C	Esther's going to the king

---

1.   Cf. Erich Zenger, *Einleitung in das Alte Testament* (Stuttgart: Kohlhammer Verlag, 7. ed., 2008) pp. 307–8. Zenger speaks of the 'time of the fights of the Diadochi'. Cf. Jon D. Levenson, *Esther. A Commentary* (Louisville, KY: Westminster/John Knox Press, 1996), p. 26. An extensive discussion of the book's dating is found in Adele Berlin, *Esther* (The JPS Bible Commentary Philadelphia: Jewish Publication Society, 2001), pp. xli–xliii. Berlin dates the Book of Esther to c. 400–300 BCE; cf. p. xli.

2.   Zenger, *Einleitung*, p. 303.

E – after Est. (MT) 8.2	Wording of the king's counter-edict
F – after Est. (MT) 10.3	Interpretation of the dream

The additions are arranged in concentric circles as it were. Mordecai's dream and its interpretation at the end of the book function as the frame narrative. It shows right at the outset that this story is a cosmic drama. Additions B and E repeat the wording of the royal edicts cited only in MT; at the centre are additions C and D which give particular emphasis to Esther's going to the king and husband. The special theological basis of the LXX version of Esther becomes apparent in addition C: Mordecai and Esther call on God and pray for rescue.[3] Finally, addition D describes Esther's risky going to the king in much detail, with emotion, and not without erotic allusions.

The cryptic character of the Masoretic text that derives above all from its refusal to name God is resolved in Esther LXX, in 2.20, 4.18, 6.1 and 6.13 of the LXX text. Here the 'blank spot' the Masoretic text makes use of is filled in. Some exegetes fear that the radical aspect of the theology of MT is jeopardized by that procedure.[4] But the authors of Esther LXX seem to have grasped the abilities and needs of their public quite well; presumably they had good reason for their sense that Esther MT needed additional editorial work so that a Greek-speaking public would understand this text. The action of the LXX should not be written off as arbitrary artistic imagination, for the accentuation of the story of Esther has its counterpart in the rabbinic view of Purim as a timeless event. And, what is more important, the word-play 'Esther/hidden' functions only in Hebrew.

Occasionally we find a certain disparagement of the LXX in the rabbinic tradition.[5] But in relation to the version of the Esther narrative in the

---

3. Cf. Kristin De Troyer, *Die Septuaginta und die Endgestalt des Alten Testaments* (Göttingen: Vandenhoeck & Ruprecht, 2005), pp. 26–48, on the discussion of the reference to God in the Book of Esther.

4. Cf. Peter Nagel, 'LXX Esther. "More" God "Less" Theology', in *Journal for Semitics* 17, (2008): 129–55. 'The translators crafted Esther and the other characters into mere puppets confined to the strings mastered by God acting as puppet master. The Greek translators, including their "modern" counterparts, endanger the theological thrust of the text, and this needs to be addressed', p. 130.

5. The *locus classicus* for this view is found in the extra-canonical tract Soferim 1,6: 'One does not write [the Torah] in [ancient] Hebrew, in the languages of the Elamites, Medes or Greeks. Seventy elders wrote the whole Torah for King Ptolemy in the Greek language. This day was for Israel as hard as the day when they fashioned the calf, for the Torah could not be translated as necessary.' Michael Higger, *Seven Minor Treatises* (New York, 1930), p. 10.

Septuagint, it is amazing how much of the LXX additions are taken up in the early medieval midrashim on Esther[6] – a sign of the decisive literary success of the Greek Esther tradition.

The third version of the Esther narrative to be mentioned is the so-called A-Text (or Alpha Text), another Greek version. It substantially elevates Mordecai in relation to both Ahasuerus and Esther. In addition, this version identifies the Macedonians as the enemies of the Jews and also refers to Haman as a Macedonian.[7] It is sparse in details and, hence, shorter. Finally, the Feast of Purim is mentioned in the A-Text only in passing.

There are two major theories concerning the placement of this text: 1) the so-called A-Text is the translation of a hitherto unknown Hebrew document that is older than the Masoretic text; and 2) the A-Text is a redaction of the LXX version. De Troyer holds to the latter view.[8] She also proposed where this version of the Esther narrative is to be located historically; this version was prepared specifically for the Roman-Jewish King Agrippa in the year 40/41 CE on the occasion of the visit of a Jewish delegation that also included Philo.[9] The delegation's concern was the threatening situation of the Jewish community in Alexandria on whose behalf Agrippa could appeal to Caligula. De Troyer sees in Mardochaios in the A-Text an allusion to Agrippa, in Haman an allusion to the Alexandrian Prefect Flaccus, and in Ahasuerus an allusion to Emperor Claudius.[10]

The existence of this version of the text suggests that in the minds of the disseminators of Jewish tradition the story of Esther was far more amenable to change and accommodation.

---

6.   The midrash Esther Rabba (on Est. 4.7) contains a dream of Mordecai; cf. Dagmar Böner-Klein and Elisabeth Hollender, *Rabbinische Kommentare zum Buch Ester*, Vol. 2, *Die Midraschim zu Ester* (Leiden: Brill, 2000), pp. 248–9. It also contains the prayers of Mordecai and Esther and portrays Esther's appearance before the king similar to the version in the LXX; cf. Börner-Klein and Hollender, *Rabbinische Kommentare*, pp. 250–1. The book *Jossipon* (ch. 9) also has those elements, cf. Dagmar Börner-Klein and Beat Zuber (eds), *Jossipon. Jüdische Geschichte vom Anfang der Welt bis zum Ende des ersten Aufstands gegen Rom* (Wiesbaden: Marixverlag, 2010), pp. 128–40.

7.   Kristin De Troyer, *The End of the Alpha Text of Esther. Translation and Narrative Technique in MT 8.1-17, LXX 8.1-117 and AT 7.14-41*, trans. Brian Doyle (Atlanta: SBL, 2000), pp. 399–400.

8.   Cf. De Troyer, *Die Septuaginta*, pp. 87–8, and the literature relating to the different research positions.

9.   De Troyer, *Die Septuaginta*, p. 120, and 2000, pp. 400–3.

10.   De Troyer, *The End*, p. 402.

3.2. *The Story of Esther in Jewish Tradition*

3.2.1. *The Megillat Esther and Purim*

There is consensus that the Masoretic story of Esther functions above all as the legend of Purim.[11] Highly diverse theories exist about the origin of the feast which presumably established itself throughout the Jewish community only in post-biblical times. Most of the theories propose Persia-Babylon as the place of its origin. Purim is seen most often in connection with the New Year feasts that mark the transition into spring. According to Theodor Gaster, these feasts contain numerous elements that are also found in the Esther narrative: preparatory fasting; electing a king and queen of the feast; symbolic fights between two parties and an equally symbolic execution of an evil doer; and festive meals and the exchange of gifts.[12] Other authors also connect Purim with Graeco-Roman feasts such as the Bacchanalia and Saturnalia. Jeffrey Rubenstein points out that with Purim one of the feasts of reversal known in many cultures established itself in emerging Judaism.[13] One of the typical features of these feasts is the temporary suspension of class differences and other rules of conduct or even their demonstrative reversal; authorities may be mocked and hierarchical manners ignored. Boisterous gorging oneself on food and drink, disguising oneself, and playing theatre are all part of the feast – the very carnevalesque customs that characterize Purim. According to Rubenstein, this creates the *communitas* described by the renowned ritual scholar Victor Turner: the exceptional situation of communality in equality as distinct from the otherwise existing hierarchically structured *societas*.[14] Tension is present as is the risk that reverting to normality may perhaps not be accomplished at such times. It is quite understandable that such a feast is highly attractive and that once known it may not disappear again. And so it makes sense that the Masoretic narrative of Esther, with its fusion of explosive theological and political actuality, and its really quite earthy humour, was also composed to introduce this kind of festivity into the ancient Jewish context and allow it to happen

---

11.   Cf. Berlin, *Esther*, p. xv: '*Megillat Esther* establishes the Jewishness of the holiday by providing a "historical" event of Jewish deliverance to be commemorated and an authorization, through the letter of Mordecai, for the continued commemoration of the event. Just as the more ancient festivals are historicized and their observance is mandated by the Torah, so Purim is historicized and its observance is mandated by the *Megillah.*'

12.   Theodor Herzl Gaster, *Purim and Hanukkah in Custom and Tradition* (New York: Schuman, 1950), pp. 12–18.

13.   Jeffrey Rubenstein, 'Purim, Liminality and Communitas', in *AJS Review* 17 (1992): 247–77, 249.

14.   Cf. Rubenstein for the applicable literature.

there. Thus, Purim could be fitted into a biblical frame of reference[15] and related to the experiences of ancient Judaism.

3.2.2. *The special position of Purim and the Megillat Esther*

The linkage of the Masoretic Book of Esther to the Feast of Purim and its exceptional situation could explain why the story of Esther often occupied a special position in how the Bible is received in Judaism. The memory of the ambivalent relation to this book can be found in the Jewish tradition. On the one hand, the Esther scroll, the *Megillah*, is part 'only' of the Writings and 'only' of the Feast of Purim which, after all, is suspect on account of its lack of restraint; on the other hand, the story and its meaning is again and again appreciated extraordinarily highly. It is occasionally asserted that in the world to come the books that belong to the 'Prophets' (*Nevi'im*) and the 'Writings' (*Ketuvim*) will no longer have validity, only the Pentateuch (*Torah*) will – and the Esther scroll.[16] What is the point of that assertion? A much greater measure of authority is being claimed for the *Megillath Esther* than the one it has by virtue of its canonical position in the *Ketuvim*: the supra-temporal validity of the Pentateuch. And so the Esther narrative is indirectly presented as a brief and catchy version of the drama of Israel and the world. This demonstrates the remarkable popularity of this narrative; the same may be said about Purim as a meta-historical feast. One can imagine that Persian-Babylonian religiosity provided particularly good preconditions for the creation of such a paradigmatic story. Some authors point to Zoroastrian elements in the Esther scroll, focusing their discussion chiefly on the form of names and on analogies to the main characters of Babylonian deities.[17] In addition, I believe that the strong (and at times exaggerated) dualism also points to the cultural context of Persia. The number 'two' plays a virtually leading role in the Book of Esther, far beyond the dualism of good and evil: there are two queens, Esther and Vashti; two courtiers, Mordecai and Haman; twice Esther goes to the king without being summoned; several times there

15. For example, through references to the exile on the basis of Mordecai's ancestry (2.5-6) and through embedding Haman in the conflict between Israel and Amalek (3.1).

16. yMeg 1,5 and yTaan 2,12. In the midrash Mishle on Prov. 9.2, Esther is compared with Wisdom who '*has slaughtered her animals, mixed her wine*', and '*set her table*'. We read there that the days of Purim will count in this world and in the one to come, just as the day of reconciliation, the *yom ha-kipurim*. Both ideas recur in Maimonides' Mischne Torah, Hilchot Megillah we-Chanukkah 2,18.

17. Cf. James R. Russell, 'Zoroastrian Elements in the Book of Esther', in Shaul Shaked, ed., *Irano-Judaica II* (Jerusalem: Ben-Zvi Institute for the Study of Jewish Communities in the East, 1990), pp. 33–40; Manfred Hutter, 'Iranische Elemente im Buch Esther', in Hannes D. Galter, ed., *Kulturkontakte und ihre Bedeutung in Geschichte und Gegenwart des Orients* (Graz: Verlag für die Technische Universität Graz, 1986), pp. 51–66.

are two banquets and two letters; and finally two days of the Feast of Purim. The Esther scroll ends with the comment that Mordecai the Jew was 'second' in command next to King Ahasuerus (10.3). Sometimes this strikes one as a humorous, exaggerated adoption of Persian dualism.

The special position of the Esther scroll lies above all in the fact that it nowhere speaks of God or mentions God's name. We are dealing here with a very complex narrative trick, namely the use of a blank spot (German: *Leerstelle).* For example, the somewhat weak but still relatively strong King Ahasuerus may be seen as a reference to the heavenly king who, although absent, guides the whole event to a good ending.[18] Overall, the deity does not appear in the Book of Esther where one would expect it. But the authors put readers in a position where in a chain of adventurous coincidences we can see connections in advance. We begin to see something like divine providence without that having to be said explicitly. In Rabbinic exegesis (bChullin 139b) the name Esther, which means 'hiddenness', is linked to Deuteronomy 31.18: 'On that day I shall surely hide my face.' Thus, 'Esther', her name as well as her character, stands for God who only seems to be absent.

A wholly different and more praxis-related explanation for the literal absence of God from the Esther scroll would be the practical function it serves: if the *Megillah* is intended for Purim from the outset, then care is taken that the name of God is not desecrated by this boisterous activity and therefore there is this vacancy ('Leerstelle'), this present absence.[19]

3.3. *The Motifs of Eating and Banquets*

3.3.1. *The structuring of the Book of Esther by banquets*

The feature that gives the Masoretic Book of Esther its structure is the banquet (Hebrew: *mishta'ot).*[20] The structure proposed here is based on and prompted by the structure developed by Levenson.[21]

18.   The Rabbinic interpretation sometimes sees Ahasuerus in analogy to God, for example in the interpretation of Esther 6.1 found in EsthR (par. in bMeg 15a): 'sleep deserted the king' is taken to mean that 'God slept'. In support of this, EsthR refers to Psalm 121.4 and Psalm 44.24. The linking of Esther 6.1 and Psalm 121.4 is found also in Rabanus Maurus' commentary on Esther.

19.   Amos Hacham makes this observation in his *Da'at ha-miqra megillat ester* (Jerusalem: Mossad Ha-Rav Kook, 1973), p. 17.

20.   I assume that a *mishteh* is a festive meal (of good food) with wine (served afterwards), even though the root of that Hebrew is *sh-t-h* (to drink). In Esther as in the Hebrew Bible in general, the concept is often found together with words for 'feast day' and 'joy' so that drinking wine and eating well can be thought of together.

21.   Levenson, *Esther*, pp. 5–6. Levenson himself discusses the structuring proposed by Michael Fox; cf. Michael V. Fox, *Character and Ideology in the Book of Esther* (Grand Rapids, MI: Eerdmans, 2nd edn, 2001), p. 157.

1	1.2-4	Ahasuerus' banquet for the nobles
2	1.5-8	Ahasuerus' banquet for the whole people of Susa
3	1.9	Vashti's banquet for the women
4	2.18	Banquet on Esther's enthronization (tax-amnesty, donations to the people)
5	3.15	Ahasuerus' and Haman's drinking session after issuing the decree
	4.3 4.15-16	Mourning, fasting, weeping and lament among the Jews Three-day fast of Esther and the Jews in Susa
6	5.6-8	Esther's first banquet with Ahasuerus and Haman
7	7.1-9	Esther's second banquet with Ahasuerus and Haman
8	8.17	Festive meal of the Jewish population after Mordecai's counter-edict
9	9.17, 19	Celebration of Purim on the (13./) 14. Adar
10	9.18	Purim in Susa on the (13./14./) 15. Adar

In distinction from the structure proposed here, Levenson sets out an order of five double-groupings: the banquets 1 and 2 are in correspondence to 9 and 10; this creates a narrative frame; 3 and 4 are banquets in honour of the queen. Analogously he groups 5 and 8 together: the banquet celebrating Haman's seeming success and the banquet on the occasion of his obvious defeat. What remains are banquets 6 and 7 to which Esther had invited Ahasuerus and Haman. What makes this arrangement attractive is that in this form the first banquet turns out in each case to be 'more general and less conclusive' and the second 'more focused and climactic'.[22] Still, it seems to me that the triple- and double-group based structure shown here can be made less complicated on the basis of the story's content: the first three banquets take place at Ahasuerus' court before the outbreak of the actual conflict; the final three represent the situation after its conclusion. The remaining double-groups, 4–5 and 6–7, admittedly go back to the two periods of fasting that lie between them. The turning point of the Masoretic Esther narrative would therefore be marked differently than in Levenson's structure which locates it in Esther 6 (that is, between banquets 6 and 7), in the unexpected command given to Haman to elevate Mordecai.[23] However convincing and comprehensible this presentation of the Book of Esther is, it leaves open the question of why Esther's decision to appear before the king even though this was prohibited – and how this decision was implemented! – is not perceived as the turning point of the story. Our narrative would

22.   Levenson, *Esther*, p. 6.
23.   Levenson, *Esther*, p. 8.

then have a double turning point, once with Esther (5.1-2) and once with Mordecai (6.11). And neither of them has anything to do with eating.

The large number of banquets as well as their balanced grouping raises the question of what prompted the authors to draw on this motif so often. The following literary possibilities suggest themselves. 1) The artful presentation of a banquet presumably calls forth among the readers an eager and delight-filled expectation: where will the banquet take place; how do the hosts present themselves; how generous are they; who is invited; and, of course, what food and drink will be served? To paint banquets and festive meals in words is clearly a highly rewarding literary motif; if done competently, readers are able to enter into the relaxed and exuberant mood of the feast. 2) Furthermore, banquets offer extensive possibilities concerning the constellation of their actors. The writer simply issues an invitation and instantly everyone involved in the action is already gathered and can add to the course of the action.[24]

And if we take the *Megillah* to be the text of the Feast of Purim, a further perspective opens up, namely the actual festive meal following the reading of the text. According to this perspective the real aim of the banquets related in the *Megillah* would therefore be the banquet that the community celebrates in accordance with the *Megillah*.

3.3.2. *Eating as a necessity of life*

As I see it, there is a rather obvious and banal reason why there are so many meals in the Book of Esther: eating and living are inseparable. Surviving is the issue of this narrative and the concomitant tension is made real in the juxtaposition of eating and fasting.

In the middle of the Esther narrative, between the first five and the second five banquets, the Masoretic text has two periods of fasting. In the first instance, the Jewish population, frightened by the edict of its destruction, turns to fasting (4.3); this clearly shows the connection between eating and living. In the second instance, Esther together with all Jews in Susa fasts so that they can resist the threatening disaster (4.15-16). Thus, in the first instance, we hear of fasting as a spontaneous reaction born out of mortal agony and then, in the second, as a conscious act of self-examination weighing how to meet the danger. The counterpart to these fasts is the celebratory meal of the Jews after Mordecai's counter-edict which secured their survival. Incidentally, the LXX links the double-fasting with the double-prayer of Esther and Mordecai which is said to have supported the fasting.

---

24.   I am indebted to Salavatore Ortisi here for his input on the literary function of meals.

The Midrash Esther Rabba,[25] interpreting verse 5.12, depicts the existential character of eating by creating a situation in which eating and remaining alive are connected to one another. In Est. 5.12, Haman, certain of his victory and having been invited already for a second time to a banquet, declares 'even Queen Esther let no one but myself come with the king to the banquet that she prepared'. The midrash now focuses on the fact that, after this second invitation, Haman ordered that the wood on which he planned to execute Mordecai be made ready. The interpretation establishes a connection between Haman's cocksure feeling of victory and the king's unrest of which Est. 6.1 speaks. 'That night, sleep deserted the king.'

> After he had finished getting the wood ready, he went to Mordecai and found him in the house of study with children sitting before him. They wore sackcloth about their hips and were busy studying the Torah, weeping and crying. He [Haman] counted them and found 12,000 (22,000) children there. He had iron chains put on them, called for guards to watch them and then said: 'Tomorrow I shall first kill these children and then hang Mordecai!' Mothers brought their children bread and water, saying: 'Our sons, eat and drink before you die tomorrow so that you don't die hungry!'
>
> Thereupon the children laid their hands on their books and swore this oath: 'By the Life of Mordecai, our teacher! We will not eat and we will not drink but die during our fast!' They all burst into crying until their cries ascended to the heights and the Holy One, blessed be His name, heard their crying, at about the second hour of the night.
>
> In that hour, the Holy One, who is blessed, showed mercy; He arose from the throne of justice and sat down on the throne of mercy and said: 'What is that loud voice I hear, like that of baby goats and lambs?' Then our teacher Moses stood before the Holy One, blessed be He, and said: 'King of the universe, it is not baby goats and lambs you hear but the little ones of your people who today are already in the third day of their fast and tomorrow the enemy will slaughter them like little goats and lambs.' At that hour, the Holy One, blessed be He, took the letters in which he had judged them and which he had sealed with clay and tore them up. In that night terror overwhelmed Ahasuerus. That is what is written (6.1) '*That night, sleep deserted the king.*' (EstR 9,4)[26]

In this midrash, Haman is so sure of his intent that he seeks to kill not only Mordecai but also his underaged Torah pupils as soon as the opportunity to do so presents itself. After the fate of these children appears to be sealed, mothers come bringing food. This can hardly be understood in any other way than as a sign of hope that the children will survive nonetheless. The children decide otherwise: they will fast and be ready to die; their determination causes God to cancel the fate imposed on Israel. The king intuits this, which is why he becomes restless and sleep deserts him. Here again we have the motif of intentional fasting that protests against the fate of destruction. But there is also the completely practical action of mothers providing nourishment

---

25.   Cf. Börner-Klein and Hollender, *Rabbinische Kommentare*, Vol. 2, p. 153, on the assembly and dating of the text of which they provide a translation and commentary, pp. 153–266.

26.   Translation from the Vilna edition of 1887. That edition cites both readings that give the number of children in the house of study.

who thereby indicate that they will resist to the very end the killing of their children.[27]

3.3.3. *The condemnation of Vashti: the banquet that gets out of hand*

Among others things, banquets are also a depiction of an exceptional situation beyond control. Antiquity is acquainted with festive meals where a conflict arises and eventually erupts and blood is shed. They are known as anti-banquets; Anja Bettenworth deals with them in her dissertation on banquet scenes in the epic poetry of antiquity. These are 'occasions of hospitality that are not managed in a more or less normative fashion to their conclusion but turn unexpectedly into a bloody fight'.[28] We do not have exactly such forms of a banquet turning into a bloodbath in the Book of Esther which is surely because of the tragic-comical aspects of the narrative. Still, two banquets end with condemnations or even executions: Ahasuerus' second banquet ends with Vashti being condemned; and Esther's second banquet with the king and Haman concludes with the unexpected-expected condemnation of Haman.

I consider the second banquet in the Book of Esther as a comical variation of the anti-banquets. No specific incidents are mentioned in connection with the first banquet, held for the royal establishment, which lasted 180 days, whereas the second banquet, held for the common people, gets out of hand and ends in a conflict which is narrated in an altogether burlesque fashion. The male guests, including the host, are drunk and the king proposes to have Queen Vashti present her beauty in front of the guests.[29] But she refuses,

---

27. The midrash implies that the fate of eradication (now lifted again) had previously been imposed by God on Israel. Esther Rabba also connects this with a banquet, the second of Ahasuerus' banquets (1.5) which he held for the whole people in Susa. This midrash (EstR 3,9) assumes that 'the whole population' is, of course, the people of Israel and that Haman was already determined to corrupt Israel during this banquet by getting the people intoxicated and by having prostitutes in attendance. By then Mordecai had already warned his fellow Jews, but 12,500 Jews had followed the king's invitation despite the warning and had 'brought shame on themselves'.

28. Anja Bettenworth, *Gastmahlszenen in der antiken Epic von Homer bis Claudian. Diachronische Untersuchungen zur Szenentypik* (Göttingen: Vandenhoeck & Ruprecht, 2004), p. 395.

29. In his interpretation of what the name Vashti means, James R. Russell (1990, p. 37) calls attention to the connotation 'desirability, beauty' from the context of Iran (cf. the cited literature in his book). Another possible connotation exists, as Ursula Rapp has shown: in Hebrew ושתי could be the feminine imperative 'and drink'! Cf. Ursula Rapp and Maria Elisabeth Aigner, 'Texte, um das Leben zu verstehen. Exegese und Bibliolog "im Inter" am Beispiel von Ester 1', in Joachim Kügler, Eric Souga Onomo and Stephanie Feder, eds, *Bibel und Praxis. Beiträge des internationalen Bibel-Symposiums 2009 in Bamberg*, bayreuther forum TRANSIT, Vol. 11 (Münster: Ö Lit Verlag, 2011), pp. 145–72.

thereby evoking a domestic-political conflict: her action might cause all women in the Persian Empire to assume all of a sudden that they no longer had to do what their husbands tell them! The king does not know how to react and has to let seven of his highest-ranking princes give him advice. They issue an irrevocable law of the Medes and Persians which states that Queen Vashti may no longer be called before the king and that she should be replaced by a better queen. The agenda behind this is also spelt out explicitly: this legally ordered exchange of Vashti will be a lesson to women and they will immediately begin honouring their husbands! This is crude irony in every aspect that literally begs to be staged.

The Septuagint as well as the rabbinic interpreters is anxious to relativize the king's inebriated capriciousness and blame Vashti for the escalation. The rabbinic interpreters do indeed admit that Ahasuerus demanded of Vashti that she present herself dressed with nothing but the royal crown *alone*. But they also tell us that her refusal had nothing to do with good manners. No, she refused because she had a sudden attack of leprosy or because the angel Gabriel had caused her to grow a tail! Besides, they go on, Vashti, the granddaughter of Nebuchadnezzar, had been a cruel ruler who had forced the Jewish women to work naked on the Sabbath.[30] That is why Ahasuerus' demand was according to the rule of 'measure for measure'.

The strategy of the LXX is somewhat different: according to Est. 1.11 LXX, the king had ordered the queen to appear so that he might crown her! Thus, her behaviour is irrational in that she refuses her own coronation.[31] Neither the Septuagint nor the Midrash want to leave the banquet scene as it is described in Esther (MT). The same is true for the first Christian commentary on the Book of Esther that was prepared by Maurus in the ninth century CE.[32] There, Vashti, the queen that is deposed, stands for the synagogue and Esther for the church from the nations.[33] Thus, throughout the interpretations we discern the intent to interpret the crude Vashti scene theologically and thus to legitimate it.

3.3.4 *Esther and the dietary laws*

The fact has been discussed repeatedly that the Masoretic Book of Esther not only contains no explicit talk of God but also no religious-cultic practice. This gives rise to the question of how the authors present their protagonist

---

30.   bMeg 12a-b; Targum Scheni on Est. 1.12.

31.   Marie-Theres Wacker, 'Das Ester-Buch in der Septuaginta', in Klara Butting, Gerard Minaard and Marie-Theres Wacker, eds, *Ester* (Wittingen: Erev-Rav, 2005), pp. 73–7, 74.

32.   Rabanus Maurus, *Expositio in Librum Esther*, PL 109, from column 635C on.

33.   *Librum Esther*, Caput II, columns 642–4B.

Esther in relation to the Jewish dietary laws. Are we faced here possibly with a Jewish heroine who does not eat kosher? In my view, the MT intentionally leaves this question open, leaving it to the readers as to what conclusions they might draw. In a longer, midrash-like section on the Book of Esther, the Babylonian Talmud (bMeg 10a-17b) indicates that all options are possible:

> *[H]e advanced her and her maids to the best place in the harem* (2.9).
> Rav said: (This means) that she was given Jewish food to eat.
> Shmuel said: (This means) that she was given pork to eat.
> Rabbi Yochanan said: Vegetables, for Scripture says (Daniel 1.16): *So the guard continued to withdraw their royal rations and the wine they were to drink, and gave them vegetables.*
> (bMeg 13a)

The section explores what may be concluded from Est. 2.9 about the food Esther was given to eat when the verse says that she and her servants were favourably treated by the royal harem's supervisor. Such favour could indicate that she received food she had asked for but it could also mean that it was food especially favoured at the court. Rabbi Yochanan proposes finally that Esther be compared to Daniel. For it might be that like Daniel, Esther succeeded in persuading her guards of the advantages of the diet of vegetables. The intertextual connection made here goes beyond the mere use of the word 'vegetables': after ten days on a vegetarian diet, Daniel looked 'better and healthier' (Dan. 1.15) than his fellow prisoners who had been allowed to eat what was served at the table of the king of Babylon (cf. Dan. 1.8-16). Thus, the Talmud finds a solution for how Esther might have observed the dietary laws at Ahasuerus' court.

The LXX also favours this solution but presents it in a very different manner. The following verses from Esther's prayer preceding her first appearance before Ahasuerus provide the key (Est. LXX, C 26-28):

> You have knowledge of everything and you know that I abhor the bed of the uncircumcised one and hate the glory of the lawless one and of any alien.
>
> You, O Lord, know my predicament, that I abhor the sign of proud position that is upon my head, and I do not wear it except on days when I appear in public. I abhor it like a cloth of a woman that sits apart.
>
> And your slave has not eaten with them at their table, and I have not honoured the king's banquets nor drunk the wine of libation.

Esther LXX, addition C, puts the question of the dietary laws into a broader context in that the matter of Esther's marital relations with Ahasuerus is raised together with the concern for dietary laws. Both of these topics are considered to be connected by the LXX, and the authors – different from the Masoretic version – think it appropriate that they be addressed openly. But they add a third topic – that of the political power in opposition to God.

Addition C notes that Esther had not married Ahasuerus voluntarily.[34] According to the LXX, her abhorrence is due to the fact that Ahasuerus is a man uncircumcised and without the law. This observation is not an exclusively cultic-religious one, but also an ethical one. The king's indifference towards the divine laws – according to the logic of the narrative – goes along with his claim of glory and honour that are not due to him. Ahasuerus' anti-godly arrogance is a mirror of his cultic difference. Both of these become unmistakably apparent in that this king does not shy away from wanting to destroy Israel. That is why both, marital relations and sharing meals with him and his 'tool' Haman, are inconceivable and offensive. The concept of 'Haman's table' may be read here almost like the designation of an 'anti-sacrament', food that would pollute one equally in an ethical as well as cultic sense.[35] Thus, when the LXX asserts that Esther observed the dietary laws, this should not be understood only as an expression of individual religiosity but also as a statement of opposition against power politics hostile to life and to God.

3.4. *Summary: A Spectrum of Life*

The Book of Esther is structured by banquets, and the reading of the text finds its continuation in the festive banquet on the Feast of Purim. The themes of 'banquets' and 'eating' comprise a broad spectrum of different motifs in the book. There are banquets that depict affluence and reputation: the first three banquets celebrate the political presence of the ruling couple, Ahasuerus and Vashti. Mirror images of these are the three banquets of Purim related last: here the Jewish community celebrates its presence which, as had once again been shown, exists because God wills it. There are banquets where conflict erupts and escalates and others where, through clever politics of invitation, decisions are reached and new courses set. But fasting, too, is

---

34.   The rabbinic interpretation also deal with this matter extensively; cf. Barry D. Walfish, 'Kosher Adultery? The Mordecai-Esther-Ahasuerus Triangle in Talmudic, Medieval and Sixteenth Century Exegesis', in Sidnie White Crawford and Leonard J. Greenspoon, *The Book of Esther in Modern Research* (London: T&T Clarke International, 2003), pp. 111–36. Both the rabbinic interpretation and the LXX are familiar with the notion that Esther was married to Ahasuerus. This is indicated in Est. 2.7 LXX. Some of the dramatic formulations in the (Masoretic) Esther narrative are given thereby a completely different significance, such as Est. 4.16; Esther's voluntary going to the king is seen to be a public consent to her marriage to him that she had hitherto only 'tolerated' (cf. bSanh 74b). That also puts her marriage to Mordecai at risk for the sake of rescuing her people (cf. Walfish, 'Kosher Adultery?', p. 117).

35.   I am reminded here of Heinrich Böll's novel *Billard um halb zehn*, in which he describes those who got corrupted by inhumanity and brutality during the Nazi regime as those who had eaten from the sacrament of the buffalo (Köln: Kiepenheuer&Witsch, 1959).

of great importance. Paradoxically, it appears at the centre of the narrative, which may at the same time be taken as a sign of its seriousness as well as of its cryptic humour. The refusal of nourishment may be due to terror and fear but also to a determination and readiness to take risks. Esther's decision to take just such a risk and to act accordingly is an important turning point in the narrative. She fasts so that she can make this decision. But she is not alone in her fast: the Jewish community in Susa fasts with her. The change of the fast into a festive meal becomes even more obvious when the goal has been achieved, when – to put it simply – the enemy has been defeated. And so, the banquets in the Masoretic Book of Esther are on the whole an expression of vitality and confidence.

The Septuagint as well as the rabbinic tradition both deal particularly with questions of identity and affiliation in connection with the banquets. Those questions arise in exemplary form from Esther's sojourn at the Persian court, a tailor-made constellation for reflecting on the coexistence of Jews and non-Jews and on whatever possible and thinkable chances and dangers are associated with that.

Translated by Martin Rumscheidt

Chapter 4

YOU ARE HOW YOU EAT:
HOW EATING AND DRINKING BEHAVIOUR IDENTIFIES
THE WISE ACCORDING TO JESUS BEN SIRACH

Ursula Rapp

4.1. Introduction: 'Decisive Meals' and the Symposium in Ecclesiasticus

There is a lot that can be decisive about a shared meal: it is not only who can partake in it, but also what is being served at table and how that is eaten and drunk, by whom and how the food is prepared, the sequence of courses or certain rites, what is and what is better not said, how one sits or reclines (or nowadays, often, also how one stands or walks). Most of the time, these are decisions influenced consciously or unconsciously by conventions that clarify who belongs to a community that arranges its meals according to particular conventions and who does not belong to it because they are not familiar with the conventions. Those who do not know how to conduct themselves in accordance with them are quite clearly 'alien' and thus do not belong. Everyone who studies how meals were understood in antiquity and the customs associated with them recognizes this feature of 'alienness'.[1] Eating meals, whether alone or in company, yields information about the conventions and, thus, about the groups with whom one identifies oneself. And so, eating meals *decides* about *identity* in general. *Writing* about 'eating' means to render conventions explicit; it can also be an indication that what had been taken for granted about eating meals has been upset. The rich literature of antiquity on symposia and syssitions, therefore, shows that the symposium was the widespread praxis of taking meals, but that the form of its concrete arrangements relating to the choice of guests, frequency and location, the order or courses served, the erudite subjects of conversation and

---

1. This becomes clear, for example, in the significance eating together had in ancient times, which caused eating alone to be 'frowned upon' (Matthias Klinghardt, *Gemeinschaftsmahl und Mahlgemeinschaft. Soziologie und Liturgie frühchristlicher Mahlfeiern* (TANZ, 13; Tübingen: Francke, 1996), p. 31). In today's Western industrial societies, however, it is not uncommon at all to eat alone during the workaday week.

one's conduct during the meal are aspects of the shared praxis of individual groups, of actual existing clubs, and reflect their identity.[2] Inasmuch as the symposium was a central component of community life, reports and descriptions of it reflect the group's praxis and an essential aspect of what constituted its communal spirit.[3] Thus, eating meals determines the praxis of a certain group, its *aims,* and its religious, social and economic *values.*

What does this mean in relation to what is decisive in what the Book of Jesus Ben Sirach says about eating meals?

Ecclesiasticus, composed by a wise Scripture scholar between 190 and 175 BCE in Jerusalem, is a complex reflection on Jewish and Hellenistic religion and culture. In several places,[4] the author discusses the topics of eating and holding common meals; this is not to be taken as a matter of his individual culinary interests – it has to do with the significance of the common meal in antiquity and particularly also in Hellenistic culture.

In 31.12–32.13, Sirach describes how one is to behave at a banquet (31.12-31) and at the symposium following it (32.1-13).[5] In exegetical literature, this text is said to be instruction for young men on how they are to conduct themselves at such social occasions as far as proper behaviour is concerned. A pithy example of this is Georg Sauer who says that this text is about 'conduct at table in the context of an urban culture'[6] and an easily comprehensible depiction of table manners in antiquity.[7]

But now we ask whether Jesus Sirach's description of table manners is not also a kind of identity portrayal which does not describe the course of a symposium but people's behaviour there and their social and economic position. Sirach 31.12–32.13 may possibly be a reflection in the wisdom tradition on identity that is more concerned with religious, economic and social values than with good manners.

This would have to be established by more accurate analysis of the concepts used in the Book of Jesus Son of Sirach and others. To date,

2. On the significance of clubs for the Christian meal praxis and for some examples of how group identity was manifest in meals, cf. Klinghardt, *Gemeinschaftsmahl,* pp. 35–43.

3. Klinghardt thinks that the common meal provided the orientation for the life of the association and gave it its profile (*Gemeinschaftsmahl,* p. 43).

4. Parenetic texts on common meals are found, e.g., in 10.27; 14.10; 29.21, 24-28; 30.16-25; 31.12–32.13; 34.25; 41.12. In the hymns of wisdom, Wisdom is said to nourish those who seek her; Sir. 1.16-20; 6.19 (H); 15.3; 24.17.

5. The concept of symposium in literature refers sometimes to the entire banquet and then again only to the second part, the bacchanal, as in Sir. 31.31; 32.5 (or, e.g., in Prov. 23.30; Qoh 7.2). The precise formulation for the bacchanal is πότος /commissatio whereas symposium comprises the entire meal. On πότος cf. Klinghardt, *Gemeinschaftsmahl,* pp. 113–14; Martin Ebner, 'Mahl und Gruppenidentität. Philos Schrift *De Vita Contemplativa* als Paradigma', in Martin Ebner (ed.), *Herrenmahl und Gruppenidentität* (QD, 221; Freiburg et al.: Herder, 2007), pp. 65–90, p. 73 n. 29.

6. Georg Sauer, *Jesus Sirach / Ben Sira* (ATD.A, 1; Göttingen: Vandenhoeck & Ruprecht, 2000), p. 223.

7. Cf. Sauer, *Jesus Sirach,* p. 224.

research has not yet undertaken this task to any extent since it seemed that the most important matters had been clarified by the understanding that the text is a set of behavioural rules. But interest was shown, and rightly so, in the similarity of the Sirach text to Greek symposia texts, especially with what Theognis had written on the subject.[8] The following will, accordingly, examine central concepts of the Hebrew texts, their use and semantic field in order to determine whether they do not point beyond the perception that this text is a code of conduct.

I shall show that Sirach opts not only for appropriate table manners, but that in describing behaviour at meals he provides an image of the wise person or, even, of a community of wise persons. In describing people's behaviour at meals, Sirach – quite in accordance with the contemporary symposium literature of antiquity – would actually *mirror his teaching,*[9] *or better: picture a kind of ideal society.* For the manner in which symposia were conducted represented an essential component of a group's and its members' identity and indicated which philosophical or religious identity they had made their own.[10]

From this perspective the symposium Jesus Sirach addresses in our text is also a 'decisive meal' since it functions, *ad intra*, to create and sustain groups and communities and, *ad extra,* to mark lines of differentiation. The decisive issue is not whether one behaves 'well', but whether one does or does not belong to this group of wise people.[11]

In ancient times, describing behaviour at meals was not only a specification of identity. Common meals were a very widespread custom.

8. Cf. Hans-Volker Kieweler, *Ben Sira zwischen Judentum und Hellenismus. Eine Auseinandersetzung mit Theophil Middendorp* (BEAT, 30; Frankfurt am Main: Lang, 1992), pp. 179–189; and his 'Benehmen bei Tisch', in Renate Egger-Wenzel and Ingrid Krammer (eds), *Der Einzelne und seine Gemeinschaft bei Ben Sira* (BZAW, 270; Berlin et al.: de Gruyter, 1998), pp. 191–215.

9. Cf., e.g., the description of the meal of the female therapeutics in Philo's *Vita Contemplativa* 64–89 and Ebner's article 'Mahl'.

10. Cf. Matthias Klinghardt and Thomas Staubli, 'Essen, gemeinsames', in Frank Crüsemann, Kristian Hungar, Clausia Janssen and Luise Schottroff (eds), *Sozialgeschichtliches Wörterbuch zur Bibel* (Gütersloh: Gütersloher Verlagshaus, 2009), pp. 116–22, p. 120. Ebner, 'Mahl', p. 67, emphasizes that Philo's move 'to describe the exceptional features of a group in terms of how their members behaved at banquets ... was by no means unusual at his time'. Cf. also the self-descriptions of clubs in Eva Ebel's discussion of meal customs, '... so that we may be able to dine undisturbed and cheerfully on feast-days'. 'Die gemeinsamen Mähler in griechisch-römischen Vereinen', in Judith Hartenstein, Silke Petersen and Angela Standhartinger (eds), *Eine gewöhnliche und harmlose Speise? Von den Entwicklungen frühchristlicher Abendmahlstraditionen* (Gütersloh: Gütersloher Verlagshaus, 2008), pp. 34–56.

11. I deliberately do not talk about a community of men because Sirach assumes that women participated in the symposia (cf. Sir. 9.7-8). This was customary in later times (cf. Angela Standhartinger, 'Frauen in Mahlgemeinschaften. Diskurs und Wirklichkeit einer antiken, frühjüdischen und frühchristlichen Praxis', *lectio difficilor* 2 (2005); Klinghardt and Staubli, 'Essen', p. 118.

Whenever possible, eating alone was avoided.[12] The formation of groups or the institutionalization of dining clubs was not a matter of leisure-time organization; clubs and (meal) communities helped find one's social identity. This was particularly important in times when once readily manageable social 'entities and options for identity-formation' of urban regions were dissolving in Hellenism. 'The search for new forms of community and for possibilities of social identity-formation betwixt and between *domus* (or οἶκος) and *provincia* (or πόλις) becomes plausible then and ought not to be discredited as pure pleasure-seeking.'[13]

For that reason, a text about the behaviour at a common meal may have had very much to do with identity and group-affiliation, particularly in relation to the much discussed and fragmented Jewish identity in Hellenistic times.

4.2. *The Text*

My study is based on the Hebrew text which has come down to us in relatively good condition. I draw on Vattioni's reconstruction[14] of the text, which was synoptically arranged by Beentjes.[15] The Greek translation follows the edition of Josef Ziegler which will be referred to only selectively due to the brevity and focus of the topic. It is not possible within the scope of this essay to discuss the variants of the text extensively.[16]

The passage of Ecclesiasticus 31.12–32.13 lies in the book's second half: 25.1–42.14.[17] In addition to paraeneses that counsel caution toward

12. Cf. Klinghardt, *Gemeinschaftsmahl*, p. 30.

13. Klinghardt, *Gemeinschaftsmahl*, p. 35.

14. Cf. Francesco Vattioni, *Ecclesiastico. Test ebraico con apparato critico e versioni greaca, Latina e siriaca* (Publicazioni del Seminario di Semitistica, 1; Napoli: Istituto orientale di Napoli, 1968).

15. Cf. Pancratius C. Beentjes, *The Book of Ben Sira in Hebrew. A Text Edition of All Extant Hebrew Manuscripts and a Synopsis of All Parallel Hebrew Ben Sira Texts* (VT.S, 68; Leiden: Brill, 1997).

16. The discussion of the text and the particular passage we are considering is found in, e.g., Rudolf Smend, *Die Weisheit des Jesus Sirach* (Berlin: G. Reimer, 1906), and in Patrick Skehan and Alexander A. Di Lella, *The Wisdom of Ben Sira* (Anchor Bible.A, 39; Garden City, New York: Doubleday, 1987).

17. There is no consensus among researchers about the structuring of the Book of Ben Sira, although it is agreed that ch. 24 is a cesura. But whether that chapter is to be ranged within the first or the second part of the book is a very different matter again. The various proposals may be found in Hans-Winfried Jüngling, 'Der Bauplan des Buches Jesus Sirach', in Hans-Winfried Jüngling, Josef Hainz and Reinhold Sebott (eds), *Den Armen eine Frohe Botschaft* (Festschrift F. Kamphaus; Frankfurt am Main: Knecht, 1997), pp. 89–105, p. 90; Skehan and Di Lella, *Wisdom*, p. 4; Sauer, *Jesus Sirach*, p. 494; Johannes Marböck, 'Structure and Redaction History in the Book of Ben Sira. Review and Prospects', in Johannes Marböck, *Weisheit und Frömmigkeit. Studien zur alttestamentlichen Literatur der Spätzeit* (ÖBS, 29; Frankfurt am Main: Peter Lang, 2006), pp. 31–45, pp. 31ff., 34–6; Jeremy Corley, 'Searching for Structure and Redaction in Ben

wealth and wealthy people (31.1-11) and their foods (29.24-28; 30.16-25), it contains admonitions and statements about health and children's education. The pericope which immediately precedes our text on behaviour at meals (31.1-11) notes that the wealthy lose weight over their financial worries and warns against wealth and greed. This paraenesis is then followed immediately by the text on how to behave at table. We will show later that the theme of this context, wealth and dealing with abundance, is further addressed in Sirach 31.12–32.13. The theme of the fear of God, a core aspect of Siracidic wisdom teaching, joins itself to our text at 32.14. But, as will be shown, this theme is already prefigured in 31.12–32.13. The critique of greed, the caution against wealth and the overabundance of goods appear to fit in with the fear of God and flow together in the passage about how to behave at meals in accordance with the teachings of wisdom.

The text can be demarcated content-wise not only because the indicated verses speak about the banquet. The Hebrew even provides a title in v. 11b: מוסר לחם ויין יחדו ('instruction (concerning) food and wine together').[18] The text then begins with the address: בני, 'my son', which in the Book of Sirach also signals the start of something new.[19]

The end of the text is marked by a reference to a prayer that concludes the symposium (31.13) and syntactically by the fourfold use at the beginning of the sentence of the same word, דורש, 'the seeker', in vv. 14 and 15.

4.3. *The Structure of the Text*

In terms of content, the text can be organized into two large segments: 31.12-31 and 32.1-13. The first is concerned with eating and drinking at a banquet (12-24: eating; 25-31: drinking wine); the second talks about speaking and singing during the symposium.[20]

A more detailed structure of the course of a banquet has recently been proposed by Zapff but he has his eye on present European customs instead

Sira. An Investigation of Beginnings and Endings', in Angelo Passaro and Guiseppe Bellia (eds), *The Wisdom of Ben Sira. Studies on Tradition, Redaction, and Theology* (Deuterocanonical and Cognate Literature Studies, 1, Berlin u. a.: der Gruyter, 2008), pp. 21–47; Johannes Marböck, *Jesus Sirach 1–23* (HThK.AT; Freiburg et al.: Herder, 2010), pp. 26–7. The division at 42.14 is signalled by the diptych of praise (42.15–44.33 and 50.1-25) that frames the third part of the book (42.15 to 50.25)

18.   Sauer's translation is 'instruction concerning bread and wine at the same time' (*Jesus Sirach*, p. 221), adding that G leaves out this title and that the Latin version transforms it into 'De continentia / Concerning abstinence'.

19.   This is not as apparent in the Book of Proverbs, nor is it an address in the Greek version. The term אם 'if' that follows indicates the description of a particular case (similarly in 31.21 in reference to delicacies).

20.   Sauer differs, *Jesus Sirach*, pp. 224–5. He sees it not as the course of a banquet as had been stated earlier but as the individual access to the meal.

of those of the ancient symposium,[21] the course of which is sketched only in rudimentary form in Sirach 31.12–32.13. The meal and the behaviour at it is dealt with in 31.12-24; reflections on the enjoyment of wine are found in vv. 25 to 31; the conduct of a conversation during the symposium is addressed in 32.1-16, and how one participates in it in vv. 7 to 10; finally, the conclusion of the symposium, the return home and the finishing praise are the subject of vv. 11 to 13.[22]

The themes of 'moderation and dealing with abundance', 'social relations' and 'wise teaching' are woven into those aspects. Schematically, the course of the meal looks as follows:

31.12-24: the meal	12-13: moderation and abundance	A
	14-18: social relations	B
	19-21: moderation and abundance	A
	22-24: *wise teaching* (22)[23]	C
31.25-31: enjoyment of wine	25: moderation and abundance	A
	26-30: *wisdom*[24]	C
	31: social relations	B
32.1-6: conduct of the conversation	*wisdom (speaking)*	C
32.7-10: participation in the conversation	*wisdom (speaking)*	C
32.11-13: conclusion, return home	11: moderation and abundance	A
	12-13: *wisdom*	C

The themes of 'moderation and abundance' and 'dealing with abundance', social relations and 'wisdom and wise teaching' determine the Siracidic statements about behaviour at banquets. Thus, eating and drinking are dealt with in terms of these aspects. And so, the issue is not simply eating itself or how it is organized, who prepares, distributes and finances it, when it takes place, who can take part in it,[25] and how to conduct oneself there. Rather, the banquet demonstrates how moderation and abundance, social relationships and attentiveness to wisdom are concretized. And, conversely, these aspects are supposed to be lived out at the banquet as the sort of

---

21.   The course of the banquet was relatively fixed. It consisted of a cleansing, a meal, a religious ceremony (libation), a session of wine drinking with a programme of teachings, riddles or performances, and a concluding religious ceremony, a common prayer (thanksgiving or eulogy). Cf., e.g., Klinghardt and Staubli, 'Essen', p. 119. Symposia can be held by private persons or as regular gatherings of groups and associations.

22.   Cf. Skehan and Di Lella, *Wisdom*, p. 388, subdivide the text into 31.12-21 (moderation in taking food), 31.22-31 (the blessing and misuse of wine), and 32.1-13 (behaviour at a banquet).

23.   The theme of 'wise teaching' is woven into a reflection on meal behaviour.

24.   The theme of wisdom is incorporated into the reflection on the enjoyment of wine.

25.   On these issues, cf. Ebel, '... damit wir ...' and her discussion of the clubs of Lavinium near Rome and the association of Iobakchen.

'bonhomie' and community that is being described here. How a meal is celebrated determines the group's identity. The following is to show how exactly this comes about.

4.4. *Dealing With (Super)Abundance*

The text begins with an admonition about how to deal with abundance on the table (31.12).

12 ἐπὶ τραπέζης μεγάλης ἐκάθισας μὴ ἀνοίξῃς ἐπ᾽ αὐτῆς φάρυγγά σου καὶ μὴ εἴπῃς πολλά γε τὰ ἐπ᾽ αὐτῆς	בני אם על שלחן גדול ישבתה אל תפתח עליו גרנך אל תאמר ספוק עליו

12 My son, if you are sitting at a grand table
do not lick your lips
and exclaim, 'What a spread!' (NEB)

The description of the table as גדול/μέγας, 'great', already signals that this is not an everyday family table. The translation of שלחן גדול/ τραπέζης μεγάλης, 'great table, the table of someone great', strongly shapes the understanding of the rest of the text. It is frequently translated as 'the table of someone great / of a great man'[26] and pictures the invitation from a rich person which fits in well with the topic of dealing with wealth and superabundance.

But it does not have to be an invitation to a private meal at a rich man's house,[27] for it may just as well be a symposium of a group whom one of its members has invited or who together organize the meal.[28] What is important

---

26. Cf. BM has גדול איש (Vattioni, *Ecclesiastico*, p. 165). Victor Ryssel, '"Die Sprüche Jesus", des Sohnes Sirachs', in Ernst Kautsch (ed.), *Die Apokryphen und Pseudepigraphen des Alten Testaments, I: Die Apokryphen des Alten Testaments* (Tübingen: Mohr, 1900), pp. 230–475 (387, note 12b), proposes – in accordance with Av V15 – 'at the table of someone great'. Cf. Kieweler, 'Benehmen', p. 197. The EÜ and the NSRV ('Do you sit at the table of the great?') go with the translation 'the table of some great person', but not the King James Apocrypha ('If thou sit at a beautiful table ...').

27. For example, Kieweler, 'Benehmen', p. 197; Sauer, *Jesus Sirach*, p. 221; Burghard Zapff, *Jesus Sirach* (NEB, 39; Würzburg: Echter, 2010), p. 198. Zapff seems to follow the interpretation of the EÜ and thinks that 'some great person' wants to show off his wealth in the abundance of his banquet.

28. If the table is understood to be 'the table of someone great' then it is more likely the invitation of a private man who chooses his guests as he sees fit and from social-political considerations. But a symposium would include all of a group's members: group-membership and not private invitation allows access to the meal. Klinghardt emphasizes that the distinction between a private and a community or group meal is a modern differentiation that does not describe the phenomenon of the meal itself but its organizational status, that is, who issues the invitation.

is that one does not have to take 'the table of some great person' to indicate where the meal took place for it can also be read as a great and overabundantly bedecked table.[29] Then it would refer to a rich, sumptuous banquet of a group or club. The text that follows would then not be about good behaviour at the table of a noble person but about wise behaviour in face of the overabundance at a banquet.

But this leaves open the question of whether the text has the behaviour of an entire corporation at its symposium in mind, that is to say, a group's self-understanding, or whether it is about rules of conduct for individuals at a symposium.

There is no reference in the Book of Sirach to a concrete corporation such as a group of wise persons meeting for common meals. Perhaps Sirach simply portrays the behaviour of an ideal group, a kind of utopia.[30]

The greatness of the table hardly refers to the size of a piece of furniture since only small tables were used at symposia. People took their places on recliners placed along the walls of a room in the banquet-house where apparently those present were served food and drink on small tables next to the recliners.[31]

The phrase 'grand / great table' expresses more about the abundance of the food and drink served. This is confirmed in v. 12b which warns against applauding this abundance: '... do not lick your lips and exclaim, "What a spread!"'.[32]

Most commentators see this as an admonition to individuals to show good upbringing and not let their speech, or as v. 13 puts it, their eyes, express greed or passion.[33] The question arises again whether good behaviour, in the sense of polite appearance, is at issue here or whether wise demeanour is being counselled that is at least restrained, if not critical, in face of the

Even when an individual issues the invitation, the meal still has a certain official significance. The structure of the *oikos* and its hosting of meals independently provided the clubs and their meals with a basic pattern. Klinghardt also describes the numerous intermediate forms between private and community meals. Guests also could bring the food to a 'private communal meal' when the one issuing the invitation was not able to raise the necessary finances him or herself (cf. *Gemeinschaftsmahl*, p. 31). But such a case is what Sirach precisely does not address. It is not possible to deduce even from our text of Sir. 31.12– 32.13 how the meal was organized and what social-historical background one has to assume behind the meal. The key issue is the behaviour at a common meal where abundant food is being served.

29.   *Gemeinschaftsmahl*, pp. 29–30. Text G also understands גדול/μέγας,, 'great', as an adjective to שלחן/τράπηζα, 'table'.

30.   Cf. Klinghardt and Staubli, 'Essen', p. 121, on ideal communities in texts on symposia.

31.   Cf. Klinghardt and Staubli, 'Essen', pp. 119–20.

32.   גרון: mouth, throat.

33.   Cf. Kieweler, 'Benehmen', p. 197; Skehan and Di Lella, *Wisdom*, p. 388, suggest that it might not be customary in the Orient for a guest to praise the meal because that was incumbent on the host.

overabundance of food. The stylistically artful construction of the verse about the 'greedy eye' and the theological argument following the admonition stands out in the overall flow of the passage and is most likely placed deliberately at the beginning:

Remember	זכור
it is a vice to have a greedy eye	כי רעה עין רעה
God hates the evil of the eye.[34]	רע עין שונא אל
There is no greater evil in creation than the eye	ורע ממנו לא ברא
that is why it must shed	כי זה מפני כל דבר תזוע עין
tears at every turn.	מפנים דמעה תדנע

The text expands the opening admonition with a very severe judgement of the eye which is understood here most often as a 'greedy' eye.[35] Hans-Volker Kieweler, in tandem with Georg Sauer, characterizes the text as being 'overloaded' on account of the length and complexity of its formulations.[36] But next to its length what stands out is that, apart from the concluding praise, this is the only place in this text that God is mentioned.[37] The admonition concerning greed and the behaviour in relation to the abundance on the table is theologically grounded: God hates this greedy eye and it goes against the order of creation. From the perspective of wisdom, nothing can speak against overabundance more clearly that to judge it as contradictory to God's creation and its order. Thus, Sirach does not necessarily overload the text; rather, with the diverse means of his art, with theology, and his unique style he puts considerable emphasis on his assertion, thereby giving it weight. Its placement at the beginning of the text may indicate that what is to follow should not be read without this theology.

We should make two observations about the first two verses. First, in reference to moderation and abundance, Sirach accentuates the theological right at the beginning: this is not only about behaviour. How the partakers receive food and drink (with their eyes) has something to do with God. Greed

---

34.   Difficult to translate clearly since רע does not correspond to the gender of עין and also is not an obvious construct.

35.   Cf. Georg Sauer, *Jesus Sirach (Ben Sira)* (JSHRZ III, 5; Gütersloh: Gütersloher Verlagshaus, 1981), p. 580; Kieweler, 'Benehmen', pp. 197–8; Otto Kaiser, *Weisheit für das Leben. Das Buch Jesus Sirach übersetzt und eingeleitet* (Stuttgart: Radius, 2005), has 'greedy eye'; Zapff, *Jesus Sirach*, p. 198. The connection with greed is quite justified when one considers the instances of the use of ὀφταλμός πονηρός in the Book of Sirach: Sir. 14.8, 9,10 or also in Prov. 23.6; 28.22 (Zapff, *Jesus Sirach*, p. 198). But this holds really only for those three texts. It is therefore appropriate not to restrict 'evil eye' only to greed.

36.   Cf. Sauer, *Jesus Sirach* (JSHRZ), p. 580.

37.   What stands out in particular is that God is named as creator and as one who hates. The evil eye is the most evil part of creation and of its order. To praise God as creator and to be attentive to the blessing contained in this praise is the highest form of wisdom according to the Book of Jesus Sirach (cf. Sir. 16.24–17.10; 39.12-35; 42.15–43.33).

for abundance goes against the order of creation. Second, that placement indicates that the text clearly understands its admonition theologically and that what follows goes beyond mere rules of conduct.

This theological reference is connected above all else with the theme of 'moderation and abundance', and its purpose is to show that the question of abundance at a symposium is not decisive for its theological meaning. Moderation, restraint in face of abundance, is what matters theologically, rather than abundance itself.

This becomes important for the next verses that take up the theme of 'dealing with over-abundance', 31.19-21. The concept of איש כסיל, 'glutton, someone lacking understanding' (NEB), in v. 20 introduces wisdom conceptuality and intimates that the matter of dealing with abundance has something to do with wisdom and not merely with bodily well-being or decent behaviour. The Hebrew text of v. 21, available only fragmentarily, is to be translated as follows:

and you will find rest
And even if delicacies cause you discomforts[38]
wait, wait,[39]
and you will find relief. (author's translation)

This 'causing discomforts', in Hebrew אנס, appears only once in the Hebrew Bible; it is in the equally late Hebrew Book of Esther, 1.8:

והשתיה כדת אין אנס
כי־כן יסד המלך על כל־רב ביתו
לעשות כרצון איש־ואיש

The NEB translation, slightly altered is: 'The law for drinking was that there should be no compulsion, for the king had laid it down that all the stewards of his palace should respect everyone's wishes.' In the JPS Tanakh translation it is rendered: 'And the rule for drinking was, "No restrictions!" For the king had given orders to every palace steward to comply with each man's wishes.'

How are we to understand the rule for drinking? The problems are indicated by some of the attempted translations: compulsion, 'Unbequemlichkeiten' (discomforts; so Schlachter), 'kein Zwang' (no coercion, Unity Translation), or 'without etiquette' (Bibel in gerechter Sprache). The following possibilities may be considered:

---

38. From אנס 'creating discomforts' (Kieweler, 'Benehmen', p. 202).

39. Etymological figure: an infinitive absolute and a masculine singular imperfect qal. (Kieweler, 'Benehmen', p. 202, but it is not clear to me where he detects the imperfect.)

1. Compulsion in relation to quantity: 'no restrictions' in Esther 1.8 means that there is no limit imposed on how much someone may drink (as the translations of the Book of Esther in the JPS Tanakh, the Unity Translation – EÜ – and Schachter suggest). That may also apply to Sirach.[40]
2. Compulsion in relation to quality: 'no restrictions' concerning *how* one eats and how one interacts with the stewards who are referred to in the next moment. This is how the translations of the *BigS*, JPS Tanakh, Unity Translation and Schachter may be read.
3. 'Compulsion' may mean that, for reasons of politeness or because of certain regulations, one must eat, although Esth. 1.8 states that that is precisely what one does not have to do (NEB, JPS Tanakh). In light of the second half of Esth. 1.8, it may also be that one ought not to compel one another in any way at all, be it to eat or to drink. At issue is the conduct of eating and drinking, even if food and drink are available in abundance, as was the case at Ahasveros' banquet in Esther 1. This corresponds to Sir. 31.21 when it talks of compelling someone to eat something.

But we can not determine this on the basis of the two references in Sir. 31.21 and Esth. 1.8 alone. The notion that one is forced to eat something only because of one's affiliation with a group, because of one's culture or according to a certain matter of etiquette, shows how powerful some orders and connections are which is possibly what Sirach critiques here.[41]

The term מטעמים (delicacies) in Sir. 31.21 suggests something similar. This concept is used only for the deceptive food that Jacob prepared for his father Isaac so that he might obtain the blessings of the first-born, albeit fraudulently.[42] In Prov. 23.3, 6, the word designates the tempting foods at the ruler's table:

> 3. Do not crave for dainties, for they are counterfeit food. 4. Do not toil to gain wealth; have the sense to desist. 5. You see it, then it is gone; it grows wings and flies away, like an eagle, heavenward. 6. Do not eat of a stingy man's food; do not crave for his dainties.

In both Genesis 27 and Proverbs 23,[43] these delicacies, these dainties, have something to do with deception. Both concepts signal that one should not

---

40.   Philo also offers a critique of the fact that at pagan meals one may eat *ad nauseam* and then encourage one another to keep eating (cf. Ebner, 'Mahl', p. 70). It is quite possible that Sirach too offers a critique here of the habits of the symposia of his time.

41.   The Greek translation G I corroborates this when it translates אנס as βιάζοομαι (coerce, dominate); cf., e.g., Deut. 22.25, 28 for sexual assault and, revealingly, also in Esth. 7.8; in 2 Macc. 14.41 it is used for violence. Somewhat less severe is the usage in Gen. 33.11; Judg. 19.7; 2 Sam. 13.25, 27; Sir. 4.26.

42.   Gen. 27.4, 7, 9, 14, 17, 31.

43.   The Greek concept ἔδεσμα is used only in Sirach and does not carry the aspect of deceit.

let oneself be led astray by fine foods and by abundance itself, ought not to compel one another, and ought not exploit wealth. Behind this lurks the question of power, the power that comes from wealth, good food and boasting, as does the question of the power to compel others to enjoy consumption. Perhaps this is a warning against the compulsion to subordinate oneself to the order of abundance, wealth and good foods. In vv. 19 and 20 as well as in vv. 23 to 25, moderation is held up against this. The purpose of moderation is to maintain one's own physical and psychological integrity.[44] Integrity orients itself by the teaching of wisdom, as v. 22 emphasizes.

Finally, we note that Sirach does not begin his text on banquet behaviour with mere etiquette, but with an admonition for moderation and critical behaviour in face of abundance at banquets and symposia. He warns against greed and excessive consumption because they go against the good order of God's creation and not because they are 'not proper'. He stresses this theological significance throughout the long and complex verse 13, and by asserting that God 'hates' an evil eye. He extends his critique of the enjoyment of abundance with a warning against submitting to coercion and a further warning against 'delicacies' and deceptive foods. In so doing, he obviously addresses what in Jewish circles must have been hot topics at the time, such as what is eaten and with whom. This clearly has something to do with one's integrity and political-social as well as religious identity. How one behaves while eating and drinking, what one enjoys and consumes, is not a matter of behaviour but of identity. The significance of identity and eating is made clearer not only in the texts of the Books of Daniel, Judith and Esther we have referred to; symposium texts themselves discuss questions of identity per se.[45]

It could be that Sirach, in his admonitions concerning how to deal with the superabundance of foods at symposia, criticizes pagan symposium customs prevalent at the time or that he calls for wise demeanour, in accord with creation, when attending such a banquet.[46] The admonitions in connection with social relations also show this understanding of the symposium.

44. Here Dan. 1.8 comes to mind where Daniel refuses the delicacies offered by the king. Here, as in Dan. 1.5, 13, 15, the concept of *patbag* from Old Persian is used; it occurs only at the places in Daniel cited. Even though the meaning of *patbag* has to be left open, it is plain that Daniel refuses the royal food because he does not want to ally himself with the king, that is, maintain his identity and integrity. (Cf. Luzia Sutter Rehmann, 'Abgelehnte Tischgemeinschaft in Tobit, Daniel, Ester, Judit. Ein Plädoyer für Differenzierung', *lectio difficilor*, 2008.) Sutter Rehmann also refers to Dan. 11.26-27 where the royal table is presented as a place of corruption. She also refers to Jdt. 12.1-2 or Add. Est. C 28 (14.7) where refusal of food is a matter of preserving identity.

45. Cf. Ebner, 'Mahl', pp. 67, 76–7; Klinghardt and Staubli, 'Essen', p. 120.

46. Philo states his critique of the boozing of pagan meals and their excessive luxury even more clearly, and deliberately juxtaposes them with the ascetic meals of the Therapeutics, *De Vita Contemplativa*, 40 (cf. Ebner, 'Mahl', p. 70 on this).

4.5. *Social Relations*

In the symposium text of Ecclesiasticus, the theme of social relations is at the very core. It begins already in 31.14 where a 'he' is introduced (in the form of the verb in 14a: יביט; and in the suffix of עם in 14b).[47] The concept רע (neighbour) and the threefold 'not to be despised' at the end of 16ab, 17a (introduced each time by פן) make this 'he' explicit.

The way the theme of love of neighbour is raised in 31.15 is reminiscent of Lev. 19.18 as well as of how it is used in Sir. 7.21 or Tob. 4.15 and Mt. 7.12: treat the other the way you wish to be treated yourself. Several times, Sir. 31.15 calls for empathy for the other, the awareness that the other is like oneself and therefore has the same needs and rights.

> Remember: your neighbour is like you (your life)
> (know your evil like yourself)
> and in whatever you hate, act with understanding!
> Know that your neighbour is like you!

This shows clearly that the symposium community is firmly committed to the *equality* of its participants and that power differences are not welcomed.[48] This is a strong assertion given that in pagan symposia rigorous hierarchy prevailed in reference to people's functions and offices which affected the size of meal-portions and where people were seated.[49] That may be why v. 16 continues deliberately with its reference to an איש נבחר, 'elected man', who, perhaps even only temporarily, exercises a certain function. But he must not be greedy and gluttonous, lest he lose social esteem. Despite all the honours bestowed on him, he is subject to the same rules of conduct as all other participants, namely, to be as attentive to the needs of others as he is to his own. This is the context where the threefold 'not to be despised' applies. The rules of social behaviour focus on mutual esteem and respect. This is achieved through moderate and considerate eating. What is striking is that right here, in v. 17, a core concept of Siracidic wisdom teaching emerges, namely, education, rule or formation: מוסר. This signals that social behaviour is to be understood within the framework of *wisdom* as

---

47. Since the subject in 14a is uncertain, Skehan and Di Lella have reversed verses 14 and 15 (cf. *Wisdom*, p. 386). That makes רע (neighbour) in 15a the logical subject of 14a.

48. On the equality of all participants, cf. Klinghardt and Staubli, 'Essen', p. 118, and on their differences, p. 121. Ebel refers to size of meal-portions, fixed seating arrangements and titles as evidence for differentiation among members of Graeco-Roman clubs, pp. 47–8.

49. Cf. Ebel, '... damit wir ungestört ...', p. 47: 'The prohibition of changing seats implies a fixed seating order at the gatherings of the Iobakchen.' This is similarly valid for another club Ebel has studied, where Diana and Antonius were revered (cf. '... damit wir ungestört ...', p. 47, note 41).

order rather than within a pagan order. The respect of those participating in the banquet orientates itself according to wisdom and wise conduct and not according to other social honours.

Once again, social relations are taken up in 31.31, the conclusion about eating and drinking at the symposium:

At a banquet do not rebuke your fellow guest	במשתה היין... אל ןתחרף] רע]ואל
Or make him feel small while he is enjoying himself.	דבר חרפה אל]תאמר לו
This is no time to take up a quarrel with him. (NEB)	ואל תנ]ן אתו לעיני בני אדם

Perhaps this refers to quarrels that occurred at symposia, especially when participants had already been heavily at their cups and felt uninhibited (cf. vv. 29-30).[50] Such behaviour would once again go against the order of creation which is presented in vv. 27-28 in the form of a 'nutritional order'.

Summing up, we note that Sirach puts conviviality during the meal, and just and needs-oriented distribution of food, at the centre. The honour of the individuals depends on their social behaviour, as the next section makes even clearer. Even though Sirach is familiar with the custom of electing men at the banquet and does not reject it (31.16; 32.1-2), the measure of behaviour is that others are given as much as one would like to have oneself. This is ultimately where the equality of all at the banquet becomes manifest. This, too, may be seen as a critique of pagan banquets where the degree of personal honour determined the portioning of food at the banquet itself and, correspondingly, the portion to be taken home.[51] In Hellenistic times, the ideal of the equality of all at a banquet is indeed no idiosyncratic idea of Sirach's. The Epicureans also valued table companionship and mutual friendship highly.[52] Sirach deals here with topics that are quite typical

50. Cf. Skehan and Di Lella, *Wisdom*, pp. 390–1; Ebel, '... damit wir ungestört ...', p. 49; Kieweler, 'Benehmen', p. 207.

51. Cf. Ebel, '... damit wir ungestört ...', pp. 41–2.

52. Cf. Karin Lehmeier, 'Verächtliche Mähler. Epikureische Gemeinschaftsmähler und Formen des Abendmahls im Vergleich', in Judith Hartenstein and Angela Standhartinger (eds), *Eine gewöhnliche und harmlose Speise? Von den Entwicklungen frühchristlicher Abendmahlstraditionen* (Gütersloh: Gütersloher Verlagshaus, 2008), pp. 57–73 (62). But this does not imply that Sirach took this idea from Epicurean writings. For one, there are numerous correspondences with the writings of Theognis on the symposium (cf. Kieweler, *Ben Sira*, pp. 186–7 and passim; Kieweler, 'Benehmen'). Second, dependence on Greek writings does not signify directly literal or intellectual dependency; rather, that Greek literature also simply influenced the thinking of Jewish savants in Hellenistic times. Kaiser speaks in this connection about a 'condition humaine' and an 'intellectual climate' in which the texts originated. (Cf. Otto Kaiser, 'Athen und Jerusalem. Die Begegnung des spätbiblischen Judentums mit dem grieschichen Geist, ihre Voraussetzungen und ihre Folgen', in Markus Witte and Stefan Alkier (eds), *Die Griechen und der Vordere Orient. Beiträge zum Kultur- und Religionskontakt zwischen Griechenland und dem Vorderen Orient im 1. Jahrtausend v. Cr.* (OBO, 191; Fribourg: Universitätsverlag et al., 2003, pp. 87–120 (112).)

in ancient literature on the symposium: 'All questions concerning social prestige (honour, places of honour, different apportioning of food, quarrel/ harmony among banquet-participants, love, etc.) play an important role here.'[53] Sirach's sympotic teaching does not emphasize hierarchy but the equality of the banquet participants and the consideration they show one another. And so, as a teaching about symposia, this is indeed not a set of behavioural rules but more likely an exploration of the identity of the community of the wise. This leads us to the third topic addressed in Sir. 31.12–32.13: wisdom.

4.6. *Wisdom*

'Banquets were the most important *Sitz im Leben* for the transmission of wisdom.'[54]

The theme of wisdom clearly marks verses 25 to 30, addressed specifically to drinking wine, as well as the passage of 32.1-13.[55] Exegetical literature regards the latter passage as a praise of wine when consumed properly.[56] Wine is said to be one of the oldest drinks of humankind; singing its praises definitely fits in with biblical tradition.[57] If one understands the text as an admonition concerning proper behaviour at banquets, then this passage is at variance with such assertions. For in vv. 26-30, the admonitions, that is, the address in the second person singular, are completely absent. They return only in v. 31 where the theme of social relations is once again taken up.

This means that there are no direct behavioural admonitions given in the passage about wine; there is a *reflection* instead and that is what concepts of wisdom express. In every instance, these concepts designate wise behaviour or what wisdom values and are used mostly or exclusively

---

53. Klinghardt, *Gemeinschaftsmahl*, p. 129.

54. Klinghardt and Staubli, 'Essen', p. 118.

55. The admonitions concerning speaking and singing also touch upon the theme of social relations in 32.3-9. But specifically appropriate speaking at the right age, at the right time and in quantities others can tolerate are central concerns of wisdom teaching and especially of Siracidic reflections and admonitions.

56. Cf., e.g., Johannes B. Bauer, '"Kein Leben ohne Wein" (Jesus Sirach 31.27). Das Urteil der Hl. Schrift', *BiLi* 23 (1955–6), pp. 55–9; Kaiser, *Weisheit*, p. 176, who refers to Ps. 104.15 and Qoh. 9.7. Kieweler 'Benehmen', pp. 204–5 and Zapff, *Jesus Sirach*, p. 202, emphasize that wine is understood there from the outset as a gift of creation which, in comparison to the other joyous praises of wine, such as in Judg. 9.13; Ps. 104.15; Qoh. 10.19; Prov. 3.16-17, in their judgement is a new idea of the Book of Ben Sira.

57. Bauer in particular stresses this point (cf. 'Leben').

in wisdom texts. What we have here is a certain 'technical jargon'.[58] In addition, no other specific concepts or phrases are used in the passages where these wisdom terms occur. The focus on the theme of wisdom shows this very clearly.

The thematization of wisdom begins in 31.17 with the 'teaching' or 'upbringing', מוסר, referred to earlier, and is not taken up again until 31.20 in the reference to איש כסיל, 'someone without understanding'.[59]

There also is wisdom terminology in 31.22, a verse that lies between the passages on 'moderation and abundance' and on 'social relations'. The demand to listen,[60] not to be contemptuous,[61] or not to ridicule,[62] make this very clear as does the concept of מוסר.

Verse 27 which, like v. 28, talks in rapturous tones about wine,[63] asks מה חיים חסר היין, 'What is life to a man deprived of wine?' (NEB). Even though the question מה חיים, 'What is life?', is not found in this formulation in the Hebrew Bible, yet it is very close to what Qoheleth asks (6.12a): כי מי־יודע מה־טוב לאד, 'Who knows what is best for someone during life?' The Book of Qoheleth (10.19) also knows the joy of wine (שמחה and יין):

The table has its pleasures
And wine makes a cheerful life;
And money is behind it all. (NEB)

Prov. 21.17 is of a different mind:

Love pleasure and you will beg your bread;
Someone who loves wine and oil will never grow rich. (NEB, altered)

The combination of שמחה, 'gladness', and גיל, 'joy', as used in v. 27, appears also in a few Psalms (43.4; 45.16; 51.15), whereas the combination of ששון, 'joy', and שמחה, 'gladness', in v. 28, is more part of the context

---

58.   For example, מוסר (upbringing) in 31.17, 22, איש כסיל (someone without understanding) in 31.20, 30, שמע (to listen), לעג (to mock).

59.   This concept also brings the first part about wisdom in 31.30 to a conclusion again.

60.   Cf. Kaiser, *Weisheit*, p. 176, where he refers to the demand in Sir. 6.23, 'Listen, my son, do not reject my advice.' Kieweler, 'Benehmen', p. 203, speaks of the 'learned' who do accept the advice; Zapff, *Jesus Sirach*, p. 200, maintains that 'to listen' is an ideal of formation in wisdom which also includes an inner listening, an appropriation (Prov. 23.22).

61.   בוז which occurs only in Gen. 22.21; 38.23; 2 Kings 19.21; 1 Chron. 5.14; Isa. 37.22; Jer. 25.23; Zech. 4.10, and 18 more times only in wisdom texts.

62.   לעג cf. 2 Kings 19.21; 2 Chron. 30.10; Neh. 2.19; 3.33; Isa. 28.11; 33.19; 37.22; Jer. 20.7; Ezek. 23.32; 36.4; Hos. 7.16, and 16 more times only in wisdom texts.

63.   שמחה (gladness) in 27b, 28a; גיל (joy) in 27c; and ששון (joy) in 28a.

of political jubilation after liberation (Est. 8.16; Isa. 22.13; 51.3; Jer. 7.34; 15.16).[64]

Verse 29 describes a counter-image to the joy of wine which is unique in its choice of words. Nowhere else in the Hebrew Bible are the consequences of too much wine addressed with the term יין, 'wine'. Numerous verses in the Bible do indeed speak of suffering from a hangover (Prov. 20.1; 23.29-35; 31.4-5; Amos 6.6; Hos. 7.5; Isa. 5.11-12; 28.1).[65] Wise behaviour is very prominent in the passage of 31.1-13.[66] Much space is devoted here to speaking at the right time and at appropriate length.[67] The reflection on speaking according to wisdom teaching is given much space in the Book of Sirach[68] as well as in wisdom literature.[69] This again shows that it is not simply conduct but wise behaviour that is at issue. Moreover, v. 2 deals with מוסר, 'formation', and שכל, 'insight'. Next to the discussion of the subject set for the banquet, the transmission of and reflection on teaching(s) is characteristic of the learned conversation at a symposium: 'Thus, the symposia are the second important place, next to the institution of public lectures, where scholarly exploration of problems took place.'[70] Sirach, too, presents his own teaching in describing meal behaviour.

While the petrological metaphoric of vv. 6-7 is difficult to comprehend and seems simply to name what is beautiful, these two verses, as well as vv. 8-9, talk about 'pleasant words' (נאים דברים) and young people's speaking. Wisdom texts not infrequently admonish young people to restrain themselves in the circle of elders (Sir. 7.14; 13.9-13; Job 29.7-9; but also Lev. 19.32).[71] Sirach's presentation of his sympotic teaching concerning

---

64.   But also in Ps. 51.15. In Est. 8.16-17, we read:

ליהודים היתה אורה ושמחה וששן ויקר:
ובכל־מדינה ומדינה ובכל־עיר ועיר מקום אשר דבר־המלך ודתו מגיע
שמחה וששן ליהודים משתה ויום טוב ורבים מעמי הארץ מתיהדים
כי־נפל פחד־היהודים עליהם

'For the Jews there was light, gladness, joy and honour. In every province and in every city, wherever the king's command and degree arrived, there was joy and gladness among the Jews, with feasting and holiday-making. Of the country's population many became Jews, since now the Jews were feared.'

65.   Cf. Kaiser, *Weisheit*, p. 176. What Theognis has to say about this matter is often cited in the literature to this place in Sirach. Theognis: 211–12, 509ff., 973–6 (cf. Kieweler, *Ben Sira*, p. 187; Kaiser, *Weisheit*, p. 176; Zapff, *Jesus Sirach*, p. 202).

66.   In what follows, I make less reference to those verses cited in secondary literature for comparison which only show that there was singing and golden bowls at carousals.

67.   The choice of words for speaking: מלל in v. 3 only in wisdom texts except in Gen. 21.7. שפך שיח (pouring out speech) in v. 4 is Psalm-language and is used only in Pss. 102.1; 142.3.

68.   For example, Sir. 5.9–6.4, 5; 19.6-7; 20.7,18; 22.27,15; 25.8, 20; 26.4; 27.13; 37.18.

69.   For example, Prov. 15.23; 25.11; 30.32.

70.   Klinghardt, *Gemeinschaftsmahl*, p. 128.

71.   Cf. Norbert Peters, *Das Buch Jesus Sirach oder Ecclesiasticus* (EHAT, 25 Münster 1913), p. 128, on the wisdom references.

wise speaking completely matches the way literature on symposia does it in transmitting its teaching by describing the banquet itself. The sympotic context is apparent also in the conduct of the carousal addressed in 32.1-2. Every symposium has called or elected someone to preside over it (symposiarch). Being a wise person, he (or she) is to be guided by the participants' needs.

A final reminder: in comparison to extra-biblical symposium texts, it is striking that the exhortation to give God praise at the end is not a common prayer of thanksgiving (*eucharistia, eulogia*)[72] as was customary at the conclusion of a symposium, but a prayer of an individual, possibly offered at home, quite general in nature and not in reference to the symposium.[73]

It is an exhortation to praise God for 'watering' the one offering praise. At least the Greek text[74] alludes to the wisdom metaphoric which claims that wisdom 'waters' those who seek her. Then, the praise offered may possibly seek to affirm that, having attended the banquet, one has received the nourishment of wisdom during the symposium and praises God for this.[75]

Sir. 1.16
Those who fear the Lord have their fill of wisdom;
she gives them deep draughts of wine. (NEB)

Sir. 24.31
I said 'I will water my garden,
drenching its flower-beds',
and at one my canal became a river
and my river a sea. (NEB)

Sir. 32.13
And one thing more: give praise to your Maker,
who has filled your cup with blessings. (NEB)

It is noteworthy that it is only in this verse, and there only cautiously, that wisdom's nourishing qualities are alluded to.[76] The banquet participants' praxis, wise and in accord with creation, and made manifest in their behaviour at table, is given prominence.

72.   Cf. Klinghardt, *Gemeinschaftsmahl*, p. 101ff.
73.   Similarly Peters, *Buch*, p. 266.
74.   The Hebrew word is difficult to translate, possibly מור, 'to exchange, to exchange (in the sense of giving)'.
75.   What is merely alluded to in Sirach is very explicit in Philo. In the Therapeutics' symposium the consumption of nourishment for the body is minimal so that it does not detract from the really essential nourishment of wisdom (cf. Ebner, 'Mahl', p. 74).
76.   Cf., e.g., Sir. 1.16-20; 16: she gives them deep draughts of her wine; 17: she stocks her storehouses with her produce; Sir. 6.19: soon you will be eating her crops (H); Sir. 15.3: for food she will give him the bread of understanding and for drink the water of knowledge; Sir. 24.17: my blossoms were a harvest of wealth and honour; Sir. 24.21: Whoever feeds on me will be hungry for more, and whoever drinks from me will thirst for more.

This restraint before wisdom as the giver of nourishment may be due to the fact that the description of eating and drinking behaviour is actually a *self*-reflection and not a reflection on wisdom and her gifts.[77] This corresponds to the context of the symposium text referred to at the beginning: it is within the framework of paraeneses about exercising caution toward wealth and wealthy people (31.1-11, directly preceding our text) and their food (29.24-28; 30.16-25), expanded by warnings and statements about health. Particularly caution toward wealth and the false enticement and power that reside in it is also found in statements that assert the absolute equality of participants at symposia (31.15-18, 23, 31) as well as where Sirach begins with warnings against praising abundance and shows his disapproval of compelling others to indulge in delicacies. The behaviour at symposia mirrors wise behaviour inasmuch as the praxis of the wise there is not determined by overabundance and the choice of food but by the values of wisdom.

4.7. *Summary: The Symposium of the Wise*

Sirach's description of wise conduct at banquets and symposia corresponds to the self-portrayal of groups and clubs contained in the symposia literature of antiquity. Behind the description of rules governing eating and drinking are references to a group's teachings and its self-understanding. In connection with Sir. 31.12–32.13, this can be represented as follows.

1. The abundance of the meal is not important (31.12-13). Praising overabundance of food highly – indeed, dignifying it at all – is rejected by Sirach. He supports this with an emphatic theological assertion which stamps greed as something against God's order of creation. What cannot be concluded from this warning is whether the author prefers the wise to eat modest meals. Wealth simply must not occupy a central place.
2. The brief reference to compulsion during a meal (31.21) makes one prick up one's ears: Sirach notes that sometimes one is compelled to indulge in delicacies. What are these delicacies? Are we to conclude that they are unclean foods or something exotic? The interpretations of this text refer only to the idea of abundance and point out that Sirach was familiar with the praxis of vomiting.
3. Eating also manifests the relation to others present at the banquet. The text deals quite extensively with social relations (31.14-19, 23, 24, 31; 32.1-12). It is essential to be aware of and acknowledge the other and not to put oneself first (the others are like you (31.15), so be like one of them

---

77.   This differs from the Therapeutics' meal in Philo; cf. Ebner, 'Mahl'.

(32.1)) and conduct yourself in a manner that allows others to accept you. Obviously, community plays an important role and mutual acceptance and respect are very prominent notions. Thus, it is not a matter of avoiding embarrassments of behaviour but instead of lusting after abundance to be attentive to the rights and the equality of others.

4. Finally, in the custom of group banquets, wisdom becomes visible. But it is not Lady Wisdom, who nourishes those who seek her, that is made visible; the wisdom seen is related to the wise behaviour of an egalitarian community whose wealth at the banquet is not the abundance of things but just relationships and the orientation to what the teacher teaches (31.22).

The symposium text of the Book of Sirach may be seen as a sketch of an ideal society that practices what it teaches in common meals, directs itself according to the order of creation, and seeks to live an order of justice among people of equal rank. Just social relations, as they are exemplified in the praxis of the symposium, bestow honour and not designated seats of honour. It could be that the author delineates his perception of the symposium over against a contemporary luxurious and unjust culture of symposia. But that has to remain hypothetical because he makes no reference to such a culture.

Translated by Martin Rumscheidt

Chapter 5

'AND ALL ATE AND WERE FILLED' (MARK 6.42 PAR.): THE FEEDING NARRATIVES IN THE CONTEXT OF HELLENISTIC-ROMAN BANQUET CULTURE

Angela Standhartinger

One might readily conclude from studying the literature on the feeding narratives that the lines of discussions were drawn long ago. There remains some controversy still as to whether the oldest version is to be found in or behind Mk 6.32-44, Mk 8.1-10 and/or Jn 6.1-15 and whether the narrative contained allusions to the last supper or not.[1] But the narrative is unanimously classified as a gift-miracle with a close tradition-historical relation to Elisha's feeding of one hundred men (2 Kgs 4.42-44) and to the feeding in the wilderness with the manna.[2] In addition, some scholars find

---

1.   That Mk 8.1-10 is the oldest version is maintained, e.g., by Sanae Masuda, 'The Good News of the Miracle of Bread. The Tradition and its Markan Redaction', *NTS* 28 (1982), pp. 191–219. Ludgar Schenke sees the oldest version in Mk 6, *Die wunderbare Brotvermehrung. Die neutestamentlichen Erzählungen und ihre Bedeutung* (Würzburg: Echter Verlag, 1983). An allusion to the last supper is to be found already in the pre-Markan version of the narrative, according to Bas van Iersel, 'Die wunderbare Speisung und das Abendmahl in der synoptischen Tradition (Mk vi 35-44par., viii 1-10par)', *NT* 7 (1964), pp. 167–94, and Paul Achtemeier, 'The Origin and Function of the Pre-Marcan Miracle Catenae', *JBL* 91 (1972), pp. 198–221. A different interpretation is that of G. H. Boobyer, 'The Eucharistic Interpretation of the Miracles of the Loaves in St. Mark's Gospel', *JTS* 3 (1952), pp. 161–71. The answer to this question also depends on the age of a Jewish pre-meal blessing which is also an issue of active discussion. See note 71 below.

2.   Cf. Exod. 16; Num. 11; Ps. 78 and elsewhere. A literary relation of the feeding narrative with 2 Kgs 4.42-44 was proposed by Alkuin Heising, *Die Botschaft der Brotvermehrung. Zur Geschichte und Bedeutung eines Christusbekenntnisses im Neuen Testament* (SBS 15, Stuttgart: Kohlhammer Verlag, 1996), pp. 17–20; Schenke, *Brotvermehrung*, pp. 94–5; and Ulrich Körtner, 'Das Fischmotif im *Speisungswunder*', *ZNW* 75 (1984), pp. 24–35, 26 n. 10. The following structural relationships can be seen: on each occasion many people are fed with few loaves of bread and condiments, and each time the man of God gives the order. In 2 Kgs 4.43 the servant (ὁ λειτουργός) expresses his doubts in his answer that the food will be enough for 100 people which makes many interpreters think of Mk 6.37-38 (8.4). Observe, however, that the Hebrew text adds in 4.44 'So he set it before them', which leaves open who the subject actually is. The result noted at the end, 'they ate, and had some left', corresponds to the word of God spoken by

the tradition of an eschatological meal 'when there will be abundant food for the righteous ones'.[3] In any case, Jesus' feeding the multitude in an uninhabited place surpasses anything that had occurred before.[4]

In the following, I would like to introduce into the discussion a neglected socio-cultural context of the feeding narratives.[5] In Hellenistic-Roman antiquity, Jesus is certainly not the only one who feeds four to five thousand people all at the same time. Other, more eminent, leaders could do so as well. After his victory over Darius, Alexander the Great is said to have invited his friends, officers and emissaries of the Greek cities to a banquet where he seated them at 100 dining couches in a tent.[6] He was trumped by Ptolemy Philadelphus who put even 130 κλίναι (dining couches) into a tent;[7] by Antiochus Epiphanes, who at times used 1,000 and sometimes 1,500 κλίναι during a banquet; and, finally, by Crassus who, after sacrificing to Hercules, treated 10,000 people to a meal, all at the same time.[8] Caesar accomplished what had never been done before: after his triumph over Gaul, Egypt, Pontus

the prophet: Φάγονται καὶ καταλείψουσιν. However, the word for word correspondences of 2 Kgs 4.42-44 and Mk 6.32-44 par. consist exclusively in imperative forms of δίδωμι and ἐσθίω. The sacrificial context is missing from Mark 6 par. as well as the motif of a divine word and its confirmation. Hence the critique of Michael Labahn, *Offenbarung in Zeichen und Wort* (WUNT II/17, Tübingen: Mohr, 2000), pp. 163–4; Adela Y. Collins, *Mark. A Commentary* (Minneapolis: Fortress Press, 2007), p. 320.

   3.   Cf. Isa. 25.6; *1 Enoch* 10.18-19; *2 Baruch* 29.5-6; *Sibyllinae* 3.744-750; *1QSa* 2.11-21. That is why some exegetes interpret the feeding narratives as an eschatological meal. Cf. Schenke, *Brotvermehrung,* pp. 90–117; Bernd Kollmann, *Ursprung und Gestalten der frühchristlichen Mahlfeier* (Göttingen: Vandenhoeck & Ruprecht, 1990), pp. 197–205; Collins, *Mark*, pp. 223–6; Peter-Ben Smit, *Fellowship and Food in the Kingdom. Eschatological Meals and Scenes of Utopian Abundance in the New Testament* (WUNT II/234, Tübingen: Mohr, 2008), pp. 53–82, 338–91. But *1 Enoch* 10.18-19, *2 Baruch* 29.5-6, and *Sibyllinae* 3.744-750 (cf. Acts 22.1-2) do not contain scenes of meals; they refer to the paradisical abundance of food that nature gives to the just in the end times. Isa 25.6-8 recounts God's eschatological preparation of wine and oil for the festive banquet with the nations, whereas 1QSa 2.11-21 describes the order of a meal with the Messiah. If there is a parallel at all, it would be with the latter text more than the others, even though it emphasizes the orderly behaviour of the participants and not the abundance of food.

   4.   Mk 6.42; Mt. 14.20; Lk. 9.17; Mk 8.8; Mt. 15.17.

   5.   Cf. Richard I. Pervo, 'Panta Kiona: The Feeding Stories in the Light of Economic Data and Social Practice', in Lukas Bormann et al. (eds), *Religious Propaganda and Missionary Competition in the New Testament World* (Leiden: Brill, 1994), pp. 163–94. In his *Offenbarung*, pp. 150–1, Labahn responds critically, above all because in his view Pervo fails to balance out the beneficial deeds and does not attend to the social differences between those who are eating. Labahn seeks to integrate the event into the life of Jesus, the oldest narration of which he sees in *Acts John* 93. This domestic multiplication of bread is reminiscent of the miraculous discovery of bread in the oven by the wife of Rabbi Hanina ben Dosa (bTa'anit 24a-25b), the showbread that never runs out (bYoma 39a), or the miraculous find of bread by the hermit Elija (Paladius, *Historia Lausiaca*, 51).

   6.   Diodorus Siculus, 17.16.4.

   7.   Athenaeus, *Deipnosophistae,* 5.25 (196b).

   8.   Athenaeus, *Deipnosophistae,* 5.22 (195d); Polybius, 30.26; Plutarch, *Crassus,* 12.2.

and Africa, he fed the citizens of Rome (τὸν δῆμον), again all at the same time, on 22,000 triklina (dining couches for three people) which corresponds to just under 200,000 guests.[9] Not only Hellenistic kings and Roman emperors manifested their benevolence through such feedings; wealthy citizens in the provinces emulated them and sponsored a multiplicity of feedings in and for their cities.[10]

The great spread of public mass-feedings, of 'public' or 'civic banquets', put Jesus' feeding of the four to five thousand into a specific context. To get an idea of the conceptions, expectations and experiences associated with these mass-feedings, we will briefly examine this phenomenon in the first century CE. Then, based on Mk 6.32-44, I want to point out connections between the New Testament feeding narratives and the public or civic banquets of the masses. Finally, I will explore what is unique to the NT mass feedings.

5.1. *Public feedings in Hellenistic-Roman Antiquity*

Male and female benefactors of Hellenistic and Roman (provincial) cities sponsored public feedings rather frequently.[11] We know this primarily from inscriptions produced by the cities' political authorities in gratitude for the benefit received. One example is the inscription honouring Cleanax of Cyme in Asia Minor (c. 2 BCE–5 CE) which I excerpt here:[12]

9.　　Plutarch, *Julius Caesar*, 55.4.
10.　　Cf. Pauline Schmitt Pantel, *La cit au banquet. Histoire des repas publics dans les cités grecques* (Rome: de Boccard, 1992) for mass-feedings in the Greek world. For the Latin context, cf. John F. Donahue, *The Roman Community at Table during the Principate* (Ann Arbor: University of Michigan Press, 2004); Konrad Vössing, *Mensa Regia. Das Bankett beim hellenistischen König und beim römischen Kaiser* (Beiträge zur Altertumskunde 193, München, Leipzig: Saur, 2004). On the emulation in the provinces of the emperors' banquets, cf. John H. D'Arms, 'P. Lucilius Gamala's feasts for the Ostians and their Roman Models', *Journal of Roman Archeology* 13 (2000): 192–200; Eftychia Stavrianopoulou, 'Die Bewirtung des Volkes: Öffentliche Speisungen in der römischen Kaiserzeit', in Olivier Hekster et al. (eds), *Ritual Dynamics and Religious Change in the Roman Empire* (Impact of Empire 9; Leiden: Brill, 2009), pp. 159–83, 181–2.
11.　　Cf. Arjan Zuiderhoek, *The Politics of Munificence in the Roman Empire* (Cambridge: Cambridge University Press, 2009), pp. 76–7.
12.　　SEG 32:1443. First publication by Ren Hodot, 'Déret de Kym en L'honneur du Prytane Kléanax', *The Getty Museum Journal* 10 (1982): 165–80; cf. R. Merkelbauch, 'Ehrenbeschluss der Kymäer für den Prytanis Kleanax', *Epigraphia Anatolica* 1 (1983): 33–7. For the following, cf. also Pauline Schmitt Pantel, 'Public Feast in the Hellenistic Greek City: Forms and Meanings', in *Conventional Values of the Hellenistic Greeks* (Aarhus: Aarhus University Press, 1997), pp. 29–47. Donahue has gathered the feeding-inscriptions of the Latin-speaking West in his *Roman Community*, pp. 163–239.

(1-3) On the motion of the generals, recorded by the Three chosen by lot, viz.: Asklapon son of Dionysos, Hegesandros son of Herakleidas, Athenagoras son of Dionysus, and the secretary to the Assembly, Heraeus son of Antipater:

(4-21) Whereas Cleannax son of Serapion, but issue of Philodamus, *prutanis*, possessed both of noble birth through his ancestors on either side and of unsurpassably ambitious benevolence towards the city of his fathers, has all through his life been a generous benefactor to the city, permitting himself no momentary neglect of his solicitude for the people, in act and utterance true counsellor to the city; for which reasons [not only] does the people now pay tribute to him in respect of the zealous execution of his present office of prutanis, its gratitude is expressed also in numerous official minutes and through earlier decrees: for example his contribution as priest of Dionysus Pandamos to the associated mysteries instituted by the city; his disbursements for the quadrennial celebration of the mysteries, where the scale of his outlay pays witness both to his determination to put on a fitting spectacle and to his piety, as the very first to discharge the office; and [when] he caused bills to be posted inviting the citizens of Cyme, the Italian residents, the resident and non-resident foreigners to a public feast in the precincts of Dionysus Pandamos, and regaled them sumptuously – a feast he provides each year; and (when) he gave a feast to the whole population on the occasion of the marriage of his daughter

(30-45) first, as prutanis now, he has performed the traditional sacrifices to the gods for New Year's Day; served a glukismos to everyone in the city; provided lavish games; performed the traditional New Year's Day ceremonies and sacrifices; entertained many of the citizens and the Italians over several days in the prytaneum; second he has performed the traditional offerings to the dead on the appointed day, and distributed milk gruel to all persons, free and slave, in the city; and on the Day of the Lark on his own initiative invited the citizens, Italians, resident and non-resident foreigners by public proclamation to lunch in the prytaneum; and provided Bounty as generously as other prutaneis have provided it; and paid for the processions on Laurel Day, and provided the priests, the victors in the games, the magistrates and many of the citizens with lunch; and at the Caesarea of the province of Asia, he provided the sacrifices and festivities, as he had promised, sacrificing oxen to the emperor Caesar Augustus and his children and the other gods – from which sacrifice he entertained the Greeks, the Italians and the resident and non-resident foreigners lavishly in the agora, announcing the invitation by handbills, providing ... in abundance; and he performed other rites ...

(46-52) Wherefore the people and council resolved: that he be presented with a crown after the sacrifice [at the festival of Dionysus] before the altar of Zeus ...[13]

Magistrate Cleanax had earned the respect of his city through the series of feedings he sponsored. Because he did so in an exceptionally magnanimous and noteworthy manner, and with the consent of the city council, gratitude was owed him to which this inscription and the public crowning with a laurel wreath attest. Three locations are named where the feasts had been held. One is in conjunction with the newly-instituted mystery celebration of Dionysos Pandemos, in the sacred precinct of Dionysos (ἐν τῶ τεμένει τῶ Διννύσω, line 18), which could refer to the temple area or, possibly, also to a sacred grove. Another festive gathering, following the New Year's Day sacrifices, took place in the prytaneum (ἐν τῶ πρυτανήω, lines 43–4), the seat of the city council. Cleanax chose the market place (…ἐν τᾶ ἀγόρα, lines 43–4) for the feast on the occasion of the provincial celebration of and sacrifices

13.   Translation of Schmitt Pantel in 'Public Feast', pp. 46–7.

to the Emperor. No location is indicated for the other feedings. Sacrifices are explicitly mentioned in connection with the New Year's Day feast (lines 30–3), the city's offerings for the dead (lines 34–46), and the provincial feast for Caesar Augustus and his sons (lines 40–5); all are followed by the feeding. It is likely that sacrifices were also offered at the marriage of his daughter, and religious connotations are certainly associated with the feasts of Dionysos and the Day of the Lark. But only at the city's offering to the dead are we explicitly told that leftovers from the sacrifices (ἀοθυσία) were included in the feeding.

Many differences and distinctions were made between the particular festivals on the basis of the lists of gifts and of those invited. For the feast of Dionysos and the Day of the Lark, invitations were sent to πολεῖται καὶ Ῥωμαῖοι καὶ παροίκοι κει ξένοι, that is, to politically active citizens – at least those born free – Romans, fellow residents without civic rights, and to foreigners, possibly emissaries from other cities. Similarly, for the Emperor's feast, Greeks and Romans, resident and non-resident foreigners were invited (line 44). But the feeding is different: for the feasts of Dionysos and the Day of the Lark, the citizens were invited for 'breakfast' (ἀριστί ζειν) only, whereas for the Emperor's feast the invited guests were served a festive meal (εὐωχεῖν, line 43) after the sacrifices. That is, only in the latter case did guests actually partake in a festive banquet of several courses at dining couches.[14] Also in connection with the annual feasts of Dionysos, Cleanax invites guests to the costly banquets (πολυτελῶς εὐωχεῖν, line 18), but exactly who is invited is not specified. One may conclude from the description of the New Year Day's feast that those invited belonged above all to the upper classes. Cleanax entertained his banquet company for several days after the sacrifices, but this company consisted only of 'many citizens and Romans' (πόλλοι τῶν πολείταν καὶ Ῥωμάοι, line 34). The Prytaneum, where the feast was held, could not provide space for many. The others in the city (ἐν τᾶ πόλει πάντας) are only served sweet wine or sweets (εγλύκισσε, lines 32–3). During the procession for Laurel Day, 'breakfast' was served only to priests, winners in the holy games, and the magistrates (lines 39–40).

The more elevated the citizen-status – which in antiquity also meant greater affluence – and the greater one's contribution to the city's honour, the greater the number of invitations and the better and more lavish the banquet.

14.   Josephus tells about festive banquets of various kings of antiquity (*Ant.*, 7.60; 8.25) and, on the occasion of the rededication of the Temple (*Ant.*, 12.323), a banquet for the whole people. But for his own day he differentiates between the festive banquet (εὐωχία) the Emperor held after his triumph march celebrating his victory over Judaea, to which he invited some kings, and other meals which were to be prepared for them at home (ἑστίασις) (*Bellum*, 7.156). The people's feeding given by Archelaos on the occasion of his father Herod's death (*Bellum*, 2.1) is also called ἑστίασις. Josephus emphasizes the high costs for this formal banquet.

Only once are slaves and freed slaves explicitly invited. At the city's offering to the dead, all people in the city including slaves (τοῖς ἐν τᾶ πόλει ἐλευθέροις τε καὶ δοίλοις, line 36) receive leftovers from the sacrifices and porridge (χος δρόγαλ, line 36, literally corn gruel made with milk).[15]

Thus, different groups are fed differently in these diverse festive occasions. What was offered at 'breakfast' and how is not made clear. But it was certainly not a proper banquet, but rather something more like a snack.[16] During Rome's imperial period an epulum, a public feeding, could be arranged by distributing sportulae, small food baskets to be taken home, or, in their place, payments of money.[17] Approximately 30 years after Cleanax, a benefactor in Acraephia named Epaminondas served a small basket of wheat (κόφινος σείτου) and wine per person (κατ' ἄνδρα) to the citizens, the resident foreigners and a group of Ectemenoi during one of the 12 feasts he sponsored.[18]

Distributing food on festive occasions was, of course, also a sign of generosity (*liberalitas*) but needs to be distinguished from the distributions of corn made more or less regularly by emperors and other benefactors.[19] These distributions had been introduced to Rome by the Gracchi brothers.[20]

---

15.   Slaves are invited to such events sponsored in the context of religious events, such as the cult for Zeus Panamara (*I Stratonikeia*, 172.8; 210.8; 254.5; 205.30). Slaves of the city's elite occasionally receive something in addition as, e.g., in the feeding sponsored by Epaminondas of Acreiphia (IG 2712.68-74). Everywhere slaves receive the smallest part. Cf. also Schmitt Pantel, *La cite*, pp. 399–401.

16.   In the priests' inscriptions of Zeus Panamara it is frequently said in the context of a feeding οὐ μόνον ἐπὶ τῷ ἀρίστῳ, ἀλλὰ καὶ ἐπὶ τῷ δείπνῳ, e.g., in Stratonikeia, 256.3-5; cf. 192.4; 210.7-8. Cf. also Hodot, 'Décret', pp. 173–4. In the Roman sphere, people are occasionally invited for prandium ('lunch'). Caesar is supposed to have provided a prandium for Emperor Tiberius during his triumphal conquest of Germany. He laid it out on 1,000 tables and spent 300 Sesterces on it (Suetonius, *Tiberius*, 20). Cf. also Donahue, *Roman Community*, p. 10.

17.   Caligula (Suetonis, *Caligula*, 18.2), Nero (Suetonius, *Nero*, 16) and Domitian (Suetonius, *Domitian*, 4.5) are said to have provided for such distributions. Benefactors would sometimes distribute the *sportulae* in cash or add money to the distributed goods. Cf. August Hug, 'Sprotla', RE 2, 6 (1929), pp. 1883–6, as well as Vössing, *Mensa Regia*, pp. 193–4, 273–5, and more. See pp. 265–328 for the diverse feedings of the emperors. Cf. his 'Die sportulae, der Kaiser und das Klientelwesen in Rom', *Latomus* 69 (2010), pp. 723–39.

18.   IG 7.2712, lines 65–6. Cf. James H. Oliver, 'Epamondas of Acraephia', *GRBS* 12 (1971): 221–37: τὴν μέλλουσαν ἑορτὴν ἔδωκεν πᾶσιν τοῖς πολέταις καὶ παροίκοις καὶ ἐκτημένοις διδοὺς κατ' ἄδρα ἕκαστον κόφινον σείτου καὶ οἴνου ἡμί. On this inscription, cf. Stavrianopoulou, 'Bewirtung', pp. 159–83. This sponsord feast is also discussed in Paul Veyne, *Brot und Spiele. Gesellschaftliche Macht und politische Herrschaft in der Antike* (München: dtv, 1994), pp. 263–7.

19.   Warren Carter, *John and Empire. Initial Exploration* (London, New York: T&T Clark, 2008), pp. 218–26, places Jn 6.1-15 into this context.

20.   Cf. Hendrik Bolkestein, *Wohltätigkeit und Armenpflege im vorchristlichen Altertum* (Utrecht: Oosthoek, 1939), pp. 272–3. Next to such distributions, there were also organizations that sold grain at reduced prices or to prevent speculation. Cf. Philostratus, *Vita Appolonius*, 1.15 as well as Peter Garnsey, 'Responses to Food Crises in the Ancient Mediterranean World', in Lucile

Intended to provide basic food supplies to citizens, they also served as a means for administrative officials 'to gain the love of the people'.[21] But here, too, the chief aim was not to support the most needy, at least not in the first instance.[22] Grain was distributed according to lists in order to make sure that only eligible citizens and, thus, the rich among them received their share.[23] It was none other than Caesar, who had put on the amazing mass-feeding on 22,000 triclina on the occasion of a triumphal procession, who reduced the number of those receiving grain from 320,000 to 150,000 in a population of Rome estimated to be one million souls.[24]

It was quite possible occasionally that poor people, slaves and non-residents received something at feedings or grain-distributions but, if at all, only a fraction of the total food. That reconfigured the idea of equality which had characterized the tradition of the Greek symposium. In the Greek polis the city fed its citizens, each of whom received the same portion as an expression of equality and commonality in the polis.[25] Democratic society reproduced itself symbolically in the common meal. But the institution of mass-feedings in Roman times – irrespective of whether the feeding took place in the Latin West or the Greek-speaking eastern part of the Empire – mirrored a hierarchical order of society. The large number of feedings

F. Newman et al. (eds), *Hunger in History. Food Shortage, Poverty, and Deprivation* (Cambridge, MA: Basil Blackwell, 1990), pp. 126–46.

21.   Plutarch, *Julius Caesar*, 57.8. Whoever did not give generously enough risked being chased out of office. Q. Maximus was not re-elected because the feeding on the occasion of death of his uncle P. Africanus was not opulent enough (Cicero, *Pro Murena*, 75). Cicero adds: 'The Roman people abhor the extravagance of individuals but it looks with favour on the state's ostentation.' On the interaction between the emperors and the people in feedings and feasts, cf. Nicholas Purcell, 'Rome and Its Development under Augustus and His Successors', in Alan K. Bowman et al. (eds), *The Cambridge Ancient History X: The Augustan Empire, 43 B.C.–A.D. 69* (Cambridge: Cambridge University Press, 2nd edn, 1996), pp. 800–11.

22.   This is supported in Bowman, *Wohltätigkeit*, pp. 259–67 (Greece) and pp. 369–79 (Rome); A. R. Hands, *Charities and Social Aid in Greece and Rome* (London: Thames and Hudson, 1968), pp. 89–115; Marcus Prell, *Armut im antiken Rom* (Beiträge zur Wirtschafts- und Sozialgeschichte 77, Stuttgart: Steiner, 1997), pp. 279–87. The distribution of grain was at the same time proof of special benevolence and is mentioned as such by Augustus at the very beginning of his accountability report (*Res Gestae* 5). Garnsey provides a systematic listing of the grain distributions of the individual emperors in *Famine and Food Supply in the Graeco-Roman World* (Cambridge: Cambridge University Press, 1988), pp. 228–43. They are not to be confused, however, with alms even though there was almsgiving in the ancient world. Cf. Anneliese Parkin, 'You do him no service: An Exploration of Pagan Almsgiving', in Margaret Atkins and Robin Osborne (eds), *Poverty in the Roman World* (Cambridge: Cambridge University Press, 1996), pp. 60–82.

23.   Cicero reports an occasion when the rich also receive something, like the Senator Piso; *Tusculanae Disputationes*, 3.48.

24.   Suetonius, *Julius Caesar*, 41.3.

25.   Garnsey, *Food and Society in Classical Antiquity* (Cambridge: Cambridge University Press, 1999), pp. 231–4.

and banquets corresponds to the large number of social relationships in which the benefactor stands out: among magistrates, priests, winners in the competitive games, among Greeks, Romans, citizens, residents without civic rights and foreigners/emissaries and, of course, the freed and slaves. In accepting the invitations and showing gratitude, those groups reinforce the rank of Cleanax.[26]

The inscription of Cleanax and others alike testify to new forms of civic banqueting in comparison to that of the Greek polis. In particular they mirror the form of the Roman 'private' banquet to which were invited not only people of equal status, but also those of differing status, such as clients by a patron. What is also new in comparison to classical Athens is that female benefactors could now distinguish themselves in sponsoring feedings.[27] Some of these feedings were segregated along gender lines. For example, Emperor Tiberius, after triumphing over the Dalmatians and Pannonians, entertained the men 'partly on the Capitol (in the Senate chambers) and partly in different locations of the city'; the women were invited by Livia and Julia.[28]

Artists would depict the status of different groups at the banquets by their various positions while at table. This is how Katherine M. D. Dunbabin interprets the banquet scene on the Amiternum Relief (50 CE). Next to a group on a triclinum there is a group of people seated, presumably guests of lower status at the banquet.[29] A similar depiction is found on a sarcophagus dated 250 years later.[30] Public dining is rarely depicted in Roman art. But a

---

26. Cf. also Stavrianopoulou, 'Bewirtung', pp. 177–9: 'Die Übernahme der Organisation von bereits bestehenden städtischen Festen und Opfern durch großzügige Euergeten ... sowie die Einführung von neuen Opfern und Bewirtungen anlässlich ihrer Amtseinsetzung als eponyme Archonten, Gymnasiarchen oder Agonotheten bot diesem Personenkreis die Möglichkeit ein bestimmtes Modell von Bürgergemeinde in symbolischer Weise vorzustellen. Es ist ein Bild einer streng hierarchisch gegliederten Gesellschaft innerhalb derer sich der Kreis der Notablen nach Belieben positionieren kann ... Gerade das aber war ein Novum, denn der neue Bewirtungsmodus in den griechischen Poleis nach Gruppen und nach Rang scheint ein Abbild der römischen Kommensalität gewesen zu sein.' See also Donahue, 'Toward a Typology of Roman Public Feasting', *American Journal of Philology* 124 (2003): 423–41; Vössing, *Mensa*, pp. 253–64.

27. There is clear evidence supporting the existence of female sponsors. See Donahue, *Roman Community*, pp. 107–14. For feasts sponsored by women for women, see Donahue, *Roman Community*, pp. 114–15.

28. Cassius Dio, *Roman History*, 50.2.4. A similar distinction between men and women is to be seen in the feedings sponsored by Epaminondas of Acraephia. For the bovine offering to the gods and the Caesars he invites the sons of the best families as well as the slaves 'in the order of twenty to thirty' (κατὰ τάξις ἀπὸ εἰκάδος μέχρι τριακάδος) for breakfast, sweet wine and a meal, while his wife invited the girls and female slaves (IG 7.2712, lines 69–74).

29. Katherine M. D. Dunbabin, *The Roman Banquet. Images of Conviviality* (Cambridge: Cambridge University Press, 2003), pp. 79–85.

30. Dunbabin, *Roman Banquet*, pp. 89.

fictional portrayal is preserved in Petronius' satire about the symposium of a rich freed man, Trimalchio. We meet him commissioning an artist:

> I want you also to depict ships in full sail, and myself sitting on a dais wearing the toga with a purple stripe and five gold rings, dispensing coins from a wallet to the people at large; you know how I laid on a dinner for them at two denarii a head. If you will, incorporate dining-halls as well, and all the citizens having a good time in them.[31]

As the story tells it, Trimalchio hosted what, within the scope of his otherwise also exaggerated self-presentation, was a very magnanimous public banquet. Two denarii (eight sesterces), which corresponds to one half-drachma per person, outdoes almost every such event attested to in inscriptions in the Latin West. One half-sesterce or one sixteenth-dracma would have paid for one day's bread in Pompey.[32] But Trimalchio had invited 'the entire population' (*totum populum*) and they are enjoying themselves lounging as honoured guests on banquet couches.

Thus, the ideal of equality in common meals was not forgotten in Rome even though the satirical aspect in Petronius' portrayal of Trimalchio must not be ignored.[33] Belonging and being equal are, therefore, important aspects that the court-poet Statius emphasizes in his poem about one of Emperor Domitian's mass-feedings. The luxuriance of the golden age displayed in this December Saturnalia is made visible at the beginning of the poem in the variety of exotic fruit that Domitian has rained down on the Coliseum in Rome where the feast is taking place (Silvae 1.6.9-27). This is followed by baskets of bread, side dishes and wine (28-34). Finally, the poet praises the giver and the gift:

> (30-35) At one and the same time you satisfy the Circle where it is reformed and sobered together with the peoples of the gown; and since you feed so many folk, wealthy lord, haughty Annona knows not this day. Antiquity, compare if you will the ages of the ancient Jove and the golden time: not so freely did wine flow then, not thus would harvest forestall the tardy year. Every order eats at one table: children, women, populace, Knights, Senate. Freedom has relaxed reverence. Nay, you yourself (which the gods could thus invite, which accept invitation?) entered the feast along with us. Now everyone, be he rich or poor, boasts of dining with the leader.[34]

The notion that 'every status ate at the same table' has only scant correspondence to reality. The seating-order in the theatre alone speaks

---

31.   Petronius, *Satyricon*, 71.9–10. The translation is by Michael Heseltine.

32.   Cf. Donahue, 'Euergetic Self-Representation and the Inscription at Satyricon 71.10', *Classical Philology* 94 (1999): 69–74, 72. In his *Roman Community*, pp. 142–3, he lists nine cases in the Latin-sponsored feedings where costs for people's feedings are given, ranging between two and eight sesterces.

33.   Cf. Vössing, *Mensa,* pp. 253–64, on the paradoxes of the Roman ideology concerning the feedings.

34.   Statius, *Silvae,* 1.6.35–50. Translation by Shackleton Bailey (LCL).

against this: the crowd of 'normal' folk was permitted seating only in the uppermost tier whereas senators and knights occupied all other lower ones.[35] Suetonius seems to give a more accurate description of Domitian's food-distribution: '[He] had large food baskets distributed among senators and the nobility and smaller ones among the plebeians.'[36] But Statius wants to present the feast as the golden age not only returned but surpassed, in that equality and abundance for all had been achieved.[37] That is why Domitian is acclaimed as God. Not only that, the figure portrayed at the end of the poem is quite comparable to Jupiter.[38]

Should we, therefore, expect to find in the feasts for the gods equity in how food was distributed such that the ideals of equality have shaped the community at its meals? Dennis Smith believes that we may do so.[39] He refers to a letter of invitation from a priest of Zeus Panamaros in Caria to the Rhodians:[40]

> Since the deity calls all human beings to the feast, allowing them to share a common table where all have equal rights (καὶ κοινὴν καὶ ἰσότιμον παρέχι τράπεζαν), wherever they come from, and since I similarly believe that the city is worthy of this exceeding honour also on account of your reputation, oh Rhodians, and since our cities share a relationship and mutuality in things sacred, I call you to the deity and pray that the inhabitants of the city attend this joyous feast in his [the deity's] presence because great honour is bestowed by the deity on the Rhodians in neighboring Caria if they receive my letter joyfully and make it known to the deity.[41]

Here a god is said to invite people to come to a common table where all have equal rights. Contrary to the feasts Cleanax sponsored, the universalism of the invitation stands out: all are invited 'wherever they come from'.[42]

---

35. Cf. Donahue, *Roman Community*, pp. 21–3 and the illustration on p. 23.

36. Suetonius, *Domitian*, 4.5: *senatui equitique panariis, plebei sportellis cum obsonio distributes.* Cf. also D'Arms, 'The Roman *Convivium* and the Idea of Equality', in *Sympotica. A Symposium on the Symposion* (Oxford: Clarendon Press, 1990), p. 320.

37. The people thereupon acclaim Domitian as their lord (83); cf. also Suetonius, *Domitian*, 13.1. But the Emperor would not stand for this alone, even though from then on he mimicked god-likeness (85–92). Cf. also Martial, *Epigrame*, 8.49 (50).

38. Statius, *Silvae*, 1.6.84–102.

39. Dennis Smith, *From Symposium to Eucharist. The Banquet in the Early Christian World* (Minneapolis: Fortress Press, 2002), p. 71, 'The ideal of social equality was often related especially to religious meals.'

40. On this cult, cf. Juditha Hanslik-Andrée, 'Panamaros', *RE* 26 (1949): 450–5. For the meal, cf. also J. P. Kane, 'The Mithraic cult meal in its Greek and Roman environment', in J. R. Hinnells (ed.), *Mithrais Studies II* (Manchester: University of Manchester Press, 1974), pp. 313–51, 330–2. The inscriptions have been gathered in the meantime in Çetin Şahin, *Die Inschriften von Stratonikeia I Panamara* (Inschriften Griechischer Städte aus Kleinasien 21, Bonn: Habelt, 1981).

41. *I Stratonikeia*, 22 (BCH 51, 1927), 73.

42. *I Stratonikeia*, 22, lines 4–5: τοῖς ὁποθενοῦ [ν] ἀφικνουμένοις. Cf. Smith, *Symposium*, p. 82.

But that does not mean that there were no differences at the table of Zeus Panamoros. Even though another inscription, the records of the priest Tiberius Flavius and the priestess Flavia Mamalon, states that they had provided not only breakfast but, indeed, a complete meal to those who had come to the temple,[43] it is also emphasized that colleagues, citizens, ephebes and sons were given special treatment and that the men were given five drachmas during their feast while the women received only three.[44] There is no clear line to be drawn between civic and religious banqueting. Cleanax also sponsored among others the festive meal for Dionysos Pandemos, that is, for a deity who was known precisely for the eradication of gender and status roles.[45] Dionysos' message was not directly represented at Cleanax's feast where only (male?) Romans, fellow citizens and some others got a breakfast.

Thus, religious and political feasts cannot be sharply distinguished as far as their causes, the politics governing invitations, and the justice of distribution pertaining to them are concerned. But we can observe a tendency to invite broader levels of the population to religious feasts. If anywhere, those who had come to the temple or the sacred domain of the gods could expect to be given food in abundance without respect to their status.

It is not surprising then that with the gods and godesses, food never runs out. Dionysos, the god of banquets par excellence, is most famous for this feat. The Bacchae describe a feast of the gods:

> One of them took a θύρσος and struck it against a rock, from which a dewy stream of water leaped out. Another lowered her fennel-rod to the surface of the earth, and for her the god set up a stream of wine. Those who had a longing for the white drink scraped at the earth with their finger-tips and had streams of milk; and from the ivory θύρσοι dripped sweet flows of honey.[46]

Other sources tell of a table that magically puts food on itself being prepared in the temple. The Roman geographer Pomponius Mela writes in his Chorographia:

---

43.   *I Stratonikeia*, 192 (BCH 28, 1904) 246–7. Lines 3–4: ὑπεδέξαντ[ο ... δι᾽ ὅλου τοῦ ἔτους μεγαλοπρεπῶς πάντας τοὺς ἀφικο]μένους ἰς τὸ ἱερόν, οὐ μόνον ἐπὶ τῷ ἀρίστῳ, ἀλ[λὰ καὶ ἐπὶ τῷ δείπνῳ.

44.   *I Stratonikeia*, 192.6–7: καὶ ταῖς δημοθοινίαις ὑπεδέξαντο συναρίας τε καὶ πο]λείτας καὶ ἐφήβους καὶ παῖδας Whenever the inscriptions first emphasize the universality of the invitation but then report a highly differentiated praxis, it becomes clear that religious and political ideals are in conflict here.

45.   Cf. Judith Behnk, *Dionysos und seine Gefolgschaft. Weibliche Besessenheitskulte in der griechischen Antike* (Hamburg: Diplomiva-Verlag, 2009).

46.   Euripides, *Bacchae*, 704–11. Translation by David Kovacs (LCL).

There is a place for feasting, which always caries food for those who wish to dine. It is
called the Table of the Sun (Heliu Trapeza). Anything placed on it is considered to have
come from the gods.[47]

What the Bible says about the jug of wine when Elijah visited the widow of
Zarephath (1 Kgs 17.16) may also be said about Zeus' visit to Philemon and
Baucis. The jug never runs out; it refills itself on its own.[48]

And it is surely no coincidence that Elisha feeds 100 men with bread
of the first reaping, 20 loaves of barley bread, and some fresh grain with
gifts of offering brought to a holy place (2 Kgs 4.42-44). According to vv.
43-44, the miracle is nothing but a visible confirmation of the word of God
the prophet tells to his servant.[49] Can the feeding narratives of the Second
Testament also be described as mass-feedings in a religious context?

5.2. The Feeding of the 4,000–5,000 (Mark 6.32-44 par.)

The narrative-genre of the feeding of the 5,000 (Mk 6.32-44 par.) and
of the 4,000 (Mk 8.1-10 par.) is unanimously designated at present as
'gift miracle'. Gerd Theißen extends Bultmann's classification of these
narratives as 'nature miracles' and proposes the genre of 'gift miracle' or
'material cultural miracle' (materielle Kulturwunder), the characteristic
of which is 'that in surprising ways they make material goods available',
namely 'transformed, multiplied foods' and 'heaps of them'.[50] Theißen
lists the following distinguishing marks of the genre 'gift miracles': (1)
they happen spontaneously without any plea of the miracle worker; (2)
their unobtrusiveness in saying not a single word about the miracle's actual
technique; and (3) they are a demonstration whose emphatic feature is that
'the reader comprehends it from its results'.[51] However, the postulation
of a genre-specific typology leaves aside the observation that most of the
New Testament's miracle stories' characteristics are missing in the feeding
narratives, namely the plea that hardship suffered be alleviated, an account

47.   Pomponius Mela, *De Chorographia* 3.87. Translation: Paul Berry (Geography / *De situ
orbis* AD 43; Studies in Classics 3, Lewiston: Edwin Mellen Press, 1997), p. 139.

48.   Ovid, *Metamorphoses*, 8.611-724.679-680. There is a similar miracle described in
Pliny's *Naturalis historia*, 2.223. The narratives of the multiplication of food described in 1 Kings
17.7-14 and 2 Kings 4.42-44 also work with a fairy-tale motif, of course. Cf. Hermann Gunkel,
Das Märchen im Alten Testament (Tübingen: Mohr, 1921), pp. 69–70.

49.   Rabbinic tradition sees this as a mass-feeding in face of a famine. Cf. Ketubbot 106a,
where it is concluded that Elisha fed 22,000 people.

50.   Gerd Theißen, *Urchristliche Wundergeschichten. Ein Beitrag zur formgeschichtlichen
Erforschung der synoptischen Evangelien* (Gütersloh: Gütersloher Verlagshaus, 1987), p. 111.

51.   Theißen, *Wundergeschichten*, pp. 111–14.

of the acts performed in the miracle itself, and the awe-struck response of the people present at the miracle.[52] Theißen gives only two additional examples of this genre: the miracle of the wine at Cana (Jn 2.1-10) and the widow of Zarephath's inexhaustible jug of oil (1 Kgs 17.7-14).[53] What is not taken into account is Bultmann's note that the sudden multiplication of food or drink is, as has already been pointed out, a trans-cultural fairy-tale motif found in almost all religious contexts and cultures. In antiquity, people claiming to possess divine powers, *theoi andropoi*, can make such multiplication happen.[54]

Whether the motif of inexhaustible sources of food makes this narrative a miracle story or not, the experience of 4–5,000 people being fed all at one time is not unusual in ancient times. Can the feeding narrative then be understood to be a public or civic mass-feeding? What are the commonalities and the differences in the feasts sponsored by Cleanax and the feeding held in honour of Zeus Panamaros?

Beside all similarities and literary dependencies, the feeding narratives in the gospels are contextualized differently throughout. The point of departure of the feeding of the 5,000 in Mk 6.32-44 is Jesus' care for his overworked disciples after their return from their preaching and healing mission (6.12-13,30-31); '... they had no leisure even to eat' says v. 31. An attempt to go by boat to a deserted place (εἰς ἔρημον τόπον) failed to find the desired solitude as Mark tells it. The place of the feeding is described as being deserted (ἔρμος), dreary, lonely, or, according to Mk 8.4 (Mt. 15.33), a desert, an uninhabited area (ἐρημία). In the context of ancient mass-feedings, this means it was an outdoor banquet. Common meals, 'picnics' in nature, are spoken of especially in a religious context and in connection with

52. This is why some exegetes discount the thesis that these narratives are miracle stories. Cf. Otto Perels, *Die Wunderüberlieferung in ihrem Verhältnis zur Wortüberlieferung* (Stuttgart: Kohlhammer Verlag, 1934), pp. 52–3; Otto Schille, *Die urchristliche Wundertradition. Ein Beitrag zur Frage nach dem irdischen Jesus* (Stuttgart: Calwer Verlag, 1967), p. 35 n. 115; Karl Kertelge, *Die Wunder Jesu im Markusevangelium* (München: Kösel Verlag, 1970), pp. 131–3. See also notes 73 and 86 below.

53. Theißen does indeed also cite the Talmudic story of Hanina b. Dosa's wife and the miracle of her miraculously finding bread in her oven (bTa'anit 24b-25a) and, in a footnote, refers to the magical invocation of a food-laden table (PGM 1.96-107).

54. Celsus asserts that, according to Origen, there were professional magicians who 'could conjure up costly meals and tables full of baked goods and condiments that in truth were never there and that what looked alive was not really alive but only seemed so to the imagination'. Origen, *Contra Celsum*, 1.68. Origen does not dispute the existence of such people but argues that Jesus cannot be compared with these 'magicians' because he wanted to move his onlookers by his miraculous deeds to moral betterment and the fear of God. Apolonius is supposed to have watched Indian savants 'conjure up a delicious meal out of nothing and by a word alone' (Philostratus, *Vita Apollonius*, 3.27). We are told in the *Vita Prophetarum* that Ezekiel provided his exiled compatriots with 'an exceedingly rich fish meal miraculously by his prayer'. *Vita Ezechiel* 11. Cf. also Jamblich, *Pythagoras*, 36.

military campaigns.[55] But in Lk. 9.10, Jesus goes with the 12 to the town of Bethsaida, entering a place where civic feedings mostly took place.[56]

The crowd is compared to a flock of sheep without a shepherd only in Mk 6.34. The citation from Num. 27.19 alludes to the political metaphor of the shepherd used throughout all of antiquity.[57] Hence, right at the outset the expectation is raised that the ruling authorities, the kings and the emperors, cater to their people.[58] But in Mk 6.35-36, the disciples beg Jesus to send the crowd away since it is already late in the day, 'so that they may go into the surrounding country and villages and buy something for themselves to eat'. The words 'for themselves' (ἑαυτοῖς) is in stark contrast to Jesus' command to the disciples, 'You give them something to eat' (Mk 6.37; Mt. 9.16).

The disciples are called upon to accomplish a logistical challenge which, in the second Markan feeding narrative (8.14), is specifically emphasized. Here the crowd had had nothing to eat for three days and Jesus fears that the people could starve on their way home. But the disciples are clueless about where they are supposed to find enough food in that desolate place. They are not alone in the logistical problems of mass-feedings. For example, Caesar, when planning a feeding of similar dimensions, mobilizes not only his own slaves but also the city's cook-shops.[59]

The question of buying bread for 200 denarii comes up in the Markan and Johannine narratives. John 6.6 makes it clear right at the start that Jesus wants to test his disciples with his question about buying bread to satisfy everyone. Philip's reply that 200 denarii's worth of bread would not be enough for each person to get even a little is surely not the most brilliant. It is difficult to conclude from Mk 6.37-38 whether it was even possible to

55.   Cf. Schmitt Pantel, *La cite*, pp. 92–102, for the locations of people's banquets. For the Latin language area, cf. Donahue, *Roman Community*, pp. 30–41.

56.   And yet, Luke 9.12 calls the place 'deserted'. That is why some translations smooth it out by rendering εἰς πόλιν καλουμένην Βηθσαϊδα as 'in the direction of a town called Bethsaida'. Cf. Hans Klein, *Das Lukasevangelium* (KEK 3,1, Göttingen: Vandenhoeck & Ruprecht, 2006), p. 332; also François Bovon, *Das Evangelium nach Lukas I* (EKK 3,1, Zurich et al.: Benziger Verlag 1989), p. 466. In the Gospel of Matthew, Jesus is fleeing from Herod. In the Gospel of John, shortly before the Feast of Passover, he and the disciples ate sitting on a large mountain above the lake from where he sees the crowd approaching. It appears that he descended from there to feed the people for, according to Jn 6.15, he disappears again on the mountain. On a sponsor's ascent and descent, see Stavrianopoulou, 'Bewirtung', pp. 172–3.

57.   For the ancient Orient, cf. Joachim Jeremias, 'ποιμήν κτλ.', *THWNT* 6 (1959), p. 485; for Greek antiquity, cf., e.g., Homer. In the *Iliad*, kings are referred to with this term, above all Agamemnon: 44 times, 12 times in the *Odyssey*.

58.   Cf., e.g., Philo, *De Josepho*, 98; *De Somniis*, 2.211; Josephus, *Bellum*, 2.1; Xenophon, *Oikonomikos*, 2.5; Pisidian Lucian, *Demosthenes,* 16 et al.

59.   Suetonius, *Julius Caesar*, 26.2. For the feeding given on the occasion of his triumphal march, Caesar receives among others 6,000 muraena from a wealthy fish-farmer *free of charge!* Pliny, *Naturalis historia*, 9.171. Donahue addresses the logistical challenges in his *Roman Community*, pp. 23–30.

buy bread for that amount; that is, whether the money was available and whether it was enough for the required amount of bread.[60] Two hundred denarii is equivalent to 3,200 asses and, depending on the price of bread, would buy about 240 kg (540 lbs) of wheat bread or twice as much of barley bread.[61] But higher expenses clearly are noted in the documented feedings sponsored, such as for the magnanimous feeding of Trimalchios which gives a figure of one half-drachma per person (Petronius, *Satyricon*, 71.10) or the presumably later – and therefore not directly comparable – feeding sponsored by Tiberios, Flavios and Flavia Mamalon Heracometis which cost five drachmas for each man and three for each woman.[62] In any case, 200 denarii is considered a very large amount; more than what was on hand for bread and condiments here.

Mark 6 is the only place that describes the seating order during the feeding. Whereas Mt. 14.19 says simply, 'he ordered the crowds to sit down on the grass', and Luke has the 12 seat the people in groups of 50 persons each, Mk 6.39-40 says, 'he ordered them to get all the people to recline symposion by symposion on the green grass. And they reclined garden-plot by garden-plot in groups of hundreds and fifties.'

Symposion (literally, drinking together) refers to a formal meal that is followed by a drinking session celebrated on dining couches (triclina). The social form of the symposium itself as well as 'reclining-at-table' (ἀνακλῖναι) is a status symbol as well as a sign of luxury.[63] Thus, a symposium is a *cena recta*, a proper banquet, and not merely a distribution of sportulae, small bread baskets.[64]

---

60.   Most exegetes dealing with Mk 6.52 and 8.14-21 tend to interpret the conjunctive in the dubitative mood and take the question to be a rhetorical-sceptical one. Cf., e.g., Collins, *Mark*, p. 321; Dieter Lührmann, *Das Markusevangelium* (HNT 3, Vol. 1, Tübingen: Mohr, 1987), p. 120; Rudolf Pesch, *Das Markusevangelium* (HThKNT 2,1, Freiburg: Herder, 1976), p. 351.

61.   In the first century CE a loaf of wheat bread cost 1 as in Rome (Petronius, *Satyricon*, 44.11). It was possibly less expensive in the provinces or out in the country because the grain did not have to be imported. In Pisidian Antioch one could have bought 240 kg of wheat or 500 kg of barley for 200 denarii (cf. the calculations in Garnsey, *Famine*, p. 263, note 33). In Roman eyes, barley was judged to be of the quality of animal feed and only fit for poor people to eat (cf. Labahn, *Offenbarung*, pp. 173–4). But in Greece, barley was widely used, even as a food-offering (cf. Garnsey, *Food*, p. 119). In any case, it is not completely unrealistic actually to receive 5,000 barley loaves for 200 denarii, i.e., 3,200 asses, depending on the price of bread; cf. Jn 6.9, 13; 2 Kgs 4.42). See also Kay Ehling, 'Die Speisung der Fünftausend und die Reisekasse der Jünger. Anmerkungen zu Mk 6.35-57', *Münsterische Beiträge zur antiken Handelsgeschichte* 23 (2005): 47–58.

62.   The least expensive public feeding in Italy would have cost around one-eighth of a denarius per person; see above note 32. For money spent on sponsored banquets in Greece, cf. also Hands, *Charities*, p. 59.

63.   Dunbabin, *Roman Banquet*, p. 13. In Aristophanes' *Wasps* there is a passage where the educated son, Antikleon, lectures his peasant father, Philokleon, on how to recline properly at a sophisticated meal.

64.   Thus Suetonius, *Domitian*, 7, in contrast to Nero (Suetonius, *Nero*, 16).

The feeding takes place 'on the green grass', a place typical of Dionysos but also of some plebeian feasts in Rome, for example, the ancient Roman New Year's feast Anna Perenna where the people drank on the grassy banks of the River Tiber.[65] Even if the picnic in the open is nothing unusual, the expression πρασιά πρασιά, taking up the συμπόσια συμπόσια in v. 40, is puzzling. Πρασιά, in the strict sense of the word, means bed in a garden, garden-plot (cf. Eccl. 24.31) and in no hitherto known text does it describe a seating order at a meal.[66] The general conclusion from the context is that it describes the seating order 'in groups'.[67] The group-sizes of 100 and 50 caused many interpreters to think of the assignment of the heads over the people of God spoken of in Exod. 18.21 and 25, and Deut. 1.15. According to 1 Macc. 3.55, this arrangement describes military units; according to 1QSa 2.21-23 it is a group-organization;[68] and according to 1QSa 2.11-22, the order of Israel at its eschatological meeting with the Messiah which is followed by a festive meal.[69] Reference to a banquet occurs only in the context of this last text; nowhere does the way people were arranged describe a seating order. Elsewhere groups of 100, 50 and ten are mentioned, whereas Mk 6.40 speaks only of 100 and 50 and Lk. 9.14 only of 50. But in the context of mass-feedings in antiquity there are instructions specifying group-orders of fixed sizes. Epameinondas of Acraiphia writes, 'after (a festive procession and offerings for the Emperor

65. On Dionysos, see Dunbabin, *Roman Banquet*, pp. 50–2. On *Anna Perenna*, see Ovid, *fasti*, 3.523-542: 'On the Ides is held the jovial feast of Anna Perenna not far from the banks, O Tiber, who comest from afar. The common folk come, and scattered here and there over the green grass, they drink ...' This reference is found also in Erich Kostermann, *Das Markusevangelium* (HNT 3, Tübingen: Mohr, 3rd edn,1936), p. 63, but later exegetes did not discuss it further. For additional meals on grass, cf. Athenaeus, *Deipnosphistae*, 11.1 (459–60); 4.38 (153b); Philostratus, *Vita Appolonius*, 3.27. Pompey's money distribution for the election of Africanus takes place in a garden (Plutarch, *Pompeius*, 44.3); Caesar's feast on the 22,000 triclinae could possibly also have taken place in a garden; cf. D'Arms, 'Between Public and Private: The Epulum Publicum and Caesar's Horti trans Tiberim', in Eugenio La Rocca (ed.), *Horti Romani* (Rome: L'Erma di Bretschneider, 1998), pp. 33–43.

66. In one of Hermocrates' letters to Chairias during the first century CE, he complains from his home in Fayum that the water canals are so badly obstructed that he cannot water his fields (μόλις γὰρ μίαν πρασιὰν ποτίζει τὸ ὕδωρ, 'there is barely enough to water a garden bed'), BGU II 520, 27-28. In her commentary on *Mark*, Collins also assumes that '[t]his connotation of the word thus continues the imagery of a simple outdoor banquet', p. 324. But it appears to have a specific group order in mind, the precise configuration of which I do not know.

67. Cf. Walter Bauer, *A Greek-English Lexicon of the New Testament and Other Early Christian Literature*, on the relevant word. The source in Strack/Billerbeck II 13 for the term גנוניות גנוניות for πρασιά πρασιά is a Talmud wordbook and is, for that reason, surely not an ancient source.

68. Cf. also CD 12,22, 'order in the camps' (סרך מושב המחנ[ו]ת).

69. This was indicated the first time by Ethelbert Staufer, 'Zum apokalyptischen Festmahl in Mk 6,34ff', *ZNW* 45 (1955): 264–6.

and different sponsored feedings), he invited to breakfast the sons of citizens and slaves of corresponding age in groups of twenty or thirty'.[70] The meal-order of groups of 100 and 50 persons given in the Gospel of Mark describes an orderly process. The reference to the desert-traditions is not persuasive here.

In the context of a miracle story, everything told to this point is to be seen as exposition. The miracle does not happen until Mk 6.41 in the sixth chapter of Mark (and par.), but the action proper to the miracle itself is missing in the narrative unless one takes Jesus' looking up to heaven and his blessing to be magical acts.[71] It might be that belief in the prophets' power of prayer stands behind this.[72] Otherwise, in the final analysis we have a miracle story without a miracle proper.

Many understand the role of the disciples to be that of table servants whose job it was to distribute the food.[73] Their task would thus be comparable to that of the slaves portrayed in third- and fourth-century murals, offering food and other eating utensils to the onlooker.[74] But this role is conspicuously missing from inscriptions paying tribute and from descriptions of banquets, like that for Cleanax mentioned above. The only people whose beneficial acts are spoken of in those decrees of honour are the sponsors, even though they themselves would hardly have distributed or served the food. The disciples are therefore not only 'servants', but also, through their inclusion in an active role, comparable to the sponsors themselves. They pass on a divine gift, similar to the priestesses and priests of Zeus Panamaros who prepare vicariously for the deity a feast for those assembled from far and wide.[75]

---

70.   *IG* 27.12.68-70. Cf. also Athenaeus, *Deipnosophistae*, 4.38 (153b): a certain Herakleon from Beroia is said to have his soldiers 'lie down on the ground in the open air in groups of a thousand' for their meals. In a law governing the distribution of grain on the island of Samos, the Prytanis was to order those gathered to sit down in groups of a thousand (κελευέτωσαν τοὺς ἐκκλησιάζοντα[ς κα]τὰ χιλιαστὺν καθίζειν); cf. *IG* 12.6.1, 4f = SEG 976, 4f.

71.   Even though much discussed (cf. note 1 above), it is difficult to decide whether the verse is an allusion to the last supper (Mk 14.22-24, par.) or a typical Jewish blessing of food – which of course comes to be formulated only later, as Clemens Leonhard points out with good arguments in his 'Blessings over Wine and Bread in Judaism and Christian Eucharistic Prayers: Two Independent Traditions', in Albert Gerhards et al. (eds), *Jewish and Christian Liturgy and Worship. New Insights into its History and Interaction* (Jewish and Christian Perspectives series 15, Leiden: Brill, 2007), pp. 309–26.

72.   Cf. 1 Kings 18.42-45; Jas 5.17-18. The prophet Ezekiel, while offering food, also makes use of prayer (*Vita Ezechiel* 11), as does the king and his entourage, having eaten, before the gathered wise men of India (Philostratus, *Vita Appolonius*, 3.27).

73.   Cf., e.g., Pervo, 'Panta Koina', pp. 190–1. Klaus Berger assigns the feeding narratives to the 'mandates' since they are really about 'the continuing action of Jesus in the disciples', *Formgeschichte des Neuen Testaments* (Heidelberg: Quelle und Meyer, 1984), pp. 315–17.

74.   Dunbabin, *Roman Banquet*, pp. 100–2, 150–6.

75.   The disciples' active role in the distribution of the food is emphasized particularly in Mt. 14.19 and Mk 8.6 par.

While reclining is aristocratic, the meal itself consists of bread and fish. Bread is a basic nourishment of the elevated classes. Many of the poorer populace ate corn porridge above all.[76] Bread is eaten when possible with side dishes (ὀψάριον). This could be fish. According to their size and where it was being consumed, fish could be both poor folk's food and a luxury item depending on the context.[77] It is worth noting that the meal in Mk 8.6-7 par. has fish as the second course on the menu, thus taking up a further characteristic of the aristocratic banquet which has several courses. But what is oddly missing altogether is wine which in most of the sponsored feedings is counted among the special highlights of the meal.[78]

Mark 6.42 par. notes, 'And all ate and were filled.' This remark – which I have not found in any inscription[79] – could have been inspired by Ps. 77.29 (LXX) and alludes to the miracle of the manna from heaven (Exod. 16; Ps. 77.23-29 (LXX)). There, in the context of the feeding with quails, we read, 'And they ate and were very much filled' (καὶ ἐφάγοσαν καὶ ἐσεπλάσθησαν σφόδρα). Quite differently than in the manna feeding, however, there are leftovers that are gathered into 12 or seven baskets (Mk 6.34 par.; 8.8 par.). The words used for small baskets, κόφινος (Mk 6.34 par./Jn 6.13) and σπυρίς (Mk 8.8; Mt. 15.37), are also used for the receptacles used in food distributions.[80] Epictetus tells the young candidate to distribute little lunch baskets (σπυρίον δειπνίσαι) to the people in order to be elected as a consul.[81] Thus, other than in the feeding narratives, the *sportulae* is not distributed to the electorate but left over at the end.[82]

In inscriptions honouring sponsors of feedings, the number of people fed is one of the things almost always highlighted in first place. In such a position it demonstrates how magnanimous the benefactor is. In the feeding

76. Cf. the feasts sponsored by Cleanax above (line 63). Also Garnsey, *Food*, pp. 116–22.

77. Small fish, eaten on the seashore, may be poor people's food. Big fish, eaten far away from the sea, e.g., in a big city, are a very special luxury item. Cf. A. C. Andrews, 'Ernährung A', RAC 6 (1966), pp. 222–3; Nicholas Purcell, 'Eating Fish. The Paradoxes of Seafood', in John Wilkins et al. (eds), *Food in Antiquity* (Exeter: University of Exeter Press, 1995), pp. 132–49. Since according to Wis. 19.11, quails come from the sea, some interpreters assume a desert tradition here. According to Sifre Num. 95 on Num. 11.21, the generation wandering in the desert ate fish from the well that had been brought along.

78. Caesar is said to be the first to have donated four kinds of wine for the mass-feedings; Pliny, *Naturalis historia*, 14.97. Cf. Vössing, *Mensa*, p. 194, on wine as a regular part of an *epulum*.

79. I found the term χορτάζειν in the databank of Clauss and Slabi only in inscriptions of the fourth/fifth century, particularly in Christian contexts.

80. Cf. the feeding sponsored by Epaminondas of Acraphaeia, *IG* 2712, lines 65–6 (see note 18 above.)

81. Arrian, *Epictet Dissertationses*, 4.10.20-21.

82. It is true that there are documents confirming that the little baskets were sometimes distributed so that the people could gather the leftovers and take them home; cf. Athenaeus, *Deipnosophistiae*, 4, 4 (130a).

narratives a figure is also mentioned but only at the end in the Gospels of Matthew and Mark.[83] What seems more important is not the great deed of the sponsor but that an initially uncounted crowd of people had enough to eat to be filled. Whether the 5,000 ἄνδρες (literally, men) in Mk 6.43 (Lk. 9.14) is meant to exclude or to include women is not clear. We have seen that feedings took place in groups of both sexes as well as in groups of one sex only. In the context of religion, especially in the Jewish context, the idea of a group of women and men is more probable.[84]

5.3. *Feeding Narrative and Public Feeding: A Comparison*

I hope to have shown that the gospel feeding narratives would have been heard in antiquity as related to other narratives about public banquets. Providing food for the masses was something expected from someone in leadership, whether in a provincial city or in Rome itself. The occasions might be a triumph, an anniversary of a reign, a funeral or a religious festivity. As we have shown above, none of the occasions were truly a-religious or simply non-political and the boundaries between political and religious remained fluid. If there is any difference between civic banquets and religious ones, then there seems to have been a tendency, particularly in the context of feasts for the gods and temple-cults, to show consideration also to slaves, to ordinary people and to foreigners.

For most hearers and readers of the gospels, feeding large groups and those representing them was part of their experience, at least by hearsay. Hence, what is unique in the feeding narratives is not 'the surprising availability of material goods such as heaps of food' nor the feeding of 4–5,000 people all at the same time.[85] Nor even the fact that five loaves and two fishes were not used up is unique. Epiphanies of gods or their representatives at

---

83.   Mk 6.43/Mt. 14.21; Mk 8.9/Mt. 15.38.

84.   For an inclusive conception, similar to the one foreseen by Philo of Alexandria, cf. Angela Standhartinger, 'Mit einer verheirateten Frau schmause nicht beim Wein (Sir. 9.9). Egalitäre Tischgemeinschaften im Kontext antiker, jüdischer und frühchristlicher Symposiumskultur', in Michaela Geiger, Christl M. Maier and Uta Schmidt (eds), *Essen und Trinken in der Bibel. Ein literarisches Festmahl für Rainer Kessler zum 65. Geburtstag* (Gütersloh: Gütersloher Verlagshaus, 2009), pp. 286–300, 298. A different interpretation is provided by Zoe Terlibakou, 'The Presence of Women in the Feeding Stories in the Synoptic Gospels', in Sabine Bieberstein et al. (eds), *Building Bridges in a Multifaceted Europe. Religious Origins, Traditions, Contexts, and Identities* (Jahrbuch der European Society of Women in Theological Research 14 (2006)), pp. 175–84. She sees it as an exclusive term since Mk 6.30-44 tells about a symposium, and Lk. 9.10-17, a public feeding to which no women were admitted, whereas Mt. 14.13-21 was a family feast.

85.   Cf. Theißen, *Wundergeschichten*, p. 111.

sacred places could provide this as well.[86] And when the magnanimity of the sponsors and the overabundance of what they donate is symbolized by the collection of what is left over into baskets, this too is a component of the depiction of generous beneficence in antiquity.

It is in the details of the feeding narratives that we find what is unique to them. Ancient authors, especially in Roman times, rarely tell of 4–5,000 people reclining at table in the aristocratic position without any social differentiation, all having a two-course meal of bread and fish.[87] The amount of money and/or food available to the disciples indicates that this is not the usual milieu of benefactors and those receiving their beneficence. On the contrary, the feeding narratives present a milieu that was excluded from most other feedings and corn-distributions elsewhere. When the wine which is elsewhere regularly part of the public banquet is missing here, it becomes clear that those people told this story are more used to food distributions than taking part in a symposium. Also missing is the emphasis on the donor's generosity and how adequate the distribution was at the appropriate location in honour of a worthy cause. Instead, what is emphasized here is how necessary it was to feed the hungry people who were in danger of starving. Therefore the feeding could only with restriction be called spontaneous.[88] The crowd needs food. And again, other than in the official presentations of mass-feedings at honorary inscriptions, attention is conspicuously directed to the problems of logistics and distribution. Nowhere else do these mention who is doing the distributing. And finally, nowhere else is any outcome of the feeding stated. The statement '... and all ate and were filled' is unique in antiquity to the gospels.

The feeding narratives are, therefore, more than one type of miracle told about someone sent by God; they intend more than to tell how Jesus surpasses the miracles of Elijah and Moses or how in his lifetime an eschatological expectation was already realized. The narratives take up the political-religious praxis and ideals of public and civic banquets and mass-

---

86. Hans Joachim Held, 'Matthäus als Interpret der Wundergeschichte', in Günther Bornkamm et al. (eds), *Überlieferungund Auslegung im Matthäusevangelium* (WMANT 1, Neukirchen-Vluyn: Neukirchener Verlag, 6th edn, 1970), describes the feeding narrative as an epiphany in the presence of the disciples because Jesus was not the host of the crowd but actually of the disciples. This is why there is no awe-struck response from those present at the miracle.

87. Origen finds this so remarkable that he gives this interpretation of the added words in Mt. 14.21 (besides women and children): 'But someone might say that, while many ate and according to their due and capacity (κατ᾽ ἀξίαν καὶ δύναμιν) participated in the loaves of blessing, some worthy to be numbered were men, but others who were not worthy of such account and numbering were children and women' (*Commentary on the Gospel of Matthew*, XI, 3).

88. In his *Wundergeschichten*, pp. 111–12, Theißen lists spontaneity as the first characteristic of the gift-miracles: 'The spontaneity of the miraculous action which is never caused by requests'.

feedings. From here they developed the underlying expectation and hope that the common meal of all turns out to become really the (u)topia where indeed all become truly 'filled'.

Translated by Martin Rumscheidt

Chapter 6

THE VARIOUS TASTES OF JOHANNINE BREAD AND BLOOD: A MULTI-PERSPECTIVE READING OF JOHN 6[1]

Esther Kobel

6.1. *Introduction*

It seems safe to say that John 6.51-58 is one of the most disputed passages of the Fourth Gospel.[2] In this passage of the 'Bread of Life Discourse', Jesus tells his audience that they must consume bread, blood and body. Jesus then identifies the bread that he will give for the life of the world with his own flesh (σάρξ). He further declares that, in order to have eternal life, it is a condition that they eat (φάγητε) the flesh of the Son of Man and drink his (Jesus') blood (Jn 6.53). Jesus elaborates on this by explaining that the one who chews (τρώγων, Jn 6.54, 56, 57, 58) his flesh and drinks his blood will have eternal life.[3] Believers will be raised on the last day. Jesus' flesh is

---

1.   This article draws on my doctoral thesis *Dining with John. Communal Meals and Identity Formation in the Fourth Gospel and its Historical and Cultural Context*, submitted at the University of Basel, Switzerland, 2010; published in the Biblical Interpretation Series, Leiden: Brill, 2011.

2.   For decades, scholars have argued over whether the passage is 'originally' Johannine or whether it is an interpolation by a later author, and if so, whether there is a conflict with the preceding verses. However hard anyone tries to solve the question, the issue ultimately remains unsolvable, or as Burge notes, 'Literary studies which have attempted to set apart this passage (along with trying to identify a uniform "Johannine style") have run aground, while the authentic character of 6.52-58 has all but been confirmed.' G. M. Burge, *The Anointed Community: The Holy Spirit in the Johannine Tradition* (Grand Rapids: Eerdmans, 1987), p. 183. See here also for further literature on the question of authenticity and coherence of Jn 6.51-58.

3.   Translations of τρώγων include: to bite or chew food, eat (audibly), F. W. Danker, W. Bauer and W. F. Arndt, *A Greek-English Lexicon of the New Testament and Other Early Christian Literature* (Chicago: University of Chicago Press, 2000), p. 1019; cf. Goppelt, 'trōgō', in Bauernfeind and Kittel (eds), *Theologisches Wörterbuch zum Neuen Testament* (Stuttgart: Kohlhammer, 1949–73), Vol. 8, pp. 236–7. The term τρώγω can signify 'gnaw, nibble, munch' and is used primarily for herbivorous animals in the sense of the German 'fressen' but also for humans. H. G. Liddell and R. Scott, *A Greek-English Lexicon* (Oxford: Clarendon Press, 1996), p. 1832.

the true food (ἀληθὴς ἐστιν βρῶσις, Jn 6.55) and his blood the true drink (ἀληθὴς ἐστιν πόσις, Jn 6.55).

The repeated use of the verb τρώγων in John 6, instead of the commonly used ἐσθίειν, draws attention to the reality of the physical eating, and it invites the reader to hear allusions of various kinds.[4] A number of themes of which the passage is possibly allusive will be discussed in the following pages.

An allusion is one of a range of forms of intertextuality.[5] Intertextuality is understood here in its post-modern sense. It refers to the sheer unlimited connections that a reader may make between a given text and other texts, traditions and concepts.[6] Texts in themselves do not contain meaning; it is the reader who finds meaning in relationship to other texts or traditions.[7] I follow Culler's observation that, 'Intertextuality thus becomes less a name for a work's relation to prior texts than a designation of its participation in the discursive space of a culture.'[8]

My interest lies in exploring the intertextual space of the Gospel of John by taking inventory of the cultural codes within which the Gospel passage operates and of which it is a manifestation. In other words, I wish to explore a number of 'tastes' or surplus meanings that the Johannine verses about the consumption of Jesus' flesh and blood in John 6.51-58 may have had when savoured by its original audience.

---

4.   Apart from the four uses in John 6 (vv. 54, 56, 57, 58) this lemma appears only twice in the New Testament – Jn 13.18 and Mt. 24.38 – and nowhere in the LXX or Philo or Josephus.

5.   Note that the terminology for elements of intertextuality such as quotation, allusion and echo (and other terms) is used in different ways by various literary theorists and biblical scholars. S. Porter, 'The Use of the Old Testament in the New Testament', in C. Evans and J. Sanders (eds), *Early Christian Interpretation of the Scriptures of Israel. Investigations and Proposals* (Sheffield: Sheffield Academic Press, 1997), p. 80.

Often the distinction between allusion, reference and echo is defined by the 'disputability' or 'indisputability' of a marker's reference to cultural tradition. This distinction, however, lacks a solid criterion, for it is impossible for a modern reader to decide to any certain degree whether a text is indisputably referring to another text or not. Identification of any type of reference less explicit than direct quotations, therefore, requires the participation and judgement of the reader. For 'criteria for testing claims about the presence and meaning of scriptural echoes' (i.e., availability, volume, recurrence, thematic coherence, historical plausibility, history of interpretation, and satisfaction), see, R. B. Hays, *Echoes of Scripture in the Letters of Paul* (New Haven: Yale University Press, 1989), pp. 29–32.

6.   In this study, 'text' is understood in a broad sense. It may refer to written documents, but also to concepts and traditions. Cf. Z. Ben-Porat, 'The Poetics of Literary Allusion', *PTL* 1 (1976): 105–28 (107–8, n. 5).

7.   T. Rajan, 'Intertextuality and the Subject of Reading/Writing', in J. Clayton and E. Rothstein (eds), *Influence and Intertextuality in Literary History* (Madison: University of Wisconsin Press, 1976), pp. 61–74 (62).

8.   J. Culler, *The Pursuit of Signs: Semiotics, Literature, Deconstruction* (London: Routledge, 1981), p. 103.

6.1. *Taste I: A Eucharistic Taste*

The most obvious and most often discussed tradition that potentially informed the readers of the Johannine text of a surplus meaning in the passage is the 'Eucharist'.[9]

As is well known, the Fourth Gospel contains its own account of a last meal before Jesus' crucifixion and it differs in a number of ways from its Synoptic parallels. Instead of an institution of the Eucharist, John portrays Jesus washing his disciples' feet. A number of reasons could stand behind the absence of a eucharistic institution in the Fourth Gospel. While unlikely, it is possible that the author of the Fourth Gospel was not familiar with any eucharistic tradition. Another option is that John consciously omitted a specific account of the Eucharist or that a eucharistic tradition is presupposed without being explicitly mentioned.[10] I will undertake a comparative analysis particularly on the semantic level in order to assess whether any words, objects, phrases in John 6.51-58 are reminiscent of eucharistic traditions.

In order to assess the likelihood and character of eucharistic allusions in the passage, I will compare the passage to the words of institution. There is a scholarly consent that the Johannine parallel to the words of institution is to be found in Jn 6.51-58 if anywhere at all.[11]

---

9.   While the verb εὐχαριστέω appears three times in John (Jn 6.11, 23; 11.41), the corresponding noun 'Eucharist', εὐχαριστία, is absent in John and the Synoptics. The use of the term 'Eucharist' is nevertheless widespread in New Testament scholarship and will be used in the following discussion. Retaining the term is a way of expressing that there is something more to the consumption than just the intake of calories. This does, however, by no means imply that there was a ritual with a fixed form that corresponded to the term at the time that the Gospel of John was written.

10.   Cf. S. Petersen, 'Jesus zum "Kauen"?: Das Johannesevangelium, das Abendmahl und die Mysterienkulte', in J. Hartenstein (ed.) *'Eine gewöhnliche und harmlose Speise?': Von den Entwicklungen frühchristlicher Abendmahlstraditionen* (Gütersloh: Gütersloher Verlagshaus, 2008), pp. 105–30 (106).

11.   A majority of scholars suggest a eucharistic interpretation of John 6.51-58. In their view Jesus' exhortations for his flesh to be eaten and his blood to be drunk indicate, or at least hint at, the eucharistic elements to be consumed by participants in the Eucharist. For example, P. Borgen, 'The Unity of Discourse in John 6', *ZNW* 50 (1959): 277–8; J. M. Perry, 'The Evolution of the Johannine Eucharist', *NTS* 39 (1993): 22–3; J. H. Hodges, 'Food as Synecdoche in John's Gospel and Gnostic Texts' (PhD thesis, University of California, 1996), pp. 15, 96–7; B. Chilton, *A Feast of Meanings: Eucharistic Theologies from Jesus through Johannine Circles* (Leiden: Brill, 1994), pp. 132–3.

Few scholars deny any eucharistic meaning to John 6 as a whole or to John 6.51b-58 in particular. For example, C. R. Koester, 'John Six and the Lord's Supper', *LQ* 4 (1990): 419–37 (433). And even in such cases it is usually suggested that there is some kind of eucharistic language in the background. Indeed, it seems hardly possible to argue otherwise. Thus, for example, it has been claimed that, though John 6.51c-58 uses eucharistic language, the primary emphasis of the passage is christological or anti-docetic. For example, M. J. Menken, 'John 6:51c-58: Eucharist

The words of institution as conveyed in variations by Paul in 1 Cor. 11.23-26 and the Synoptic writers in Mt. 26.26-29, Mk 14.22-25, and Lk. 22.15-20 are taken as points of reference to identify possible eucharistic allusions in the Fourth Gospel. It is not necessary to presuppose that John knew the Synoptic Gospels or the Pauline epistles in written form. Whether the author of the Fourth Gospel was familiar with these texts is uncertain. The fact, however, that a text as early as 1 Corinthians offers an account of the words of institution strongly suggests that some form of eucharistic ritual was practised in early communities. Furthermore, all gospels obviously share common traditions. It is likely, therefore, that John shares with the Synoptics the tradition of Jesus' last meal even if John departs from the Synoptics in notable ways. Both parallels and differences between John and the Synoptic and Pauline passages are numerous. Elements of the Johannine text that may have been reminiscent of eucharistic texts, concepts or traditions for the original audience can now be discussed.

First, Jesus states that the *bread* that he will give is his flesh, offered for them and for the life of the world, ὑπὲρ τῆς τοῦ κόσμου ζωῆς (Jn 6.51). The notion that Jesus gives his body for others strongly alludes to the eucharistic institution.[12] Despite the obvious parallels there is an equally obvious difference in wording: while the Synoptics and Paul use the lemma σῶμα, John uses σάρξ.[13]

Second, the *blood* (αἷμα), which the Johannine Jesus orders his audience to drink (Jn 6.53), is reminiscent of the blood referred to in the Synoptic and Pauline words of institution (Mt. 26.28, Mk 14.24, Lk. 22.20, 1 Cor. 11.25, 27). In these verses, the cup, or its content, which is wine or at least a product of the vine, is equated to Jesus' blood.[14] In John 6, the blood appears here without previous reference. There is no mention of a cup, or of wine, or of any other drink. Nevertheless, it is obvious that the blood could easily have been associated with the wine and its ritual function, thereby paralleling the connection between bread and body.

or Christology', in R. Culpepper (ed.), *Critical Readings of John 6* (Leiden: Brill, 1987), pp. 183–204; J. D. Dunn, 'John 6. A Eucharistic Discourse?', *NTS* 17 (1971): 328–38 (337).

A number of scholars adopt an intermediate position, as, for example, Raymond E. Brown. Rejecting theories that the entire discourse is either referring solely to Jesus' teaching or solely to the Eucharist, Brown suggests that 'The combination of "flesh" and "blood" in 6.53-56, and the use of the realistic verb trōgō ("to feed on") are other eucharistic indications. Thus we must see both doctrinal and eucharistic themes in Jn 6.' R. E. Brown, 'The Eucharist and Baptism in John', in R. E. Brown (ed.), *New Testament Essays* (Garden City, NY: Image Books, 1965), pp. 77–95 (82).

12. Cf. τοῦτό μού ἐστιν τὸ σῶμα τὸ ὑπὲρ ὑμῶν (1 Cor. 11.24; ἔνοχος ἔσται τοῦ σώματος καὶ τοῦ αἵματος τοῦ κυρίου (1 Cor. 11.27); τοῦτό, ἐστιν τὸ σωμά μοῦ (Mt. 26.26; Mk 14.22; Lk. 22.19).

13. καὶ ὁ ἄρτος δὲ ὃν ἐγὼ δώσω ἡ σάρξ μού ἐστιν, Jn 6.51; repeated in different forms in the rest of the discourse, Jn 6.52, 53, 53, 54, 55, 56, and again in 6.63.

Third, both the Johannine verses as well as the Synoptic passages mention the act of eating. Again, however, there is a notable difference in wording. The Synoptics use various forms of the more common lemma ἐσθίω, while John peculiarly employs the verb τρώγω in its participle form τρώγων. The use of this verb instead of the more familiar one may be understood as a linguistic means of emphasizing the intention of the passage. According to this interpretation, from Jn 6.51c onwards, the eating does not mean the taking on of Jesus' self-presentation through faith, but the taking on by means of physically eating, that is, partaking of the Eucharist.[15]

Besides these striking parallels and allusions to the institution of the Eucharist, a number of central elements of these accounts are absent.[16] As Petersen points out, in Jn 6.51-58 there is neither any mention of community, κοινωνία (cf. 1 Cor. 10.16), or of a covenant, διαθήκη (cf. Mk 14.24; Mt. 26.28), or new covenant, καινὴ διαθήκη (cf. 1 Cor. 11.25; Lk. 22.20). The notion that the eating and drinking should be repeated in remembrance of Jesus is missing (cf. 1 Cor. 11.24-26; Lk. 22.19), as is the connection to unworthiness of potential consumers (cf. 1 Cor. 11.27). John 6 is possibly a mere speech while in the Pauline and Synoptic scenes the words are accompanied by symbolic actions (i.e., the taking and breaking of bread, the taking of the cup).

John 6 positively values the consumption of Jesus' flesh and blood by true believers. Those who eat and drink of it will attain eternal life. It seems necessary, however, to take into account the few verses following Jn 6.51-58, for they complement the sayings in a peculiar way. The disciples react negatively to Jesus' 'hard' sayings (Jn 6.60) and trigger a clarification of the enigmatic discourse on behalf of Jesus. Jesus now states that the flesh is of no use and that it is his words that are the spirit and the life (Jn 6.63). The true ingestion of Jesus, therefore, is not the flesh and the blood but the belief in Jesus. The positive portrayal, even salvific necessity, of consuming Jesus' flesh and blood as a means of eternal life (Jn 6.53) seems to be contradicted by Jn 6.63. A closer look, however, reveals that Jn 6.63 likely does not contradict Jn 6.53, for the manner in which σάρξ is employed in those two verses is categorically different. First, the combination of πνεῦμα / σάρξ in Jn 6.63 differs from σάρξ / αἷμα in Jn 6.53. Second, the σάρξ in Jn 6.51-56 is always qualified as Jesus' σάρξ. In all other occurrences in the Fourth Gospel, however, σάρξ (without article) is established as flesh as such and as the opposing pole to the spirit (πνεῦμα). It can be said, therefore, that Jn 6.63

14.	Mt. 26.27, Mk 14.25 and Lk. 22.18 mention wine explicitly; as for 1 Cor. 11.25 it seems likely that here also wine is the content of the cup.

15.	L. Goppelt, 'τρώγω', in G. Kittel (ed.), *Theologisches Wörterbuch zum Neuen Testament*, Vol. 8, pp. 236–7.

16.	Petersen, *Jesus zum 'Kauen'*, pp. 115–17.

does not refer to 6.53 in order to create ambivalence but rather belongs to the framework of opposition as it is familiar, for example, from the talk between Jesus and Nicodemus (Jn 3.6).[17] The eating of the flesh and the drinking of the blood is not an end in itself. John 6.63 emphasizes that it is the spirit that gives life, the flesh is useless. Ultimately the word, that is, what Jesus has spoken to his audience, is the goal of the discourse.

The numerous markers alluding to eucharistic traditions allow for the judgement that Jn 6.51-58 has a notable eucharistic theme even if some elements from the texts of reference are missing. While the consumption of body and blood is valued highly in the bread of life discourse, the true way to partake in Jesus is through faith and spirit (6.27-29, 35, and especially 63). The allusive presence of eucharistic elements and the emphasis on faith and spirit invite the audience to focus on Christ's death, the salvific revelation of God in Jesus, and not just to the symbols that point to it.[18] Whether or not the community performed a ritual containing bread and wine, possibly after the meals, however, cannot be discerned from the Johannine text.

6.2. *Taste II: A Taste of Mystery*

The second taste of Jn 6.51-58 to be explored is the taste of mystery. The Gospel of John is undoubtedly rooted in a Jewish matrix. It is shaped by its Jewish roots, such as, for example, the Jewish Scriptures, and is influenced by the more recent and highly formative belief in Christ. At the same time, as is well known, the gospel emerged from a highly hybrid context, a peculiarity shared by all Mediterranean regions in antiquity. Thus it is possible that the Fourth Gospel was additionally influenced by other traditions found in the Mediterranean area, for example by mystery cults that were widely spread and practised by many at the time of the emergence of the gospel.[19] It therefore seems appropriate to assume on the part of author and readers a general familiarity with the main ideas of various mystery cults. I will explore Jn 6.51-58 for possible meanings that may have been associated from the world of mystery cults by a first- or second-century audience.

17.   The parallels between John 6.63 and John 3.6 are not confined to the parallel wording of the opposition between flesh and spirit. In both verses the theme is how to attain eternal life and the explanations correspond. The revelatory aspect of speech is marked in both cases by the statement that flesh and spirit are harshly opposed as human and divine possibilities. Both verses deal with the paradoxical combination of Jesus' coming down to earth and his elevation. G. Bornkamm, 'Die eucharistische Rede im Johannes-Evangelium', *ZNW* 47 (1956): 161–9 (166–7).

18.   Cf. C. S. Keener, *The Gospel of John: A Commentary* (Peabody, MA: Hendrickson Publishers, 2003), pp. 689–91.

19.   For an introduction to mystery cults, see F. Graf, 'Mysterien', in M. Landfester, H. Cancik and H. Schneider (eds), *Der neue Pauly. Enzyklopädie der Antike* (16 vols; Stuttgart: J.B. Metzler, 1996–2003), Vol. 8, pp. 615–26.

The cult of Dionysus in particular offers a backdrop against which the passage can fruitfully be illumined. During the Hellenistic period the cult of Dionysus was well known and was practised in various forms all over the Mediterranean area, especially in the border regions of the Greek world, that is, Asia Minor.[20] The known literary sources go back to the early fifth century BCE and reach well beyond the Hellenistic period.[21]

The importance of mystery cults as a reference for the last supper traditions has been thoroughly researched by New Testament scholars.[22] Also, it has been convincingly demonstrated that not only the Cana account, but very likely the entire Gospel of John, engages in a subtextual discourse with Dionysian tradition.[23]

As has already been discussed, the graphic nature of John's language in the passage is underscored by two terms in particular: the term for 'eating' and the term for 'body'.[24] The nuance of chewing, munching, and so on, in the verb τρώγειν is usually lost in modern translations. Nevertheless, we may suggest that original audiences would have been aware of, and struck by, the particular nuances given its meanings in Greek. It is therefore likely that the Johannine use of τρώγειν here is not just a variant, but a deliberate emphasis on the reality of physical eating.[25] Furthermore,

---

20. F. Sokolowski, *Lois sacrées de l'Asie Mineure* (Paris: Boccard, 1955), p. 125.

21. The richest literary source is certainly Euripides' play *Bacchae*, probably written around 407 BCE. T. Paulsen, *Geschichte der griechischen Literatur* (Stuttgart: Philipp Reclam, 2004), p. 131. For an investigation into the literary and epigraphical evidence for Dionysian cults, see H. S. Versnel, *Ter unus: Isis, Dionysos, Hermes* (Leiden: Brill, 1990), pp. 134–46.

Literary sources are complemented by iconographical and archaeological evidence and a considerable number of inscriptions. For example, Livy's report on the 'Bacchanalian Affair' in his *Ab urbe condita*, p. 39; T. Livius, P. G. Walsh (ed.), *Book XXXIX* (Warminster: Aris and Phillips, 1994). Iconography is found, e.g., in the Villa Farnesina and the Villa dei Misteri in Pompeii. Grave finds stem from Olbia, Hipponium, Crete and Cumae. For photos of the bone tablets from Olbia, see M. L. West, *The Orphic Poems* (Oxford: Clarendon Press, 1983), first page of appendix. On inscriptional material, see R. Seaford, *Dionysos* (London: Routledge, 2006), p. 60.

22. H.-J. Klauck, *Herrenmahl und hellenistischer Kult: Eine religionsgeschichtliche Untersuchung zum ersten Korintherbrief* (Münster: Aschendorff, 1982); Petersen, *Jesus zum 'Kauen'*.

23. Reading the Fourth Gospel against the backdrop of mystery cults in general, and Dionysian traditions in particular, has a long tradition. For a good overview and the argument about the subtext, see P. Wick, 'Jesus gegen Dionysos? Ein Beitrag zur Kontextualisierung des Johannesevangeliums', *Bib.* 85 (2004): 179–98.

24. Notably, John does not employ a distinctive term for the drinking. The terms καταρροφέω or ἀναρροιβδέω that express slurping or sipping would have been possible options.

25. Cf. Bultmann, 'Andrerseits wird in V. 54 der Anstoß dadurch gesteigert, daß das φάγειν durch das stärkere τρώγειν ersetzt ist: es handelt sich also um reales Essen, nicht um irgendeine geistige Aneignung.' R. K. Bultmann, *Das Evangelium des Johannes* (Göttingen: Vandenhoeck & Ruprecht, 1986), p. 176.

instead of the otherwise frequently employed σῶμα,[26] John uses σάρξ in this passage.[27] Usually σῶμα is translated as 'body' – referring to either a corpse or a living body[28] – while σάρξ is usually the flesh, the material that covers the bones of a (human or animal) body.[29] The idea of physically eating Jesus' flesh is, therefore, emphasized in this passage and culminates in v. 57. Here Jesus states that whoever eats or chews him will live through him.[30]

This passage's peculiar vocabulary can be illumined against Dionysian traditions. In order to undergird the argument that this passage is allusive of Dionysian traditions and not the result of chance, the discussion opens up its view to the entire gospel and adduces further striking parallels between the Johannine Jesus and Dionysus.

Dionysus is the most visible of all Greek gods, polymorphous in nature, and present in myth, literature and art. While his characteristics are manifold, the best known is Dionysus as the God of wine. Indeed, Dionysus is even identified with wine.[31] According to Teiresias, Dionysus is responsible for the gift of wine to humankind, 'Himself a god, he is poured out in libations to the gods, and so it is because of him that men win blessings from them' (*Bacchae* 284–5).[32]

26. For example, in the words of institution (τὸ σῶμά μου, Mt. 26.26; Mk 14.23; Lk. 22.19, and τοῦ σώματος, 1 Cor. 11.27.)

27. καὶ ὁ ἄρτος δὲ ὅν ἐγὼ δώσω ἡ σάρξ μού ἐστιν, Jn 6.51; and repeated in the rest of the discourse in different forms, Jn 6.52, 53, 53, 54, 55, 56, and later again in 6.63.

28. Danker et al., *Greek-English Lexicon*, p. 983.

29. Danker et al., *Greek-English Lexicon*, pp. 914–15. In the Fourth Gospel, the word σῶμα occurs in five instances, in four of which it clearly signifies the dead body/corpse of Jesus (on the cross: 19.31, 38, 40; in the tomb: 20.12). The only possibly ambiguous occurrence of σῶμα is in Jn 2.21 when the narrator informs the readers that Jesus is talking of the temple of his body (ἐκεῖνος δὲ ἔλεγεν περὶ τοῦ ναοῦ τοῦ σώματος αὐτοῦ,, Jn 20.12). From the context it is obvious, however, that in this instance σῶμα is a reference to the dead body, the corpse that will be resurrected after three days.

30. The incarnatory aspects of Jesus as flesh and blood appear also in the works of Ignatius. In *Tral.* 8.1 Ignatius relates the renewal of faith to the flesh of the Lord and love to the blood of Christ (ἀνακτήσασθε ἑαυτοὺς ἐν πίστει ὅ ἐστιν σάρξ τοῦ κυρίου καὶ ἐν ἀγάπῃ ὅ ἐστιν αἷμα Ἰησοῦ Χριστοῦ, *Tral.* 8.1). In *Rom.* 7.3 he states that he desires the bread of God, the heavenly bread, the bread of life, which is the flesh of Jesus Christ, the Son of God; and that he desires to drink of God, namely his blood, which is incorruptible love (ἄρτον θεοῦ θέλω ὅ ἐστιν σάρξ Ἰησοῦ Χριστοῦ...τοῦ ἐκ σπέρματος Δαυείδ καὶ πόμα θέλω τὸ αἷμα αὐτοῦ ὅ ἐστιν ἀγάπη ἄφθαρτος, *Rom.* 7.3).

31. For the equation of Dionysus with wine and further sources for this idea in antiquity, see W. Burkert, *Homo necans: Interpretationen altgriechischer Opferriten und Mythen* (Berlin: Walter de Gruyter, 1997), pp. 248–9, esp. n. 42.

32. οὗτος θεοῖσι σπένδεται θεὸς γεγώς, ὥστε διὰ τοῦτον τἀγάθ' ἀνθρώπους ἔχειν; Euripides, *Bacchae*, D. Kovacs (ed.), (Cambridge, MA: Harvard University Press, 2002), pp. 36–7. Cf. also the parallel in Pauline literature: 'I am poured out, as a sacrifice' (σπένδομαι ἐπὶ τῇ θυσίᾳ, Phil. 2.17).

The association of wine with blood appears frequently. The juice of the grapes associated with blood is well known in many traditions, Jewish and pagan alike (for example, Gen. 49.11; Deut. 32.14; Rev. 17.6; Achilles Tatius 2.2.4). The idea of Dionysus being torn apart and pressed into wine appears in songs that are sung when grapes are pressed (for example, Clement of Alexandria, *Scholia in Protrepticum et Paedagogum* 2.3).[33]

Parallels to our passage are quite obvious. Just as Dionysus has brought wine to humankind, Jesus is the provider of wine at the wedding in Cana (Jn 2.1-11) and even calls himself the true vine (Jn 15.1). Nevertheless, John 6 does not mention wine, but only bread, blood and body. The chewing of the flesh is a necessary act for attaining eternal life. But if flesh and bread are associated with each other and blood shall be drunk along with it, then it is not a great leap to associate the blood with wine.

Aside from the association of Dionysus with wine and other plants, he was often identified with animals, especially a bull.[34] Particularly interesting is the ritual of eating a bull's flesh in Dionysian rituals, seemingly a widespread custom.[35] Such rituals apparently included the tearing apart of the living creatures, the so called *sparagmos*, and a subsequent feast of raw flesh, known as *omophagy*. A *sparagmos* of Dionysus himself appears in the famous myth about Dionysus Zagreus.[36] According to the myth, the Titans killed the infant Dionysus and tore him apart limb by limb.[37] The myth about Dionysus Zagreus is connected with Dionysian *omophagy* in a scholion on Clement of Alexandria on Protrepticus (Scholion Clem Al Prot 119.1).[38] According to the scholiast, the initiates to Dionysus ate raw meat to imitate the tearing apart of Dionysus by the Maenads. Evidence from an inscription from Miletus referring to ὠμοφάγιον suggests that participants actually

---

33.   ἀγροικικὴ ᾠδὴ ἐπὶ τῷ ληνῷ ᾀδομένη, καὶ αὐτὴ περιεῖχεν τὸν Διονύσου σπαραγμόν. Clemens Alexandrinus, *Scholia in clementem alexandrinum (scholia recentiora partim sub auctore Aretha): Scholia in protrepticum et paedagogum*, U. Treu et al. (eds), *Die griechischen christlichen Schiftsteller der ersten Jahrhunderte*, Vol 12 (Berlin: Akademie Verlag, 3rd edn, 1972).

34.   For plants, see J. E. Harrison, *Prolegomena to the Study of Greek Religion* (Princeton: Princeton University Press, 1991), p. 426; for animals, see Seaford, *Dionysus*, pp. 23–5.

35.   For example, *Bacchae* 135–9, 735–47, 1125–43; Plutarch, *Moralia* 417C; Euripides, *Fragments* 472.9-15. See also W. Burkert, *Ancient Mystery Cults* (Cambridge: Harvard University Press, 1987), p. 110.

36.   This son of Zeus may originally have been a distinct god, but he was soon identified and merged with Dionysus; O. Kern, 'Dionysos', in G. Wissowa (ed.), *Paulys Realencyclopädie der classischen Altertumswissenschaft* (83 vols; München: Alfred Druckenmüller, 1893–1980), Vol. 5.1, pp. 1008–46 (1014).

37.   S. I. Johnston, 'The Myth of Dionysos', in F. Graf and S. I. Johnston (eds), *Ritual Texts for the Afterlife. Orpheus and the Bacchic Gold Tablets* (London: Routledge, 2007), pp. 66–93.

38.   Klauck, *Herrenmahl*, p. 111.

performed the ritual of eating raw flesh.[39] According to this inscription no one was allowed to lay the ὠμοφάγιον down before the priestess.

In summary, there is a well-known tradition that followers of Dionysus cut up the sacrificial animal into pieces and ate of the raw flesh. They believe that by ingesting the bloody flesh they substantially absorb the god. *Sparagmos* and *omophagy* are the vehicles through which the believers appropriate the living power of the god who is present within the victim. The notion of ingesting Dionysus is inherent to the consumption of wine, which represents the blood of this god, and to the consumption of raw meat from a bull that has been torn apart and also represents Dionysus. The boundaries between god, human and sacrifice blur.[40]

Since the traditions of *sparagmos* and *omophagy* appear in several sources over a long period of time within several areas of the Graeco-Roman world, it seems reasonable to assume that the gospel writer(s) and audience were very likely familiar with these ideas. The peculiar wording in Jn 6.51-58, according to which true followers of Jesus need to chew his flesh and drink his blood in order to attain eternal life, may well have been allusive of the idea of Dionysian traditions for the earliest gospel audience.

While Dionysian followers consumed raw flesh dripping with blood, be it in reality or merely in literary depiction, John takes the notion of consuming the divine to a more abstract level.[41] After exhorting his audience to chew his flesh, Jesus equates himself with bread. Thus, those who chew the bread eat Jesus, a sign of true belief in him.

Reading the strikingly peculiar and graphic vocabulary of Jn 6.51-58 in light of Dionysian traditions suggests that the passage is likely allusive of them. Whoever chews Jesus' flesh and drinks his blood, and thereby demonstrates that he believes in Jesus, is said to attain eternal life. It is a post-Easter community to whom these words about chewing Jesus are addressed. The allusions may well function as a means of reassuring the believers that Jesus is present among them, even within them, and provides life for them even after his own death.

---

39.   For example, H. Jeanmaire, *Dionysos: Histoire du culte de Bacchus* (Paris: Payot, 1951), pp. 264–5. Klauck suggests that the meat referred to in this inscription consisted of small pieces of raw flesh that was distributed to the celebrants, commemorating the bloody *sparagmos* that was not actually performed any longer. The originally wild proceedings were reduced to a tame ritual. Klauck, *Herrenmahl*, p. 112. Henrichs argues against the idea that this inscription refers to actual performances of *omophagy*. He suggests instead that it was not the Maenads that received the animal or its raw flesh as food, but Dionysus himself who is known as the eater of raw flesh. A. Henrichs, 'Greek Maenadism from Olympias to Messalina', *Harvard Studies in Classical Philology* 82 (1978): 121–60 (151). On the inscription, see especially Henrichs, *Greek Maenadism*, pp. 148–52; Sokolowski, *Lois sacrées*, pp. 123–5.

40.   Cf. Klauck, *Herrenmahl*, p. 111.

41.   Cf. Petersen, *Jesus zum 'Kauen'*, p. 125.

6.3. *Taste III: A Bonding Taste*

The third and last taste to be explored is the bonding taste. The graphic language of Jn 6.51-58 not only alludes to eucharistic traditions, but also raises the uncomfortable possibility that the Johannine Jesus may be inviting his listeners to engage in 'cannibalism'.[42] It seems to me, however, that the earliest audience may have heard this passage not in an exclusively metaphorical manner but that they may well have picked up allusions to cannibalistic behaviour.

A number of sources from the early centuries CE accuse Christ-believers of ritual murder followed by the consumption of human flesh and incestuous intercourse.[43] The rumours about immoral behaviour by Christ-believers stem from as early as the first century CE. As is well known from Tacitus, Christ-believers were already hated in Nero's time for their (alleged) crimes (*flagitia, Ann.* 15.44), their destructive superstitions (*exitiabilis superstitio, Ann.* 15.44), and their hatred of humankind (*odium humani generis, Ann.* 15.44). [44] Some scholars have interpreted this source as pertaining to Christ-believers' meals, in which cannibalism was allegedly performed.[45] A more reliable source is the famous letter that Pliny the Younger sends to the

---

42.   Interestingly enough, only a few commentators care to discuss this possibility. Usually they dismiss it as a mere metaphor with no correspondence to real life. For example, H. Thyen, *Das Johannesevangelium* (Tübingen: Mohr Siebeck, 2005), pp. 365–6.

43.   Over the last century several attempts have been made to interpret the sources from the first few centuries CE concerning the reproach of thyestean feasts and oedipal incest. The most important are: J. P. Waltzing, 'Le crime rituel reproché aux Chrétiens du IIe siècle', *Bulletins de la classe des lettres de l'Académie Royale Belge* (1925): 205–39; E. Bickermann, 'Ritualmord und Eselskult', *MGWJ.NF* 35 (1927): 171–87; 255–64; F. J. Dölger, 'Sacramentum Infanticidii. Die Schlachtung eines Kindes und der Genuß seines Fleisches und Blutes als vermeintlicher Einweihungsakt im ältesten Christentum', *AuC* 4 (1934): 188–228; W. Speyer, 'Zu den Vorwürfen der Heiden gegen die Christen', *JAC* 6 (1963): 129–35; R. Freudenberger, 'Der Vorwurf ritueller Verbrechen', *ThZ* 23 (1967): 97–107; A. Henrichs, 'Pagan Ritual and the Alleged Crimes of the Early Christians. A Reconsideration', in P. Granfield, J. A. Jungmann and J.Quasten (eds), *Kyriakon. Festschrift Johannes Quasten* (Münster: Aschendorff, 1970), pp. 18–35; R. M. Grant, 'Charges of "Immorality" against Various Groups in Antiquity', in R. van Broek, M. J. Vermaseren and G. Quispeln (eds), *Studies in Gnosticism and Hellenistic Religions. Presented to Gilles Quispel on the Occasion of his 65th Birthday* (Leiden: Brill, 1981), pp. 161–70; M. J. Edwards, 'Some Early Christian Immoralities', *AnSoc* 23 (1992): 71–82; F. G. Downing, 'Cynics and Christians, Oedipus and Thyestes', *JEH* 44 (1993): 1–10; A. McGowan, 'Eating People. Accusations of Cannibalism against Christians in the Second Century', *JECS* 2 (1994): 413–24.

44.   Tacitus, *The Annals Books XIII–XVI* (1991), pp. 282–5.

45.   First Hans Achelis (H. Achelis, *Das Christentum in den ersten drei Jahrhunderten* (Leipzig, 1912), p. 294) followed by Waltzing, *'Le crime rituel'*, p. 210. According to Lanzillotta, *superstitio* and *odium humani generis* were normally attributed to the Jews, thus the suggestion that Tacitus considered Christians to be a Jewish sect: L. R. Lanzillotta, 'The Early Christians and Human Sacrifice', in J. N. Bremmer (ed.), *The Strange World of Human Sacrifice* (Leuven: Peeters Press, 2007), pp. 81–102 (83–4).

Emperor Trajan in the very early second century.[46] From this source it becomes obvious that Christ-believers defend their doings by emphasizing that their meals are ordinary and harmless (*ad capiendum cibum, promiscuum tamen et innoxium*, X.96.7). Behind this may well lie rumours about murderous actions connected to meals.[47]

In the course of the following centuries, the reproaches became more explicit and much more colourfully described. Incest, ritual murder and cannibalism originally appeared separately from each other only to be linked over time and eventually becoming inseparable.[48]

Accusatory language alluding to cannibalistic banquets would have been recognized and understood immediately in the Graeco-Roman milieu.[49] With regard to the Gospel of John, Albert Harrill has recently explored this topic in an article about cannibalistic language in John and Greco-Roman polemics of factionalism.[50] He argues that 'We should interpret the cannibalistic language in John 6.52-66 in the social context of this firing back and forth of invective between the synagogue authorities and the sectarian Johannine community,' and he claims that 'the Johannine author revaluated the cultural taboo of cannibalism in positive terms as a means of self-definition for his community, to throw outsiders off the scent and to weed out those insiders "who did not believe" (6.64)'.[51]

Harrill may be right in presupposing that accusations of cannibalism against the Johannine Christ-believers are reflected in the text and even

46.   G. C. S. Plinius, *Letters and Panegyricus in Two Volumes*, B. Radice (ed.), (London, Cambridge: Heinemann, Harvard University Press, 1969).

47.   S. Benko, *Pagan Rome and the Early Christians* (Bloomington: Indiana University Press, 1984), p. 70.

48.   It is in Athenagoras' *Legatio* 3.1, dating from 177 CE, that the threefold charge of atheism, Thyestean meals and Oedipal intercourse appeared in its familiar form for the first time. Athenagoras, *Legatio pro Christianis* (Berlin: Walter de Gruyter, 1990), p. 26. Cf. the threefold charge in the letter from the Greek-speaking Christ-believers of Vienne and Lyons to those in Asia and Phrygia concerning the martyrdoms. Eusebius has preserved this testimony in which persecutions of the Christians in 177 CE are recorded: *Hist. Eccl.* 5.1.3-63; Eusebius, *Die Kirchengeschichte*, F. Winkelmann and E. Schwartz (eds), (Berlin: Akademie-Verlag, 1999), pp. 403–27. The fully developed portrayal of felonious Christian rituals of initiation with all the necessary preparations and disgusting details is found in the works of the apologetics Tertullian (*Apol.* 7–9) and Minucius Felix (*Octavius* 9.5-7) (both second to early third century CE); Tertullianus, *Quinti Septimi Florentis Tertulliani ad Nationes libri duo*, J. G. P. Borleffs (ed.), (Leiden: Brill, 1929); M. Minucius Felix, *Octavius: Lateinisch-deutsch*, B. Kytzler (ed.), (Darmstadt: Wissenschaftliche Buchgesellschaft, 1993).

49.   B. S. Billings, 'The Disputed Words in the Lukan Institution Narrative (Luke 22:19b-20). A Sociological Answer to a Textual Problem', *JBL* 125 (2006): 507–26 (516).

50.   Lanzillotta, *Early Christians and Human Sacrifice*.

51.   J. A. Harrill, 'Cannibalistic Language in the Fourth Gospel and Greco-Roman Polemics of Factionalism (John 6:52-66)', *JBL* 127 (2008): 133–58 (156, 136).

more so that John 6 is about factionalism.[52] The text of the gospel, however, lacks supporting evidence for the claim that John is responding to Jewish accusations of Christian cannibalism at the time of the gospel's composition. As an alternative I suggest reading the passage against another backdrop: that of groups in the Graeco-Roman world whose members engaged in human sacrifice followed by the drinking of the sacrificial blood and eating of the sacrificial flesh.

Sources from as early as the first century BCE testify to communal consumption of human blood and body in order to attain or solidify a bond among participants. According to Diodorus of Sicily, Apollodorus, in his aim for tyranny, invited a young man in order to sacrifice him and offer him to the gods (*Universal History*, XXII.5.1).[53] In order to create a bond with his companions, Apollodorus gave them the victim's blood to drink and his vitals to eat.[54]

Three sources roughly contemporary to the Gospel of John refer to members of a group who deal with human blood ritually. They touch or even consume parts of a human corpse in order to seal or renew their communal bond. (1) Plutarch reports (75 CE) that youths came to confer with the Aquilii and that the decision was taken that all conspirators should swear an oath, pour in libation the blood of a slain man and touch his entrails (Publicola 4.1).[55] (2) According to Publius Papianus Statius, Charops' wife offered her son as a sacrifice, and his blood served to seal an oath (Thebaid V.159).[56] The participants greedily stretched out their hands, presumably in order to touch the victim's body, and it is said that they bonded in the sweet crime 'in living blood' (*ac dulce nefas in sanguine vivo coniurant*, Thebaid V.159).

---

52.   'The charge of cannibalism was a commonplace in polemics against factionalism, and the synagogue authorities who faced the religious dissent of what would become the Johannine community likely Othered [sic!] such messianic sectarians as "cannibals".' Harrill, *Cannibalistic Language*, p. 150.

53.   Diodorus of Sicily, *Fragments of Books 21–32*, F. R. Walton (ed.), (London: Heinemann, 1957).

54.   Conspiracies and assassinations were part of Roman history from its very beginning. In several conspiracies in the Roman Empire, sacrifice of a human being and the subsequent drinking of its blood and devouring of the flesh play a decisive role. V. E. Pagán, *Conspiracy Narratives in Roman History* (Austin: University of Texas Press, 2004), pp. 10–11.

The Greeks seem to have renounced the use of blood for their acts of fraternization at a very early stage, and sources are therefore very sparse in the classic period. Nevertheless, traces appear in Aeschylus' *Septem Contra Thebas* 42–6. Even though the blood is not drunk, it still serves as a means to bind the leaders to the oath. Aeschylus, 'Septem Contra Thebas', in D. L. Page (ed.), *Aeschyli septem quae supersunt tragoedias* (Oxford: Clarendon Press, 1972), pp. 45–87. Cf. K. Kircher, *Die sakrale Bedeutung des Weines im Altertum* (Giessen: Töpelmann, 1910), pp. 78–80.

55.   Plutarch, *Plutarch's Lives: Publicola*, B. Perrin (ed.), (Cambridge, MA, London: Heinemann, 1993), pp. 510–11.

56.   P. P. Statius, *Thebaid, Books 1–7*, D. R. S. Bailey (ed.), (Cambridge, MA: Harvard University Press, 2003). Life dates: * c. 40 in Naples, † c. 96 ibid.

The probability that the stretching of the hands was done in order to drink the blood and eat from the corpse is strongly suggested by the notion that she (i.e., *umbra,* the shadow, the new ghost, born through death) hears the sound of biting (*audit concurrere morsus*, Thebaid V.159). Interestingly, in this case, the group devours the flesh and blood of a family member, that is, of an in-group person. (3) Josephus reiterates various ridiculous slanders concerning the temple of Jerusalem in his defence of Judaism against Apion (*Contra Apionem* 2.91-96). Human sacrifice appeared as the worst of all calumnies of which the Jews were accused. Further sources continued to portray descriptions of communal feasts of the entrails of a victim and a sacrificial oath for binding newcomers into the group.[57]

Yet another group that used human blood and flesh in order to create a bond among its members is that of Catiline (c. 108–62 BCE) and his fellow conspirators. The accounts about Catiline are an excellent example of the development of a legend and of growing exaggeration in the course of the tradition.[58] They grew from a drink of blood mixed with wine in the earliest sources into human sacrifice, and eventually to the killing of a young person, possibly infanticide, in the later sources.[59]

The members of the Johannine community would have been familiar with this kind of food-related ritual. Given that the bonding over blood and body was a widespread *topos* in antiquity, the members of the Johannine community would easily have recognized allusions to such practices when they heard or read John 6 at their communal meals.

From these sources it becomes clear that a comparable set of actions appears in different sources in the Graeco-Roman world over a period of several centuries. It is possible, therefore, to speak of a *topos*. In each case, a particular group of people kills a person, or at least takes a dead body or parts of a dead body, and the members of the group perform actions of a ritual

---

57. Thus in a collection of papyri from the second half of the second century BCE, containing the fragments of a novel by Lollianus (*PColon* 3328, B1 recto, lines 9–21); S. A. Stephens and J. J. Winkler, *Ancient Greek Novels: The Fragments* (Princeton: Princeton University Press, 1995), pp. 338–41.

58. For a thorough investigation of the narrative and rhetoric of Catiline's conspiracy as well as others in Roman history, see Pagán, *Conspiracy Narratives*.

59. Gaius Sallustius Crispus (86–35/34 or 27 BCE) was the first to tell the legend about the drinking of human blood (De coniuratione Catilinae 22). G. Sallustius Crispus, *De Catilinae coniuratione*, D. Flach (ed.), (Stuttgart: Franz Steiner Verlag, 2007), p. 56. Florus comments on the act in *Ep. Hist. Rom.*, 2.12.4 (*Bellum Catilinae*), L. A. Florus, *Epitome of Roman History*, E. S. Forster (ed.), (Cambridge, MA, London: Harvard University Press, Heinemann, 1984), pp. 262–3. Plutarch, a contemporary of Florus, develops the story further in his *Life of Cicero* 10.3. Plutarch, *Plutarch's Lives: Cicero*, B. Perrin (ed.), (Cambridge, London: Heinemann, 1986), pp. 106–7. Finally, Cassius Dio (c. 163–229 CE) portrays the sacrifice of a boy (*History* 37.30); Cassius Dio, *Dio's Roman History: In Nine Volumes*, E. Cary (ed.), (London, Cambridge, MA: Heinemann, Harvard University Press, 1960–90), pp. 148–9.

character. In each case, the ritual expressly serves to seal or renew an oath or binding purpose. The *topos* of consuming blood and parts of a dead body appears in accounts of groups that seal a bond, or it appears as a practice repeated periodically in order to consolidate an existing group and to renew its boundaries against outsiders.

In light of these sources, there are striking parallels between John 6, in which the consumption of Jesus' flesh and blood is the precondition for being a member of Jesus' group, and the *topos* of practices attributed to certain circles in the Graeco-Roman world. In the Fourth Gospel, those who dare to eat the flesh and to drink the blood of their leader and founder eventually form an exclusivist group, a faction that distinguishes itself from 'the Jews'.

The literal meaning may allude to groups in the Roman world that drank human blood in order to consolidate their group identity or that ate the flesh of their founder, thus creating union with their founder and attaining eternal life. Chewing the flesh of Jesus ultimately serves to distinguish those who have the courage to join and to remain in Jesus' group as described by John, and those who do not. In light of this, John 6 may be declaring that the true followers of Jesus are those who chew the flesh of Jesus and drink his blood in order to attain eternal life.

The *topos* of enclaves in the Graeco-Roman world that bond by eating human flesh and drinking human blood proves to be a valid context of interpretation. A literal reading of the passage allows the possibility of identifying allusions to the bonding function of communally devouring flesh and blood and the positive evaluation of the victim as the group's founder, an idea which is familiar from the earliest tradition of Christ-believers.

In a broader perspective, the use of such language has a number of possible implications. The audience may well contain former 'Jews' who had already distanced themselves from Judaism, or the addressees may have come from a pagan background. An audience that was familiar with the *topos* of bonding over human flesh and blood would likely have detected these allusions. This, however, by no means implies that the members of the audience actually did consume human blood or flesh. Bread and wine that are associated with Jesus may well have served as placeholders; after all, Jesus equates himself with the bread that has come down from heaven. The discourse may serve to assure those who are already part of the group that 'chews the flesh of Jesus', persuading them that they are doing the right thing, and that it is important to maintain the communal bonding around their leader.

6.4. *Conclusion*

A number of backdrops against which Jn 6.51-58 can be read have been explored. Allusions to eucharistic traditions have been identified and echoes of motifs from mystery traditions have also been singled out. The same passage may be read against Dionysian traditions and striking correspondences emerge from sources about enclaves bonding around the consumption of human flesh and blood. More and other backdrops against which the gospel passage may fruitfully be explored are always possible.[60]

The fact that one and the same text can adopt so many diverse meanings – or tastes – indicates that there is a wide scope for interpretation. At the same time and, to express it negatively, it demonstrates that it is possible to completely misunderstand the author's intention.

When reading the Gospel of John we enter into a world which constituted the natural background for the original readers, but which is only partially known to us and which is distant from us in many respects. Each and every attempt to understand what John meant and what his original audience may have heard necessarily includes a reconstruction of the context from which the text emerged and the symbolic world to which the text refers. Unfortunately, we are quite restricted in our ability to enter the 'true' world of John and his contemporaries. A good measure of insecurity is and has to be the point of departure for any interpretation. The result can never be regarded as more than a tentative construction, certainly not a definitive reconstruction.

This somewhat deflating insight, however, has a positive aspect to it. The wide range of possible allusions may well have had an integrating effect on John's original audience. No matter what background the addressees came from – be it Jewish or pagan – they would have been able to notice markers in the Johannine text that would have allowed for associations to one or more ideas, traditions and concepts familiar to them from other, perhaps earlier, affiliations. This may have enabled them or decisively facilitated it for them to connect and bond with Johannine Christ-believers. The multifaceted character of the Fourth Gospel with regard to its manifold intertextual relationships suggests that the gospel has the quality and ability to address people not only from a Jewish background (as suggested by many) but also from pagan backgrounds. In other words, the Fourth Gospel has the capacity to bring out a number of flavours, thus attracting and satisfying a wide range of people with possibly very different tastes.

---

60.   For example, rabbinic or wisdom traditions to name only two. For rabbinic traditions, cf. the highly influential study by P. Borgen, *Bread from Heaven: An Exegetical Study of the Concept of Manna in the Gospel of John and the Writings of Philo* (Leiden: Brill, 1965). For wisdom traditions, see, e.g., R. E. Brown, *The Gospel According to John* (Garden City, NY: Doubleday, 1966–70), pp. 269, 273–4; A. Strotmann, 'Die göttliche Weisheit als Nahrungsspenderin, Gastgeberin und sich selbst anbietende Speise', in J. Hartenstein (ed.) *'Eine gewöhnliche und harmlose Speise'? Von den Entwicklungen frühchristlicher Abendmahlstraditionen* (Gütersloh: Gütersloher Verlagshaus, 2008); D. R. Burkett, *The Son of the Man in the Gospel of John* (Sheffield: JSOT Press, 1991), pp. 129–30; for a reading of John with Isa. 55.1-3, 10-11, as background, see ibid., pp. 130-4.

Chapter 7

What Happened in Caesarea?
Symphagein as Bonding Experience (Acts 10–11.18)

Luzia Sutter Rehmann

'Those of us who were never hungry will never understand hunger.'[1]

The way to my topic leads through the praxis of eating: eating in order to live.[2] How differently that sentence reads in times when food is scarce than when there is more than enough or people are sated. We are in danger of reading from an abundance of food, overlooking the signals the text sends out to the hungry. I would like to address the blindness of readers and enable them to recognize hunger in the text even when they are themselves sated. The question is how we can recognize hunger in the text today. We have to be on the lookout for signals in the text, for markers that show what lies beneath its surface.

Therefore, seeing the shadow of eating – hunger – is a hermeneutical problem. But it is only the shadow that gives the picture its contour, its depth-dimension. In the gospels, there are numerous references to hunger and scarcity. It can be no coincidence that the story of the miraculous feeding is told six times in the gospels.[3] Obviously the story of everyone eating and being filled could not be told too often and was preserved in diverse variations next to one another.

I want to show in the following, the ways of survival recorded in the Book of Acts. Eating together is a necessity of life and gives foundation to

---

1.   Elie Wiesel at the Petra Conference, June 2008: http://www.eliewieselfoundation.org/petraconferences.aspx.

2.   Cf. Andrea Bieler and Luise Schottroff, *Das Abendmahl. Essen, um zu leben* (Gütersloh: Gütersloher Verlagshaus, 2007), ET: *The Eucharist. Bodies, Bread and Resurrection* (Minneapolis: Fortress Press, 2007).

3.   The story of the miraculous multiplication of bread in Mk 6.30-44 is told altogether six times. 'This accumulation alone shows how important the story was for the first Christian generations.' *Abendmahl*, p. 113.

a community that without common meals would break apart. In Acts 10–12, we see how the small community of Joppa unites itself with the household of the centurion and how this bonding experience becomes interpreted as an incident of God's good creation shining forth.

You went to the uncircumcised and ate with them. Acts 11.3

But in Acts 10–11.18 we do not hear anything about Peter's eating in Caesarea.

We do hear about Cornelius' good deeds (vv. 2-4), Peter's vision in Joppa (vv. 11-16) and his going on a journey to Cornelius (v. 23), what he says there (vv. 34-43) and how the whole household spoke in tongues and extolled God (vv. 44-46). Not a word of a common meal.

However, συμφάγειν does appear in Peter's speech, 'After he had risen from the dead, the Risen One appeared to those who *ate* and drank *with him*' (10.41). In addition, the verb φάγειν (without prefix) appears in Peter's vision in Joppa and in his reaction to it (10.13, 14; 11.7). Yet, it cannot be denied that the people Cornelius had sent to Joppa were received by the people there just as the latter were received into Cornelius' house and fed there.[4]

But what determines the sense of συμφάγειν in this context? What is meant by συμφάγειν with the Risen One (10.41)? And what does συμφάγειν with Cornelius and his household mean (11.3)? Surely it is not a coincidence that one and the same verb connects both meals.

In what follows, I shall try to show the decisive event in Caesarea that caused questions to be raised in Jerusalem. I will follow signals within the text and put them into the context of the food scarcity that had fallen upon the people in the later years of the fifth decade of the first century CE. A further aid in reading the text is given by the fact that it repeats everything: first, as events in Joppa and Caesarea, and second, in Peter's narrative report. Thus, we can understand the 'corrections' in his report in Jerusalem as further signals of how Peter, that is, Luke, intends the reader to understand the events in Caesarea.

7.1. *Processes of Fixing Border Lines*

In 11.3, those 'circumcised' (οἱ ἐκ περιτομῆς) ask whether Peter ate with 'men who have their foreskin' (ἄνδρας ἀκροβυστίαν ἔχοντας). These are the coordinates that preoccupy the history of interpretation: obviously,

---

4. According to Jervell, the brothers in Jerusalem interpreted what happened in Caesarea as 'eating together', although Peter had spoken of κολλᾶσθαι (10.28). Κολλᾶσθαι signifies entering upon a close relationship, to associate oneself closely with someone, living together with someone (Acts 5.13; 9.26; 17.34; Lk. 15.15). Jacob Jervell, *Die Apostelgeschichte* (Göttingen: Vandenhoeck & Ruprecht, 1998), p. 308.

border lines were crossed in Caesarea and that caused conflict in Jerusalem. 'The issue is the acceptance of the first gentiles into the community hitherto composed only of Jewish Christians.'[5] Interpreters here speak of the conversion of Cornelius, of a 'paradigmatic conversion of gentiles'.

Furthermore, some interpreters seek to establish clearly who belongs to Judaism and who does not, yet the text itself is not interested in doing so. The narrative in Acts does not present Cornelius as a 'gentile' but, rather, as 'a devout man who feared god' (10.21). He was a man of generosity and prayed to the deity of Israel. He had close connections to the synagogue in Caesarea, *how* close exactly is left open in the text. Nor do we learn whether Cornelius let himself be circumcised as a result of the meeting with Peter or whether he observed the Torah from then on or not.[6]

Concentrating on the Jewish–gentile relation gives semblance to numerous interpretations, manifesting a fascination with discourses about border lines and their establishment.[7] Jews and gentiles, that is, Pharisaic Jews (in Jerusalem) and gentiles (those who fear God), are discussed repeatedly as two groups confronting each other in this narrative and whose relation requires closer elucidation.

Most of the time eating together is studied in terms of that focus' parameters,[8] namely that Jewish dietary laws prevented table fellowship.

5. Franz Mussner, *Apostelgeschichte* (Würzburg: Echter Verlag, 1984), p. 62.

6. But some interpreters explicitly occupy themselves with this matter, e.g., Ben Witherington, *The Acts of the Apostles. A Socio-Rhetorical Commentary* (Grand Rapids: Eerdmans, 1998), pp. 340–1. He emphasizes that Cornelius would not let himself be circumcised or observe the Torah subsequently. Nor was he regarded as a Jewish convert.

7. It swirls unswervingly around the Jewish–gentile relation. For example, 'Peter is the primary figure of the narrative; even though resisting it, he is led to cross over the separation barrier between Jews and gentiles – and that is the chief theme of the text.' Rudolf Pesch, *Die Apostelgeschichte. Evangelisch-katholischer Kommentar zum Neuen Testament* (Neukirchen-Vluyn: Neukirchener Verlag, 1986), p. 333. Or '10.34-35 not only justifies the association of the Jewish Peter with the Gentile Cornelius, but opens the way for the mission to the Gentiles, allowing any Jewish believer to receive hospitality and share meal fellowship with any God-fearing and upright Gentile.' John Paul Heil, *The Meal Scenes in Luke-Acts. An Audience-Oriented Approach* (Atlanta: Society of Biblical Literature, 1999), p. 254. Or '... that God himself forced the mission to the gentiles and their acceptance into the church against a reluctant Peter and a resisting community in Jerusalem ...'. Jervell, *Apostelgeschichte*, p. 316. Cf. Wilfried Eckey, *Die Apostelgeschichte. Der Weg des Evangeliums von Jerusalem nach Rom*, Part I (Neukirchen-Vluyn: Neukirchener Verlag, 2000), pp. 235–6. Bruce J. Malina and John J. Pilch, *Social-Science Commentary on the Book of Acts* (Minneapolis: Fortress Press, 2008). Darrel L. Bock, *Acts* (Grand Rapids: Baker Academic, 2007), pp. 380–1.

8. In this context exegetes also reflect on the polluting contact with gentiles and connect it with table fellowship even though fellowship is not described in the text. For example, Jervell notes that although there was no prohibition against Jews associating with gentiles, it still was quite customary. The kind of association the text depicts is expressed in the word κολλᾶσθαι, a close relationship, a close attachment to someone : 'As 11.3 puts it, Peter eats together with an uncircumcised man, that is, shares table fellowship with him, which strictly speaking was seen to be polluting.' Jervell, *Apostelgeschichte*, p. 308.

And in this text, those laws are thrown overboard. Rudolf Pesch writes, 'To all appearances the accent of the Cornelius narrative rests not on the admission of gentiles to baptism without preceding circumcision, but on the question ... of table fellowship between Jewish and gentile Christians ...'[9] Pesch understands Peter's vision of the sheet coming down from heaven and the animals on it as a renunciation of Jewish dietary laws. According to him the distinction between permitted and forbidden foods in *kashrut* is being annulled personally by God. What Peter learns here is that these distinctions are no longer important for Christians. And so, the Peter whom we meet in this interpretation is a Jew who slowly lets go of his resistance to contact with unclean gentiles.

What this interpretation ignores is that the text of Acts 10–11 leaves open what food might possibly have been eaten. In addition, Pesch links the question in 11.3 to Gal. 2.12 (eating with people of other nations, μετὰ τῶν ἐθνῶν συνέσθιειν): in Caesarea, Peter disregarded the separation of Jewish and gentile Christians the Jerusalemites had observed hitherto.[10] But one must explore more closely why Gal. 2.12 uses συνέσθιειν while Acts 11.3 uses συμφάγειν.

This interpretation is interested in a clarification that the text cannot provide. The clarity sought after seems to be something interpreters experience as an intellectual need not shared by the narrating text. It leaves much unsaid, yes, but, at the same time it sends out signals which this interpretation overlooks. I shall return to them later.

The history of discourse about establishing border lines in connection with the interpretation of this text is a long one.[11] Identities are constructed, border lines proposed and defended, giving rise to traditions of border-line-fixing. I have my doubts about how useful they are in understanding a concrete text like Acts 10–11.18. All the more since usage of – in many ways – fluid concepts was widespread in the first century CE.[12] Shaye J. D. Cohen's remark, that it was not that simple to tell a Jew when you saw one, is apropos here.[13] He shows what diverse degrees of distance from or closeness to the

9.   Pesch, *Apostelgeschichte*, p. 335.
10.   Ibid.
11.   Cf. Judith Lieu, *Image and Reality. The Jews in the World of the Christians in the Second Century* (Edinburgh: T&T Clark, 1996), p. 11.
12.   Even Ben Witherington concludes that we are not dealing here with fully developed concepts. For Luke uses concepts such as proselyte, God-fearing people, God-worshippers, in order to portray gentiles who venerate the deity of Israel and belong to the synagogue, while not using them with clarity. This corresponds to the image of open and as yet unestablished border lines. In: *The Acts of the Apostles. A Socio-Rhetorical Commentary* (Grand Rapids: Eerdmans, 1998), pp. 340–1.
13.   Shaye J. D. Cohen, *The Beginnings of Jewishness. Boundaries, Varieties, Uncertainties* (Berkeley: University of California Press, 1999).

Jewish community can be found in texts of antiquity. In any case, who is and who is not a Jew is not really clear until the *Mishnah* (around 200 CE) codifies the conversion-ritual. But how many Jewish communities at that time were in compliance with the *Mishnah* is an open question. Paula Frederiksen therefore seeks for a basically new approach concerning our vocabulary.[14] The definitions and presuppositions[15] that shape our reconstructions of antiquity derive from the historical victors and do not mirror the situation in which the texts developed and to which they reacted.[16]

7.2. *Defining What is Clean*

The discussions about border lines find support in Acts 10.15: Καὶ φωνὴ πάλιν ἐκ δευτέρου πρὸς αὐτόν, Ἃ ὁ θεὸς ἐκαθάρισεν σὺ μὴ κοίνου. 'What God deems to be clean you must not deem unclean.' Is this about which food is or is not deemed clean – and therefore about the dietary laws – or about human beings deemed clean?[17] This leads naturally to the question about what clean and unclean means, that is, by what categories that is to be understood.

In order to avoid the pitfall of the previously described hermeneutic of border-line-fixing, I stay as close to the text as possible. A perusal of the

14. Paula Frederiksen, '"What Parting of the Ways?" Jews, Gentiles, and the Ancient Mediterranean City', in Adam H. Becker and Annette Yoshiko Reeds (eds), *The Ways that Never Parted. Jews and Christians in Late Antiquity and the Early Middle Ages* (Tübingen: Mohr Siebeck, 2003), pp. 35–64.

15. Peter J. Tomson, 'The Wars Against Rome, the Rise of Rabbinic Judaism and of Apostolic Gentile Christianity, and the Judaeo-Christians: Elements for a Synthesis', in Peter J. Tomson and Doris Lambers-Petry (eds), *The Image of the Judaeo-Christians in Ancient Jewish and Christian Literature* (Tübingen: Mohr Siebeck, 2003), pp. 1–31.

16. Frederiksen and others even consider the model of 'the parting of the ways' a wholly false route because it misconstrues the social and intellectual history of Judaism and Christianity as well as much of Mediterranean culture up to the seventh century. Daniel Boyarin accepts this view and develops a sketch of how the two 'ways' that later became known as Judaism and Christianity only came into existence through self-descriptions that set each apart from the other. Daniel Boyarin, *Border Lines. The Partition of Judaeo-Christianity* (Philadelphia: University of Pennsylvania Press, 2004), p. 6.

17. 'God himself declares the hitherto unclean animals clean (καθαρίειν, declarative sense) and bade [Peter] to eat them (Acts 10.15; 11.9). This implies that it is God himself who in the new redemptive time abrogates the old distinction between clean and unclean. Peter has to draw a different conclusion from this concerning animals on the one hand and the religious respect due to gentile human beings on the other.' So writes Friedrich Hauck in 'καθαρός', *Theologisches Wörterbuch zum Neuen Testament*, Vol. 3 (Stuttgart: Kohlhammer Verlag, 1990), p. 428. 'Peter's vision is about food ... God commands Peter to kill any of these creatures and eat it ... of course, the reference is to Israel's Torah rules of prohibited foods (Leviticus 11). The strong statement disavowing Israel's food laws about what foods are appropriate ...' Malina-Pilch, *Social-Science Commentary*, p. 77.

Septuagint reveals no relation between καθαρίζειν and the dietary laws.[18] Foods deemed unclean are nowhere declared clean in Leviticus 11. This transformation of what – in the Pentateuch – is deemed clean never relates to food. With the exception of Leviticus 14.48, which speaks about a house infected with leprosy, a priest only declares human beings to be clean. Hence, the concern of Leviticus is the cultic cleanliness of human beings and not the transformation of unclean foods into clean ones.

The location of the narrative in Acts 10–11 is Caesarea, where going to the temple is not a simple option. All Jewish people in Caesarea, as everywhere in the Diaspora, are therefore in a constant status of cultic impurity but which is not to be understood as a problem. Before going up to the temple they would have to undergo the appropriate ritual cleansings (Num. 5.5-7; cf. Mt. 5.23-24). But a visit to the temple is not envisaged here.

As shown by Le Cornu and Shulam, the understanding of κοίνος as 'profane' corresponds to this view.[19] It is unlikely that Peter claims the state of lifelong cultic cleanness for himself here. Κοίνος does not refer here to that cultic category but, rather, to a moral one: Peter makes the claim that he never ate together with morally unclean or violent people and evil-doers or ever ate anything unclean;[20] in other words, that he lived according to the Torah's dietary laws.

The words κάθαρτον and κοίνος bring into view the basic category of *kashrut*, the distinction between clean and unclean, allowed and forbidden, albeit in a moral and not a cultic context. But this refers in no way to the determination of border lines between Jews and others; it is, rather, that Peter seeks to present himself in his reaction as a Jewish person. Whenever possible he thinks and lives according to the dietary laws of the Torah. But the question is how Peter is going to respond to this dilemma.

---

18. Καθαρίω appears in the Pentateuch only in Exod. 20.7: do not make wrongful use of the Lord's name; in Lev. 12.7, 8, in connection with the priest's cleansing actions; in Lev. 13.6, 13, 17, 23, 28, 34, 59, where in case of leprosy priests pronounce cleanness/uncleanness; and in Lev. 15.13 and 28 relating to male discharge or menstruation.

19. 'Whatever is written in the Torah and in traditional lore about the rules relating to things unclean or clean is only in connection with the temple and its sacred objects, heave-offerings and second tithe. The Torah warns those who are unclean against entering the temple or eating anything that is hallowed, or terumah or tithe, while in a state of uncleanness. But no such prohibition applies to common food; and it is permissible to eat common (i.e. non-consecrated) food and to drink things that are unclean.' Hilary Le Cornu with Joseph Shulam, *A Commentary on the Jewish Roots of Acts*, Vol. 1 (Jerusalem: Academon, 2003), p. 565.

20. Bringing cultic uncleanness upon oneself was not too problematic. But moral uncleanness was not washed off with ease. Murderers, adulterers and idol-worshippers could not take a bath and thereby become 'clean'. They had to seek genuine forgiveness, to go to those whom they had caused suffering and to God, seeking to repent and make a new beginning. Cf. Jonathan Klawans, *Impurity and Sin in Ancient Judaism* (Oxford: Oxford University Press, 2000).

7.3. *Some Necessary Hermeneutical Clarifications*

When the dissolution of the polar terms 'Jews-Christians' or 'Jewish Christians-Gentile Christians' into a vague plurality is taken seriously, serious repercussions arise for the interpretation of Acts 10–11.18. If border lines were in fact drawn in Caesarea, we have to reconsider their nature. For it is quite possible that they were different border lines than those usually proposed as the boundaries between Jews/Gentiles/Christians, respecting the abrogation of the dietary laws for the emerging Christian community. The search for a determined border line or for one that had been trespassed is possibly misleading. If it is so, a new hermeneutical access to the text is required.

As a feminist theologian, I am interested in permeable processes, in to-and-fro movements between groups and am prepared to problematize the perspective of domination that resides in numerous discourses where border lines are drawn up. My exegetical work is nourished by a deep yearning for peace. Religions were always used when it came to exclude groups of people, when power was to be legitimated. I live in Switzerland under the shadow of many catastrophes (well-protected, to be sure, but marked by the shadows nonetheless). The Holocaust in Europe has left behind ineradicable marks and shaped theological thinking. I observe how politics of destabilization work worldwide to make the rich even richer while plunging the poor into yet deeper poverty. I look upon economic globalization as a war against poor countries, against working women and men who can barely defend themselves, a war with devastating consequences.

The Book of Acts was written after the Jewish-Roman war. How did the first readers, as people who had been displaced by and survived that war, receive the story of the feast in Caesarea in the house of a centurion in the army of Rome? Roman soldiers were the political and military enemies of Palestine's population. Here I want to consider how the text deals with these burdensome experiences. I imagine that the text has more to say about these experiences than the border-line discussions of the second, third or fourth century CE.

7.4. *Hunger as the Point of Departure in Acts 10–12*

Hunger is easily ignored by those who have enough to eat because they have no inkling how hunger haunts and rages, what hunger exacts from a human community. In Acts 10.10, the text confronts the readers with Peter's hunger (ἐγέετο δὲ πρόσπεινος). A clear signal is given here. When we look at the subsequent context of the narrative, we note that a famine (λιμός) is at the centre of chapters 10–12 (11.28) which forces the community to look for ways of surviving. It would, therefore, be cynical to regard Peter's hunger as something of no meaning for the remainder of the story, to treat his hunger as if he just felt like getting a snack.

During the reign of Emperor Claudius (41–54 CE) there was a food shortage in Egypt, Judaea, Syria and Greece. It was aggravated by the fact that several neighbouring regions had supply shortfalls. It became harder and harder to buy grain. Hunger grew stronger and lasted for extended periods of time. As transportation routes became more and more extended, it took longer and was less safe to move food. Flavius Josephus writes about this shortage and points out that Jerusalem had to send to Alexandria and Cyprus in order to get food.[21]

Again and again hunger led to uprisings, destabilizing entire regions. This is true also for our narrative. Unrest and persecution pervade these chapters of Acts; the port cities of Tyre and Sidon come under extreme threat (12.20).

According to Peter Garnsey,[22] everything depends fundamentally on how a community was able to handle a food shortage given that the state laid claim on whatever surplus farmers had but did nothing in bad times to help the population. In Acts 12.20, we see that the community had to find allies in the royal court because their region was dependent on other regions (that is, on royal regions) for food. The support from people out of solidarity with the hungry was another means of surviving; it took the form of a collection that was sent to Judaea (11.29).

In times of shortage the wealthy played a key role. On occasion, some from among them would open their granaries and sell grain instead of hoarding it to be sold at inflated prices. There were several occasions when euergetics stepped in; those benefactors would sell food cheaply or help people out.[23]

Inscriptions testify that the cities in the provinces had to fend for themselves in times of famine, that is, they had to depend on wealthy citizens. An inscription from Sala (Morocco) from 144 CE is an exception in that it honoured a Roman prefect (and not one of the citizens) as the

---

21.   'Now her coming was of very great advantage to the people of Jerusalem; for whereas a famine did oppress them at that time, and many people died for want of what was necessary to procure food withal, Queen Helena sent some of her servants to Alexandria with money to buy a great quantity of corn, and others of them to Cyprus, to bring a cargo of dried figs ...' Flavius Josephus, *Ant.* 20, 2, 5. In *The Works of Josephus. Completed and Unabridged*; New Updated Edition, William Whiston, transl. (Peabody, MA: Hendrickson Publishers, 1996).

22.   Peter Garnsey, *Famine and Food Supply in the Graeco-Roman World. Responses to Risk and Crisis* (Cambridge/New York: Cambridge University Press, 1988), p. 21.

23.   'Euergetism is also (almost) absent from the documents. Here the case is different. It is a legitimate suspicion that hoarding and speculation in necessities by wealthy landowners and traders were standard occurrences that were soft-pedaled by the upper-class sources, and rarely formed the subject of an annalistic note. The public display of generosity, however, was not compatible with Roman political practice.' Garnsey, *Famine and Food Supply*, p. 176.

benefactor of the city for protecting the inhabitants against habitual injuries and theft of cattle, and in times of distress he provided food supply from his own troops; thanks to his intervention the Roman prefect prevented uprisings in Salla.

The local commander, M Sulpicius Felix, is introduced in accordance with his military career: he is named prefect of the First Germanic Cohort and the cavalry of the Second Wing of Rome's Syrian citizens. Then his actions are described in lines 15 and 16

> ... 15 minimo sumtu ambiendo, seu annonae avaris difficultatibus ex copiis armaturae suae plurima ad nostrum 16 utilitatem, nihil ad militum damnum commodando...
>
> 'During the harshest tribulations (*avaris difficultatibus*) he provided food from the replenishments of his troops and very often acted to our advantage yet never to the detriment of his soldiers ...'[24]

Cornelius, too, is introduced in accordance with his military career: a centurion of the Italian cohort; his actions too are mentioned (Acts 10.1-2). He was the leader of a 100-man unit[25] and therefore had access to its food replenishments in the harbour-city of Caesarea. Having this powerful centurion for a friend of the synagogue, a man who was ready in hard times to help the Jewish community, was therefore quite significant. It provides another way of securing survival for the small community of Joppa that had already come to experience hunger (10.10).

7.5. *The Vision and Audition in Joppa*

Peter saw something like a linen sheet coming down from heaven (v. 11) and heard a voice (v. 13). We are told about a vision and an auditory message.

Since Peter clearly experienced hunger (10.10) it is not surprising that he is served many animals. But here exegesis immediately focuses itself on the

---

24.   Cf. Stephane Gsell et Jérôme Carcopino, 'La base de M. Sulpicius Felix et le décret des décurions de Sala', in *Mélanges d'archéologie et d'histoire*, 48 (1931), pp. 1–39.

25.   Karl Jaroš, *Das Neue Testament und seine Autoren: Eine Einführung* (Köln: Böhlau, 2008). He does not deem the reference to the Italian cohort an anachronism. Several inscriptions of the first and second century CE give testimony to the cohort in Syria (cf. E Meyer, II, 1923, p. 147, n. 2). The epitaph of Optio (an aid to a centurion) Proclus, son of Rabilus of the Cohors II. Militaria Italica Civium Romanorum Voluntarium, is the oldest attestation to this unit (Inscriptiones Latinae Selectae 9168). This special unit of the Cohort II, to which this Proclus belonged, consisting of archers, is dated from the year 69 CE. Tacitus refers in his Histories II 83 to an army that included 13,000 archers; it had marched under the Syrian legate to Italy in support of Vespasian against his rival Vitellius. These two pieces of evidence firmly locate this unit in Syria in the year 69 CE. No further dating on the basis of these pieces of evidence is possible.

issue of uncleanness/cleanness. For according to Leviticus 11, the animals served him are not on the kosher menu – at least not in their entirety.[26]

A voice commands Peter to get up, offer sacrifice, and eat. His reaction is one of shock; he is very distraught. The message of Acts 10.13-14 is retold by him in 11.8. His distress may be compared, on the verbal as on the performative level, with that of Ezekiel when he is told of war, siege, hunger, and death to come.

Acts 10.14-15

Ὁ δὲ Πέτρος εἶπεν μηδαμῶς, κύριε, ὅτι οὐδέποτε ἔφαγον πᾶν κοινὸν καὶ ἀκάθαρτον. Καὶ φωνὴ πάλιν ἐκ δευτέρου πρὸς αυτόν ἃ ὁ θεὸς ἐκαθάρισεν, σὺ μὴ κοίνου.

Acts 11.8

Εἶπον δέ· μηδαμῶς, κύριε, ὅτι κοινὸν ἢ ἀκάθαρτον οὐδέποτε εἰσῆλθεν εἰς τὸ στόμα μου.

Ezek. 4.14

Καὶ εἶπα Μηδαμῶς, κύριε θεὲ τοῦ Ισραηλ· ἰδοὺ ἡ ψυχή μου οὐ μεμί αντ‌αι ἐν ἀκαθαρσίᾳ, καὶ θνησιμαῖον καὶ θηριάλωτον οὐ βέβρωκα ἀπὸ γενέσεώς μου ἕως τοῦ νῦν, οὐδὲ εἰσελήλυθειν εἰς τὸ στομα μου πᾶν κρέας ἕωλον.

Peter's retelling no longer uses ἔφαγον but εἰσελήλυθειν εἰς τὸ στόμα μου. This aligns Peter's vision with Ezekiel's. He puts Ezekiel's words into his mouth, so to speak, thereby building on the common frame of reference of the Scriptures, helping the sisters and brothers in Jerusalem to understand what took place in Caesarea.

Like Ezekiel, Peter rejects what he is told to do by the angel. The voice that he, like Ezekiel, addresses as 'Lord' becomes more insistent and re-emphasizes that 'what God has said to be clean, you must not declare unclean' (10.15). This dialogue recalls the horrified reaction of Ezekiel when told of affliction, war, siege, persecution and hunger to come in Ezek. 4.14 and 15.[27]

---

26. For example, 'To eat all these unclean things would be a violation of the law (Lev 10.10; 20.25; Ez 4.14; Dan 1.1–2.2; Macc 5.27; 6.18; Tob 1.10-11; Jdt 10.5; 12.2).' 'The vision symbolizes that what separated Jews from Gentiles is now removed.' Darrell L. Bock, *Acts* (Grand Rapids: Baker Academie, 2007), pp. 389 and 390.

27. Ruth Poser, '"Das Gericht geht durch den Magen." Die verschlungene Schriftrolle (Ez 2.8b–3.3) und andere Essensszenarien im Ezechielbuch', in *Essen und Trinken in der Bibel. Ein literarisches Festmahl für Rainer Kessler zum 65. Geburtstag*, Michaela Geiger et al. (eds), (Gütersloh: Gütersloher Verlagshaus, 2009), pp. 116–30.

The horror is related not only to what Ezekiel/Peter are told to do (eat something unclean) but very much also to the announcement that a devastating catastrophe will come (cf. Ezek. 5.15-17).'

Hunger will force Ezekiel to eat things that are dreadful and do not belong on any menu. Food shortages have always challenged communities to adapt their eating habits to the prevailing circumstances, abandon them altogether and avail themselves of whatever can be found.[28] Such adaptation made great demands on the body but also signified a huge social burden.

The oracle shows Ezekiel clearly what will happen to the community. He is cast into the role of the exemplar: he has to demonstrate to the community what is to come, what God will put it through before he turns toward it once again.

Whatever the differences between Ezekiel and Peter, Peter too is horrified by the command that he is to eat things that he despises. He quite understandably resists this outrageous demand, just as Ezekiel did. But in neither case are we dealing with an abrogation of the dietary laws; the focus is on the catastrophe that coerces people to eat abhorrent things.

Whereas Ezekiel indicates clearly which things he had never eaten, Peter is more general (κοινὸν καὶ ἀκάθαρτον); this has led to much diverse speculation concerning the dietary laws (see above). The vision of the animals on the sheet being lowered from heaven is also rather general, yes, quite encompassing: there are τετράποδα (four-footed creatures), ἑρπετα τῆς γῆς (animals crawling on the earth), πετεινὰ τοῦ οὐρανοῦ (birds of the sky). When he describes the vision later in Jerusalem, Peter supplements it with a fourth species of animals: τα θηρία (11.6).

It is important to note that these four animal species (τετράποδα, ἑρπετα τῆς γῆς, πετεινὰ τοῦ οὐρανοῦ, τα θηρία) are not listed in the dietary laws of Leviticus.[29] This should not be overlooked.

It is Peter's addition of the fourth species in particular that helps us see the connection to the good creation in Gen. 1.24, 25, and 30:[30]

28. Peter Garnsey distinguishes between five categories of foods in times of hunger: 1. livestock not in ordinary circumstances destined for slaughter; 2. inferior cereals (even damaged by pest or weather); 3. regular animal food; 4. natural products or non-foods such as roots, twigs, leaves, bark, leather; 5. human flesh. Garnsey, *Famine and Food Supply*, p. 28.

29. However, this is asserted repeatedly; e.g., 'God commands Peter to kill any of the creatures and eat it ... of course, the reference is to Israel's Torah rules of prohibited foods (Leviticus 11).' Malina-Pilch, *Social-Science Commentary*, p. 77. Also the passages Bock names substantiate nothing. They do not fit in with these four animal species. No animals are listed in Lev. 10.10, and in Lev. 20.25 τετράποδα and θηρία are not mentioned. Cf. 'To eat all these unclean things would be a violation of the law Lev 10.10; 20.25; Ez 4.14; Dan 1.8–12.2; Macc 5.27; 6.18; Tob 1.10-11; Jdt 10.5; 12.2).' Bock, *Acts*, p. 389.

30. The German text of the following Scripture passage used by the author is from the new German translation of the Bible: *Bibel in gerechter Sprache* (Gütersloh: Gütersloher Verlagshaus, 2006) and is given here in English translation (Translator's note).

24. The earth shall bring forth living creatures each of their kind, cattle (τετράποδα), creeping things (ἕρπετα) and wild animals (τὰ θηρία τῆς γῆς). 25. God made the wild animals (τὰ θηρία τῆς γῆς) of the earth of their kind, the cattle of their kind, and all the creeping things (ἕρπετα τῆς γῆς) on the earth of their kind. And God saw: Yes, it was good.

30. And every green plant shall serve as food to all animals of the earth (τοῖς θηρίοις τῆς γῆς), all birds of the sky (πετεινοῖς τοῦ οὐρανοῦ,), all that creeps on the earth (ἕρπετῷ τῷ ἕρποντι ἐπὶ τῆς γῆς), to whatever lives drawing breath. And so it was.

The animal species pictured in Peter's vision all draw breath – all have a throat with which to draw breath – according to Gen. 1.30. In addition, they all share the same food: green plants. There is no mention of predatory birds or carnivorous animals. The earth brings forth, and there is enough for all.

Thus, the vision of the different species of animals evokes peace-filled associations with God's good creation where there is no hunger.

To sum up, through the oracle in Joppa, Peter comes to understand that the hunger he is already experiencing will become even more acute. This distresses him. Later, in Jerusalem, he compares this auditory message to Ezekiel, thereby indicating that his distressed state resulted from the ominous shadow cast by hunger.

The vision of the four species points to the shared fate of the creatures in Gen. 1.24 and 30. They share *nephesh* and nourishment. The latter is said to be vegetarian, which leaves predatory animals out of the picture. The earth brings forth green plants for them to eat. This makes God's providence visible.

What Peter hears in the oracle, namely that a famine will come upon the land and force people to eat what is abhorrent to them, distresses him. He emphatically rejects the insinuation by referring to the Torah's dietary laws, *kashrut*. The rejection makes it abundantly clear that he has understood the announcement. He cannot recognize at first what he sees in the vision – the sheet with the four species of animals coming down from heaven – as God's good creation (10.17, 19). He begins to understand only in the hospitable house of Cornelius (v. 34): Cornelius had sent for the hungry sisters and brothers in Joppa and brought them into his house. All living beings share *nephesh* as well as the green plants of the earth (Gen. 1.30); the vision of the good creation becomes reality in Caesarea, around the centurion who shares food.

7.6. *Hunger and Humiliation*

All his life Peter had eaten what was morally appropriate. Now he is scandalized by the suggestion that he will have to eat what would be morally inappropriate. But the expectation is that he will do just that because of the food shortage that will grow into a famine (11.28). Hunger pervades chapters 11 and 12. There is historical evidence that hunger reigned in Egypt, Judaea, Syria and Greece around the year 48 CE.

The clear reference to common food shared by all animals drawing breath (Gen. 1.30) makes us acutely aware of hungry Peter's situation. The comparison with Ezek. 4.14 intensifies the humiliation hunger imposes and it horrifies Peter. Ezekiel must eat bread of inferior quality and which has been prepared over a fire of human excrement – during a siege, normal food and normal fuel run out in the city. This situation is life-threatening and humiliating.

When Ezekiel, in an experience of the Spirit, makes use of the verb 'to declare clean', he speaks of a human being's moral cleanness, as we can see also in Ezek. 36.29, 30 and 33:

> 29. I will save you from all your uncleanness (ἐκ πασῶν τῶν ἀκαθαρσιῶν ὑῃῶν) and I will summon the grain and make it abundant and lay no famine upon you.
> 30. I will make the fruit of the tree and the produce of the field abundant, so that you may never again suffer the derision of the nations because you must suffer hunger.
> 33. I will release you from all your entanglements in debt (καθαριῶ ὑμᾶς ἐκ πασῶν τῶν ἀνομιῶν ὑμῶν) and will let the towns be inhabited anew and the waste places will be built up with houses.[31]

Here, too, hunger and derision are linked. The hungry will be mocked by the sated (v. 30).[32] After the foretold catastrophe, God offers reconciliation through removing the moral pollution and giving abundant harvest of grain and fruit. Reconciliation manifests itself in the abundance of food so that all nations will see that Jerusalem's humiliation has ended. The wealth of food will put an end to the mocking, for all can once again eat properly, appropriate morally and in accordance with *kashrut* and in accordance with their self-perception.

The exegetes' assumption that the dietary laws are set aside in Acts 10.15 rests on the concept of 'gentile Christianity free of the law'[33] which Peter's vision is said to legitimize. But this concept is historically premature when applied to the reality of the first century CE. In addition, the verb

31.　Please see note 30 above for the translation of this passage (Translator's note).

32.　'Those of us who were never hungry will never understand hunger,' Elie Wiesel declared. 'Hunger brings humiliation. The hungry person thinks of bread and nothing else. Hunger fills his or her universe. His prayer, his aspiration, his hope, his ideal are not lofty: they are a piece of bread. To accept another person's hunger is to condone his or her tragic condition of helplessness, despair and death.' Elie Wiesel at the Petra Conference, June 2008: http://www.eliewieselfoundation.org/petraconferences.aspx.

33.　For a critique of this concept, see Luise Schottroff's '"Gesetzfreies Heidenchristentum" – und die Frauen?', in Luise Schottroff and Marie-Theres Wacker (eds), *Von der Wurzel getragen. Christlich-feministische Exegese in Auseinandersetzung mit Antijudaismus* (Leiden: E.J. Brill, 1996), pp. 227–45.

καθαρίω or καθαρίζω does not refer to the context of the Levitical dietary laws. And the assumption that contact with gentiles causes uncleanness is itself problematic. Even Witherington concedes that there was no formal Jewish law declaring gentiles to be unclean and prohibiting contact with them.[34] 'Gentiles are unclean and contact with them causes Jews to become unclean': this claim also is simply erroneous, according to Jonathan Klawans,[35] as it is based on the failure to distinguish between moral and cultic uncleanness.[36]

Instead of seeking to do away with the categories of 'permitted' and 'not permitted', Acts 10.15 actually builds upon them. The threatened catastrophe of famine takes on vivid contours and becomes dangerous in that these categories, which are utterly taken for granted, must be set aside so that one can remain alive at all. Such action impacts also on the dignity of those affected, damaging their self-respect as human beings.

Would God permit breaking the dietary laws in such times of hunger in order not to burden the starving people even further? Would God let those go free who share their food, even if they were soldiers, Rome's agents of death? Or one might ask whether sharing food in the centurion's house happened because the God of Israel had heard Cornelius' plea (Acts 10.4) and freed him from the moral entanglements that go with being a soldier.

I do not want to answer these questions here. What I do want to leave behind me is those old discussions about setting border lines which swirl around the questions of the abrogation of the dietary laws while the hunger and the concomitant humiliation of the hungry is left unacknowledged.

7.7. Symphagein *as Bonding Experience*

Acts 10–12 sketches out some ways of survival that were vitally necessary for communities:

Support is being organized for the community in Judaea (11.29).

A confidant is won in Herod's administration, allowing for fresh provisions to be sent to the community (12.20).

Another option is cited in the Cornelius narrative: there are benefactors among the foreigners who are prepared to give aid to the synagogue (10.1-2).

34.   Witherington, *Acts*, p. 353.
35.   Klawans, *Impurity and Sin*, p. 137.
36.   Cf. Klawans, *Impurity and Sin*. See above, note 20.

The communities that suffered from hunger were vitally interested in finding means of survival and in how God helps them in their efforts. Peter maintains that God takes the side of the hungry in that God opens up possibilities for their survival. For God instructs Cornelius to bring the hungry to his house.

The question raised at the beginning – which border line is being crossed here at all? – is to be answered as follows: it could have been the border line between the hungry in Joppa and the sated in Caesarea; it could also have been that between the so-called 'lowly' (Jewish craftspeople, fisher folk, tanners) and an Italian cohort. This would have been a highly significant border line at the time when the Book of Acts was written, so soon after the devastating Jewish-Roman War: the people in Jerusalem had experienced the Roman cohorts' violence, their starving the inhabitants out during the siege and then plundering them. For them, there certainly was a deadly border line between themselves and Rome's cohorts; the centurion's hospitality breaks through this separation.

Had the sisters and brothers in Jerusalem not put questions to Peter, we would not know anything about eating together (11.3). The text says nothing about whether the meals in the house were kosher or vegetarian. Nor do we hear anything about what the Risen One ate (v. 41). Rather, what is being held up high is the act of justice in the name of the God of Israel (10.2), that food is being shared with those in need and that the distance between the Roman soldiers and the community in the tanner's house in Joppa is overcome through acts of hospitality in times of hunger.

It is significant that the verb συμφάγειν is used in 11.3 and 10.41. The eating and drinking together 'after he rose from the dead' transforms those eating into a 'we'. Not all saw the murdered one after his death, only those who had eaten and drunk with him. The συμφάγειν changed those who had eaten into a 'we' who see things differently than before.

Eating together creates a deep bonding experience against the powers of death, be it against the threatening hunger or the power of the devil and of death (vv. 38-41), so that those in Jerusalem can exclaim: the peoples of the nations can also come to life (11.18).

Translated by Martin Rumscheidt.

Chapter 8

TO EAT OR NOT TO EAT – IS THIS THE QUESTION?
TABLE DISPUTES IN CORINTH

Kathy Ehrensperger

8.1. *Introduction*

Disputes in Corinth are prominent and not all of them have to do with issues around the table. However, the issues around the table were hotly disputed in the Corinthian community as they considered it necessary to write to Paul and ask for his advice.[1] Perhaps even more contentious have been the scholarly debates that the respective passages have provoked ever since. The passages in question are usually discussed under headings like *Idol Food in Corinth*,[2] *Food Offered to Idols*,[3] *Dangerous Food*.[4]

Although all relate to issues concerning idolatry and food consumption, I would like to propose in this article that there are actually three different issues around the table addressed by Paul in chapters 8–11. They have to do with three different contexts and situations:

a) 1 Cor. 8.1-13 and 10.14-22 address the participation in public meals at a sanctuary;
b) 1 Cor. 10.23–11.1 addresses a situation in the private house of a pagan host;
c) 1 Cor. 11.17-34 addresses a situation at the communal table of Christ-followers.

---

1. As indicated by περὶ δέ. Cf. also R. E. Ciampa and B. S. Rosner, *The First Letter to the Corinthians* (Grand Rapids, MI: Eerdmans, 2010), p. 368.
2. A. T. Cheung, *Idol Food in Corinth: Jewish Background and Pauline Legacy* (Sheffield: Sheffield Academic Press, 1999).
3. J. Fotopoulos, *Food Offered to Idols in Roman Corinth: A Social-Rhetorical Reconsideration of 1 Corinthians 8:1–11:1* (Tübingen: Mohr Siebeck, 2003).
4. P. D. Gooch, *Dangerous Food: 1 Corinthians 8–10 in its Context* (Waterloo, ON: Wilfrid Laurier Press, 1993).

All of these passages address issues related to meals, although in different contexts and with different issues under debate; and not all of them are actually concerned with the food on the table. I will focus on the first situation in this article although the three different situations are somewhat interlinked. I will explore firstly why problems concerning the consumption of food offered to idols and participation in cultic practices of pagans arose in the first place; I will then analyse the identity of those among the Christ-followers who seem to have had questions concerning such participation; followed by an analysis of the two arguments Paul presents against participation in pagan temple meals. It will be argued that Paul's foremost concern is with the holiness of the community. Paul sees this holiness threatened by actions which could hurt or destroy a brother/ sister, including what is seen as association with demons. The issue of food consumption is part of Paul's argument in an indirect way in that the request not to participate at public temple meals deprived people who lived under conditions of malnutrition of an important source of food provision.

8.2. *Why does the Problem arise in the First Place?*

One may wonder why the whole problem of eating in public emerged in the first place. To actively participate in pagan rituals, including eating food which had been consecrated in the ritual context of worshipping a pagan deity, was in principle out of the question for Jews, and consequently also for worshippers of the God of Israel through Christ. It is out of the question that Jews would intentionally have eaten anything that had been involved in sacrifices to pagan deities, as this would have jeopardized their unique loyalty to the One God. Paul advocates that the same applies to gentiles who have joined the Christ-movement. There is no compromise with regard to this demand, nor can there be. It would seem likely that such a fundamental consequence of becoming a member of the Christ-movement would have been rendered clear beyond any doubt by Paul upon his founding of the community and his initial teaching when he was in Corinth. If the Corinthian Christ-followers had already learned that they could not under any circumstances participate in pagan worship, of which eating at a temple table was part, why would there arise a controversy in the first place? The fact that the Corinthians do have questions concerning this is evidence that the issue which seems very clear in principle was not as clear-cut in practice as it might seem.

What actually did constitute idolatry, that is worshipping and serving a deity other than the One God, was, if not a matter of debate, at least in practice an issue of blurred boundaries among some Jews living in the

Diaspora. At a cognitive level, a certain openness towards other religious traditions can be found in, or example, the *Letter of Aristeas* where in section 16 Aristeas is depicted as saying 'the God who is overseer and creator of all things whom they (the Jews) worship is he whom all humanity worship, but we, O king, call differently as Zeus and Dis' (τὸν γὰρ πάντων ἐπότην καὶ κτίστην θεὸν οὖτοι σέβονται,ὂν καὶ πάντες, ἡμεῖς δέ, βασιλεῦ, προσονομάζοντες ἑτέρως Ζῆνα καὶ Δία⁵). The perception here is that the one God of Israel is the same just called by a different name in Jewish as well as in Greek tradition. Philo in a remarkable passage states that Greeks and barbarians actually worship the same God 'the father of gods and men and the maker of the whole universe',[6] but concludes that therefore they should refrain from inventing new deities. A Jewish inscription from Gorgippa at the Bosporus dated 41 CE (*CIJ* 690) refers to the manumission of a slave with what seems to be a clear reference to the One God (θεῶι ὑψίστωι παντοκράτορι εὐλογητῶ – to God the most high, almighty, blessed), followed by a pagan juridical formula (ὑπὸ Δία, Γῆν,῎Ηλιον – under Zeus, Earth, Sun). The dedication notes that it is made in the προσευχή which has been demonstrated as being an exclusively Jewish term.[7]

There is further inscriptional evidence that Jews did visit pagan temples, as, for example, from near the temple of Pan in Edfu in upper Egypt (dated between the second and first century BCE). Although the inscriptions do not suggest worshipping activities of the Jews named there, it is noteworthy that they placed their votive dedication within the compound of a pagan deity.[8] When it comes to the manumission of slaves, Jews in the Diaspora seem to have adopted the recognized practice that a manumission required a deity acting as a broker and the actual manumission was a handover of the slave to the deity. An inscription from Delphi (*CIJ* no. 711, 119 BCE) mentions that someone ᾿Ιουδαῖος (Ioudaios) sold his slave Ἀμύντας to Apollo, a sale which should be actualized upon the death of ᾿Ιουδαῖος. Whether these examples provide a glimpse into exceptional or common practice among Diaspora Jews is difficult to assess. But they clearly indicate that at least in some instances the boundaries between what was considered faithful adherence to the traditions of the ancestors and idolatry were blurred. Hence the boundary between what was considered idol worship and mere shared common practice seems to have been a matter of local and possibly individual perception.

5.   *Let.Aris.16.*
6.   *Spec. 2.165.*
7.   See W. Horbury and D. Noy, *Jewish Inscriptions of Graeco-Roman Egypt* (Cambridge: Cambridge University Press, 1992), p. 14; also I. Levinskaya, *The Book of Acts in its Diaspora Setting* (Grand Rapids, MI: Eerdmans, 1996), pp. 207–25.
8.   Horbury and Noy, *Jewish Inscriptions*, pp. 211–12.

Such variations in the perceptions of these boundaries could have contributed significantly to the problems Paul feels he needs to address in his letter.

Since the perception of what did and did not constitute idolatry was not as it seems, Paul has to clarify the perception of pagan deities for Christ-followers. Paul seems to refer to aspects of previous teaching, maybe repeated in the letter sent to him, when he states in 1 Cor. 8.4 οὐδὲν εἴδωλον ἐν κόσμῳ ('there are no idols in the world') and that οὐδεὶς θεὸς εἰ μὴ εἷς ('there is no God but one').[9] By referring first to the artefact representing the deity, he states a perception common also among non-Jews; it is not the statue or the image which actually *is* the deity but rather these represent the deity, although popular perception and practice may differ from this cognitive perception. Paul then changes the reference to the deity as such and seems to stress that there is actually only one. The reference in v. 5 to 'so-called gods in heaven and on earth' and 'many gods and many lords' seems paradoxical, as it is unclear whether Paul in one sweep acknowledges and denies the existence of other deities. It could be that the 'many gods and lords' should be put in quotation marks indicating that this also refers to 'so-called gods'.[10] It could be an ironic statement or the perception of deities was not a matter of clear-cut boundaries even for Paul. He was most likely not a monotheist in a modern sense. With his Jewish and gentile contemporaries he shared the perception that the heavens and earth and every sphere in between were populated if not by numerous deities, certainly by numerous spiritual beings referred to as demons,[11] or as Paula Fredriksen has eloquently formulated it, they lived in a world congested by deities.[12]

In that sense, Jews were no different from their pagan contemporaries. The difference was that their loyalty was to only One God. There was nothing strange in a deity being the deity of a particular ἔθνος/people; on the contrary, this was a key aspect of the normal role of deities, in as much as families or clans were loyal to their particular clan deities. To be part of a people and worshipping a particular deity were inseparable aspects

---

9   This may be a quotation from a letter sent to Paul by the Corinthians; if so, this would strengthen Paul's emphasis on shared knowledge.

10.   Ciampa and Rosner argue that 'Since Paul had already referred to the things worshipped by others as so-called gods in v. 5a it seems appropriate to place gods and lords in quotation marks in v. 5b' (p. 381).

11.   P. Fredriksen, '"Judaizing the Nations": The Ritual Demands of Paul's Gospel', *NTS* 56: 232–52.

12.   P. Fredriksen, 'What "Parting of the Ways?" Jews and Gentiles in the Ancient Mediterranean', in *The Ways that Never Parted: Jews and Christians in Late Antiquity and the Early Middle Ages*, ed. A. H. Becker and A. Yoshiko Reed (Tübingen: Mohr Siebeck, 2003), pp. 35–63.

of what in antiquity formed a unity. However, deities could be translated from one culture into another, and loyalty to deities was not exclusive but could be combined in innumerable ways.[13] The exclusive loyalty claim of the God of the Jews was irrational and incomprehensible from a non-Jewish perspective. Since the well-being of communities, cities and the empire as a whole depended on the benevolence of the gods, secured by loyalty rituals such as sacrifices, refusing to participate in such rituals could be seen not just as antisocial behaviour, but as threatening the well-being of communities and the empire as a whole. This is most likely where the pagan perception of Jews as being antisocial misanthropists emerged. However, in as much as Jewish exclusivist loyalty claims were considered odd, at times even bordering on treason, these were tolerated and to some extent even acknowledged as ancient traditions (mores), a concept which in Roman perspective had to be respected.

Thus it is evident from our discussion of this passage that Paul was not a monotheist and did not expect the Corinthians or any other Christ-followers to become monotheists. Such a concept was inconceivable for the period in question.[14] However, Paul did expect that the Christ-followers would show, and should be seen to show, loyalty to the One God of Israel only and exclusively. Acknowledging that there are other deities or lords who claim loyalty, Paul emphasizes that ἀλλ' ἡμῖν εἷς θεὸς ὁ πατήρ ('for *us* there is *one* God ... and *one* Lord ...', 8.6a). This exclusive loyalty to one God and one Lord affects the whole of life, in that the whole of creation is God's, and the purpose of the community is seen as being exclusively shaped by its relation to God. Although this knowledge is shared at the cognitive level by Paul and the Corinthian Christ-followers, it is not necessarily embraced by all in the community.

From Paul's way of arguing in 8.5-6, it seems that the conclusion some of the Corinthian Christ-followers drew was – because their 'real' loyalty was only to the One God of Israel, and the other deities were actually only subordinate gods or demons – that they were free to participate in certain activities related to pagan cultic practices. This included participation in public meals at Corinthian temples,[15] since they would not consider the food on the table as 'really' offered to a deity.[16] This brings us to the question of who are 'those who have knowledge' and who are those 'whose do not have knowledge'?

---

13. Cf., e.g., M. Smith, *God in Translation* (Tübingen: Mohr Siebeck, 2008).

14. P. Fredriksen, 'Gods and the One God', *Bible Review* (February 2003): 12, 49.

15. Cf. Kar Yong Lim, *The Sufferings of Christ Are Abundant in Us: A Narrative Dynamics Investigation of Paul's Sufferings in 2 Corinthians* (London, New York: T&T Clark, 2009); J. B. Tucker, *'You Belong to Christ': Paul and the Formation of Social Identity in 1 Corinthians 1–4* (Eugene, OR: Wipf & Stock, 2010), pp. 95–100.

16. Cheung, *Idol Food*, p.128; Ciampa and Rosner, *1 Corinthians*, p. 386.

8.3. *The Addressees*

Whether 'those who have knowledge' were Jewish or gentile Christ-followers or both, Paul implies that they were potentially or actually reclining 'at a table in an idol's temple' (1 Cor. 8.10). As we have noted above, there were debates about what actually should be classified as idolatry, and the boundaries were blurred to some extent, but a temple meal was such a public participation in a non-Jewish cultic practice that it is difficult to see this as anything other than an act of idolatry.[17] But at this point (8.7-13) this is not the reason why Paul strongly argues against such participation. He does not argue at the level of cognitive perception nor does he present a definition here of what constitutes idolatry. Jews did under certain circumstances participate in public meals, visit pagan temples, contribute financially to a temple building, or become involved in the manumission of a slave in a pagan temple.[18] The theoretically very clear rejection of idol worship, and the sharp criticism of participation in any cultic practices related to idolatry by writers such as Philo and Josephus, does not cover all the issues which did arise in daily life in a context which was entirely permeated with pagan cultic practices.[19] Hence Jews obviously did have to negotiate the practicalities of their lives in relation to this all-pervasive presence around them and at least some Jews did not conceive all activities related to pagan temples as actual participation in pagan cultic practice and thus equivalent to worshipping the respective deity. It seems that one of the guiding parameters was that of intention or what in Pauline terminology is called 'conscience'. The situation discussed in 8.7-13 seems to be part of this pragmatic boundary-negotiating discourse in which Diaspora Jews seem to have been involved possibly on a daily basis, rather than a discussion of idolatry per se.

Hence one possible group who 'have knowledge' could be Jewish members of the Corinthian community for whom the loyalty to One and exclusively One God would have been inherent to their identity and practice of life in the Diaspora. Being accustomed to negotiating the practicalities of life in a Diaspora context, it would theoretically be possible to find someone who would not classify participation at a temple meal as idolatry. Although I find such a possibility unlikely, since such meals were public events, it cannot be entirely ruled out.

A more likely scenario in my view involves former god-fearers who claim to have knowledge (which Paul actually confirms), and others whom

17. P. Tomson, *Paul and the Jewish Law: Halakha in the Letters of the Apostle to the Gentiles* (Minneapolis: Fortress Press, 1990), pp.153–63.

18. L. S. R. Phua, *Idolatry and Authority: A Study of 1 Corinthians 8.1–11.1 in Light of the Jewish Diaspora* (London, New York: T&T Clark, 2005), pp.180–3.

19. Phua, *Idolatry and Authority*, pp. 89–120.

Paul sees as lacking such knowledge (οὐκ ἐν πᾶσιν ἡ γνῶσις, 8.7) rather than Jews. Indication for the identity of those who are lacking in knowledge is found in v. 7b where Paul describes them as τινὲς δὲ τῇ συνηθείᾳ ἕως ἄρτι τοῦ εἰδώλου ('some who are until now accustomed to idols'), which clearly refers to former pagans rather than Jews. No clear indication for the identity of those 'who have knowledge' can be found in the text. However, there are a few indications which provide hints to the identity of the knowledgeable: the absence of any reference to the purity of the food involved; the public nature of the practice under discussion; the address 'all of us have knowledge' seems a slightly strange assertion if directed to fellow Jews who would have long-standing experience in negotiating the practicalities of Jewish life in the Diaspora as mentioned above. The reference to knowledge seems rather to be directed to people who are proud of their newly embraced insights and who are now keen to demonstrate this in their everyday life. I conclude that the key addressees here most likely are non-Jews, former pagans from the gentile nations, knowledgeable or not.[20] However, I consider it most likely that the earliest Christ-followers from among the non-Jewish nations were not just any pagans, but were gentiles who had in some form already been in touch, familiar with, or even associated with Judaism, as God-fearers.[21] The familiarity of these God-fearers with Jewish practice and Scriptures varied on a spectrum from being close to actually becoming Jews to having some occasional interest in synagogue communities, or acting as patrons supporting a building financially.[22]

However close their relationship to the Jewish community may have been, including attendance at Sabbath assemblies, characteristic for all God-fearers would have been continued participation in pagan cults and thus expressions of loyalty to other gods alongside some forms of expression of loyalty to the God of Israel. Since in the Diaspora such varied loyalty did not involve any temple sacrifices to the God of Israel, these two practices could have been seen as two different activities. To attend a Sabbath assembly could, from a non-Jewish perspective, be seen in the same vein as attending the gathering of a philosophical school rather than being compared to cultic practices at pagan temples. Such a perception in

20.   This is supported by the direct address in 12.2: 'You know that when you were pagans, you were enticed and led astray to idols that could not speak.'

21.   See, e.g., D.-A. Koch, 'The God-fearers between fact and fiction: Two theosebeis-inscriptions from Aphrodisias and their bearings for the New Testament', *Studia Theologica – NJT*, Vol. 60/1 (2006): 62–90.

22.   See, e.g., references in Josephus: '(the Antiochian Jews) were constantly attracting to their religious ceremonies multitudes of Greeks and these they had in some measure incorporated with themselves', *BJ* 7.45; also *Ant* 14.110, where he notes that 'one need wonder that there was such a wealth in our temple, for all the Jews throughout the habitable world, and fearers of God, even those from Asia and Europe, had been contributing to it for a very long time'.

conjunction with the unproblematic option of showing loyalty to numerous deities would have rendered it normal and entirely unproblematic for a God-fearer to be interested in aspects of the God of Israel and simultaneously to continue to be loyal to other deities and thus, for example, participate in public meals at temples. Although there has been debate concerning the existence and role of God-fearers in Jewish communities, Jewish sources of the Diaspora provide no indication that the participation of such gentiles who participated in both pagan cults and Jewish customs was seen as problematic by the Jewish communities. There are no indications of fear of contracting impurity from socializing with these gentiles[23] and to accept them as participating in some Jewish practices (although the extent to which this was possible is unclear), despite the fact that they remained guests and were obviously not full members of the synagogue communities. Gentiles, whether God-fearers or not, were not inherently impure. They attracted impurity through certain immoral activities, such as idolatry, but such impurity was neither contaminating nor was it an ontological status. As non-members of God's covenant with Israel they were profane.[24]

If we envisage a scenario where such gentile God-fearers joined the Christ-movement, they would already have knowledge of the Scriptures, the Law ('for I am speaking to those who know the law', Rom. 7.1; 'this was written for our instruction', 1 Cor. 10.11, etc.), but the exclusivist claim of Paul's gospel would have been alien to them. They would have known that this claim was non-negotiable for Jews, but Paul precisely emphasized that gentiles who joined the Christ-movement should under no circumstances become Jews.[25] However, without becoming Jews these gentiles nevertheless were required to adopt the exclusivist practice of being loyal, and showing loyalty, to the One God alone. This might have caused some confusion to say the least among these new Christ-followers. If they were not supposed to become Jews, why then could they not continue to practise their previous loyalty rituals? Since religion and ethnicity were inseparable, to do so would have seemed to be the logical conclusion. A gentile (non-Jew) by definition is someone who is loyal to the deities of his respective people and clan/family, or else he/she becomes a Jew. Paul in his demand for exclusive loyalty to the One God and in his emphasis that gentiles must join the Christ-movement as gentiles, that is without becoming Jews, seems to combine aspects which are inconceivable, both

---

23.   C. Hayes, *Gentile Impurities and Jewish Identities: Intermarriage and Conversion from the Bible to the Talmud* (New York: Oxford University Press, 2002), pp. 20–2.

24.   Cf. P. Fredriksen, 'Paul, Purity and the Ekklesia of the Gentiles', in *The Beginnings of Christianity*, ed. R. Pastor and M. Mor (Jerusalem: Yad Izhak Ben-Tzvi, 2005), pp. 205–17 (217).

25.   See W. S. Campbell, *Paul and the Creation of Christian Identity* (London, New York: T&T Clark, 2008), pp. 59–61.

from a Jewish as well as from a gentile perspective.

Thus I think the problem arose because of the previously acceptable practice of God-fearers who had now joined the Christ-movement, who understood that they did so as gentiles, and hence were 'in Christ' on the same terms as Jews, but without becoming Jews. These former God-fearers, although familiar with some aspects of Judaism, and possibly also understanding at a cognitive level the requirement to abstain from idolatry as Christ-followers, were not embedded in the practice of negotiating boundaries of loyalty to the One God familiar to Diaspora Jews. Hence the implications of this command, which in principle was clear to them, were less obvious in practice. To renounce participation in public meals at the temple seems to have been one of the consequences of joining the Christ-movement which was less obvious for them.

8.4. *Social and Economic Implications of Non-Participation in Public Meals*

For people who lived at or below subsistence level in Corinth to stay away from the opportunity to participate in public meals must not have been a mere issue of cultic practice. Paul explicitly notes in the opening section of the letter οὐ πολλοὶ σοφοὶ κατὰ σάρκα οὐ πολλοὶ δυνατοί οὐ πολλοὶ εὐγενεῖς ('not many of you were wise by human standards, not many were powerful, not many were of noble birth', 1 Cor. 1.26b); this certainly does not refer to the Corinthian elite.[26] Hence to assume some social and economic implications following from Paul's demand to stay away from public temple meals is not difficult to imagine.[27] For a society where poverty at or below subsistence level was the norm rather than the exception, the temple festivals, of which there must have been many, particularly in temple-congested Corinth, would have rendered Paul's demand at least incomprehensible if it did not also actually cause hardship.[28] The details of this implication cannot be explored in this contribution but this is in my view a considerable aspect of Paul's discussion and it should be kept in mind that the cultic practice and real life experience were not separate but integrated aspects of life. To deprive members of the Christ-movement of access to one of the few accessible sources of additional food would have had an impact which cannot be subsumed under the rubric 'concern for

26.   For a discussion, see J. Meggitt, *Paul, Poverty and Survival* (Edinburgh: T&T Clark International, 1998), pp. 97–9.

27.   Meggitt, *Paul, Poverty and Survival*, pp. 97–106, 166; also B. W. Longenecker, *Remember the Poor: Paul, Poverty and the Graeco-Roman World* (Grand Rapids, MI: Eerdmans, 2010).

28.   P. Garnsey, *Famine and Food Supply in the Graeco-Roman World* (Cambridge: Cambridge University Press, 1988).

the well-being of the brother/sister'. It may not be pure coincidence that the discussion about where and what to eat (at pagan temples, food, meat sacrificed to idols) is brought to a conclusion through the reference to the Lord's supper and its appropriate consumption (1 Cor. 11.17-34). To see a brother/sister hungry when coming together for this celebration is an act of humiliation not merely on the ideological level but in relation to the real life experience of malnutrition.

Given these economic implications combined with the issue of blurred boundaries concerning the perception of idolatry among some Diaspora Jews, the uncontested practice of loyalty to pagan deities and participating in aspects of synagogue life by God-fearers, Paul's rhetorical strategy, arguing for abstaining from any participation in public temple meals, must have been an uphill struggle to say the least.

8.5. *To be or not to be at the Table –* *Paul's Double-Rationale in 1 Cor. 8.7-13 and 10.14-22*

In this wider context Paul's guidance should be seen a part of the boundary-negotiating practices in the first-century Jewish Diaspora. To envisage such a context for Paul's way of arguing in the passages in question provides a rationale for the tension perceived by some interpreters between the principle stated in 8.4-6 and the seemingly contradictory guidance given in relation to eating food which was involved in pagan cultic activities in the passages which follow. Whilst in 1 Cor. 8.7-13 and 10.14-22, Paul provides two reasons why the Corinthians should abstain from any involvement in table-fellowship which involved offerings to pagan deities, he seems to give contradictory advice in 10.23-30. In this contribution I can only focus on the first two passages which both deal with participation in public temple meals, whereas the context of the third scene rather seems to be a private house.[29] Paul provides two different rationales in 1 Cor. 8.7-13 and 10.14-22, whilst 10.23-30 has some affiliations with 8.7-13 in that both passages are concerned with someone's συνείδησις.

Before we analyse 1 Cor. 8.7-13 and 10.14-22 in further detail, it is worth noting that the issue in neither passage involves the impurity of food, that is, food laws. The fact that the food on the table might not be 'allowed', that is, impure (ἀκάθαρτος) for Jews, does not play any part in this discussion of whether or not to eat. This clearly indicates that there are no so-called Jewish purity/impurity issues concerning food at stake here. If meat were involved (which is not the only option), the issue is not from which animals the meat intended for consumption comes, nor whether the food is produced according

---

29. For a fuller discussion which includes the third passage, see my *Paul at the Crossroads of Cultures – Theologizing in the Space-Between* (London, New York: T&T Clark, forthcoming).

to the food laws. Paul does not mention any such details. He also does not mention table-fellowship between Jews and gentiles here (significantly the issue concerning table-fellowship at the Lord's table in Corinth has to do with social hierarchies rather than Jewish/gentile concerns). The issue also is not whether a Christ-follower could share the table with a pagan. This is obviously presupposed as a non-debated option in 1 Cor. 10.26–11.1 where it is considered 'normal' that one might be invited to the house of a pagan gentile and accept the invitation. The host cannot be Jewish since the issue that might cause a problem in such a situation is food offered as sacrifice. The problem is not that it had been sacrificed but that in Corinth, this could only imply that it had been offered to pagan deities. (Paul is not formulating any critique of temple sacrifices as such. Temples are a given, and the temple in Jerusalem is at the centre of the Jewish symbolic universe in the first century, including sacrifices and temple meals. It is inconceivable that Paul would have challenged this Jewish practice.)

Having established that no issues concerning specific Jewish dietary laws are involved in the particular problems around the table in Corinth, a detailed analysis will be given of the two reasons Paul provides for strict non-participation of Christ-followers in pagan temple meals. I will argue here that they both have to do with Paul's concern for the holiness of the Christ-following community.

8.5.1. *To be seen at the temple table (1 Cor. 8.17-22)*

Paul argues in a pedagogically exemplary way in this chapter. Rather than beginning his reply to the question of the Corinthians by telling them that they are mistaken in what seem to have been their conclusions from his teaching, he begins with the positive acknowledgement that those who seemed to have asked the question actually do have knowledge. However, he questions their understanding of the significance of this knowledge. Paul seems to refer to different aspects of knowledge. The aspect he refers to in vv. 4-6, and the allusions he makes in vv. 2-3, speak of different dimensions of knowledge. The latter possibly resonates with 'knowledge' in the vein of ידע, that is, knowledge not confined to the cognition of certain facts, but intrinsically encompassing something which we might today refer to as emotional empathy/intelligence. Paul reminds the Corinthians that knowledge without deep empathy or compassion is not true knowledge in Christ. He acknowledges that their knowledge concerning the existence and relevance of other deities in vv. 4-6 is accurate at the cognitive level. Thus their loyalty to the One God is not questioned here; their real understanding and thus true knowledge, however, is questioned. In Paul's view the knowledge of 'those who have knowledge' has not yet reached the mature stage he had hoped for, thus he as to explain that knowing the facts is not enough ('I fed you with milk, not solid food; for you were not ready for it; and even yet you are not ready', 1 Cor. 3.2-3). Knowledge is not the recognition of facts, nor is it confined to, and beneficial for, an individual only. The decisive question is how such 'knowledge' is translated into practice, how it affects the life of a community. The 'brother or sister for whom Christ died' is the testing ground for knowledge. In relationships with others it becomes evident whether knowledge is 'true knowledge' or mere recognition of facts.

In principle, Paul acknowledges that the conclusions of 'those who have knowledge' are not entirely wrong. The existence of other deities, if not absolutely denied, is certainly declared irrelevant, hence what happens at a pagan temple is not really relevant for those who are exclusively loyal to God. From this it seems to be a short step to conclude why not enjoy a free meal and socialize with others, possibly friends at the temple, outside the Christ-following communities. Paul does not directly question this conclusion and does not question that for those who think that they do have knowledge, this might be an appropriate conclusion. Significantly Paul does not classify participation at a temple meal as idolatry per se; this is merely referred to as ἐν εἰδωλείῳ κατακείμενον (eating/reclining in the temple of an idol). The key aspect is how others, in this case, fellow Christ-followers, perceive such participation. Even though from the perspective of those who have knowledge such participation might not be seen as participation in worshipping the deity, others may perceive such participation differently.

This is Paul's concern here: not that 'those who have knowledge' commit idolatry but that Christ-followers who do not have this knowledge (8.7), may be οἰκοδομηθήσεται εἰς τὸ τὰ εἰδωλόθυτα ἐσθίειν (encouraged to eat food sacrificed to idols, 8.10b). For those who do not 'know' the nothingness of idols this would mean that they were actually eating the temple meal as 'idol food', hence they would commit idolatry. It is thus not the participation of the knowledgeable at the temple meal which is classified as idolatry and sin but rather the effect this might have on another Christ-follower. To cause him or her to commit idolatry is classified as sin by Paul. Although committing idolatry is a severe issue, the target of Paul's argument is the sin of seducing someone to commit idolatry. Such an act amounts to destroying the brother/sister and hence is threatening the community per se. The key point in the argument here is not the act of idolatry as such but the concern for the other. Out of concern for brothers and sisters 'in Christ' participation in a public temple meal is out of the question.[30] To illustrate the importance of this, Paul refers to his own

---

30.   Mark Nanos has argued that the brothers and sisters in view here might be pagan gentiles (not Christ-followers), people who are potential Christ-followers who are not yet convinced. They should not be tempted to come to the wrong conclusions concerning this

practice and explains that he himself abstains entirely from eating meat, implying that he does this so that no occasion could occur which would confuse a brother/sister to commit idolatry.

It has been emphasized that an ethical concern for the brother/sister 'in Christ' is the core of Paul's admonition. Knowledge has to be infused with a concern for the well-being of the brother/sister.[31] Although this certainly is an important aspect of the issue at stake, this is not the only focus of Paul's argument. Paul's concern is the holiness of the community.[32] Holiness is a ritual category. The ethical concern is inherently intertwined with ritual concerns. In order to come near and associate with the divine one has to fulfil certain purity requirements.[33] What is important to note with regard to the passage discussed here is that this holiness could be threatened by immoral actions against someone else. To hurt a brother/sister, that is, to cause him/her to misconceive the requirement for exclusive loyalty to the One God, would actually threaten their status as gentiles in Christ, and hence put them in danger of ἀπόλλυται γὰρ ... ἐν τῇ σῇ γνώσει ('finding destruction in your knowledge', 8.11).[34] This concern is similar to the one in Rom. 14.15, although the situation is significantly different in that in Rome the issue has nothing to do with participation in pagan temple meals.[35] But in both cases the concern for the brother/sister is centre stage and has decisive implications for the community as a whole. Unethical

new movement, but be given a clear picture of their identity. See his 'Why the "Weak" in 1 Corinthians 8–10 Were Not Christ-Believers', in *Saint Paul and Corinth: 1950 Years Since the Writing of the Epistles to the Corinthians: International Scholarly Conference Proceedings (Corinth, 23–25 September 2007)*, Vol. 2, C. J. Belezos with S. Despotis and C. Karakolis (Athens, Greece: Psichogios Publications S.A., 2009), pp. 385–404.

31.   Cf., e.g., D. W. Ellington, 'Imitating Paul's Relationship to the Gospel: 1 Corinthians 8.1–11.1', *JSNT* 33 (2011): 303–15, 306.

32.   As R. Ciampa and B. Rosner have outlined in a recent article, 'The structure and Argument of 1 Corinthians: A Biblical/Jewish Approach', *JSNT* 33 (2011): 205–18. Thiselton notes the element of 'impurity' and 'pollution' in 8.7 (καὶ συνείδησις αὐτῶν ἀσθενὴς οὖσα μολύνεται), but does not relate this to the ritual or cultic dimension of holiness: A. C. Thiselton, *The First Epistle to the Corinthians: A Commentary on the Greek Text* (Grand Rapids, MI: Eerdmans, 2000), p. 640.

33.   This perception is shared between Jews and pagans. Certain purity regulations had to be adhered to when approaching the deity, and such regulations were by no means unique to Jews. It was not only not appropriate to approach the deity in a state of impurity, or as profane – it could be dangerous.

34.   Cf. Thiselton, *1 Corinthians*, p. 653 (I find his argument for an 'active' translation of ἀπόλλυται quite convincing).

35.   For a detailed discussion of this issue in Romans 14, see my '"Called to Be Saints" – the Identity Shaping Dimension of Paul's Priestly Discourse in Romans', in K. Ehrensperger and J. B. Tucker (eds), *Reading Paul in Context: Explorations in Identity Formation* (London, New York: T&T Clark, 2010), pp.90–109. Also A. T. Cheung, *Idol Food in Corinth* (Sheffield: Sheffield Academic Press, 1999), pp. 135–6; R. E. Ciampa and B. S. Rosner, *The First Letter to the Corinthians* (Grand Rapids, MI: Eerdmans, 2010), p. 371.

behaviour conveyed impurity to the community and thus threatened its holiness.[36]

Significantly it is not the association with pagan so-called deities (which do not really exist), which according to Paul's argument here presents the biggest threat, but rather 'sinning against your brothers/sisters and wounding their conscience' (v. 12) is the major problem which is actually seen as sinning against Christ.[37] The clear implications of sinning against Christ may be open to debate but there are significant indications throughout the letter to render a reading plausible which sees this as a reference to the corporate dimension of Christ, that is, as a reference to the Christ-following communities as the 'body of Christ' (cf. 12.27).[38] Thus, the 'sinning against the brother/sister' would be a sinning against the community 'called to be holy' (1.2).[39] Earlier in the letter (3.16-17) the concern for the holiness of the community is also formulated by Paul via the metaphor for the community as God's temple. To cause a brother/sister to 'find destruction' would bring destruction to God's temple including the instigator of this negative process.[40] The concern for the well-being of the brother/sister in Christ in Paul's argument is inseparably intertwined with a theocentric concept of holiness.

8.5.2. *Participation in Christ*[41] *and participation in demons (10.14-22)*

Paul returns[42] to the issue of idolatry (10.1-13) and participation in public meals at pagan temples (10.14-22) via the example of the golden calf

---

36.   Cf. J. Klawans, *Impurity and Sin in Ancient Judaism* (New York: Oxford University Press, 2000).

37.   Thiselton, *1 Corinthians*, p. 656.

38.   Campbell, *Paul and the Creation of Christian Identity*, pp. 153–6.

39.   Indications for this can be found throughout the letter. The scope of this paper does not allow for dealing with this aspect in detail here, hence a few references must be sufficient: in the opening of the letter the addressees are named ἡγιασμένοις ἐν Χριστῷ Ἰησοῦ ... κλτοῖς ἁγίοις (sanctified in Christ Jesus ... called to be saints, 1 Cor. 1.2); they are reminded that they are God's temple, which is holy (ὁ γὰρ ναὸς τοῦ θεοῦ ἅγιός ἐστιν οἵτινές ἐστε ὑμεῖς, 1 Cor. 3.17); the body is a temple for the Holy Spirit (τὸ σῶμα ὑμῶν ναὸς τοῦ ἐν ὑμῖν ἁγίου πνεύματός ἐστιν, 1 Cor. 6.19); the focus on the community as the body of Christ (1 Corinthians 12). Since pagan gentiles are impure and profane, Paul is very concerned that those gentiles who have been sanctified through Christ do not attract impurity again.

40.   Paul's athletic metaphor passage (1 Cor. 9.24-27) is another way of referring to the implications one's own behaviour towards others has eventually on oneself.

41.   For a detailed discussion, see W. S. Campbell, 'Coventnal Theology and Participation in Christ: Pauline Perspectives on Transformation', in R. Bieringer and D. Pollefet (eds), *Paul and Judaism: Crosscurrents in Pauline Exegesis and the Study of Jewish-Christian Relations* (London, New York: T&T Clark, 2012).

42.   The two passages discussed here are significantly separated but also linked to each other by chapters 9.1–10.13, where Paul refers to his own decision not to claim his right to

incident. The narrative serves as a reintroduction of this topic and is used to exemplify the impossibility of participating in the worshipping practice for pagan deities and for the God of Israel through Christ at the same time.[43] Paul here provides a second and notably different argument against the participation of all Christ-followers, even those who are knowledgeable in public temple meals.

The admonition in v. 14 is clear and non-debatable. But again, the implications of this and what constitutes idolatry are less obvious. As in chapter 8, Paul does not imply that mere eating at a pagan temple table constitutes an act of idolatry. In 9.19 he repeats the perception of 8.4 that neither idols nor food sacrificed to idols are anything. The issue is thus not the eating of the food (and the drinking of a cup) as such. According to the arguments presented in this passage, the key element that renders participation in a temple meal impossible is the sharing of the table. Although Paul repeats here the denial of the existence of idols, he is nevertheless of the view that there are spiritual powers, that is, demons, which although not at equal level with God, are worshipped by pagans as deities. These beings were perceived as exercising power over every aspect of life, positive and negative, and hence could not be ignored, either by Jews or by gentiles. But these second-tier spiritual beings should by no means be treated with a respect which only the One God of Israel deserves.[44]

The way Paul builds up the argument here could be seen as an example of 'ritual inter-cultural communication'. He refers to two practices of ritual, in Jewish and in non-Jewish/pagan culture respectively, and compares these with the Lord's table. The point of comparison here is not the sacrifice itself. Thus Paul does not compare Jewish and pagan temple sacrifices on the one hand with the cup and the bread on the other.[45] He emphasizes, however, that when Jews participate in a temple meal (which can only happen in Jerusalem), they participate in the altar, which means they are in

---

support from the Corinthians as an example of renouncing one's freedom in Christ. He thereby actually confirms the perception of those who claim 'knowledge' to some extent, but takes them on a pedagogical journey via his own example including his 'teaching method' passage in 9.19-23. Paul thus seems to have confirmed to those who have knowledge that their knowledge is accurate, although their understanding of how such knowledge should translate into the practice of real life is not. At the end of chapter 9 the issue of freedom in Christ and how it should be lived in relation to others in the community seems clarified and Paul moves back to the issue of idolatry.

43.   It is interesting to note that Paul explicitly mentions in what ways this scriptural passage is relevant for these gentiles in Christ – as a means of learning and teaching.

44.   For a detailed discussion of demons, see G. Williams, *The Spirit World in the Letters of Paul the Apostle: A Critical Examination of the Role of Spiritual Beings in the Authentic Pauline Letters* (Göttingen: Vandenhoeck & Ruprecht, 2009); also Ciampa and Rosner, *1 Corinthians*, p. 379.

45.   Contra, e.g., Thiselton, *1 Corinthians*, pp. 771–2.

community with God and their fellow Jews. What is offered to God in the sacrifice is given back by God to the community; he thus is the host of the temple meal. This table is God's table,[46] and by participating in the meal at this table fellowship with God and fellow participants is established. There is not a hint of critique in this reference to the nature of Jewish temple worship, sacrifice and temple table fellowship;[47] this is a mere statement of what is constitutive of temple meals from a Jewish perspective.

This is a positive reference to what is perceived as a key aspect of a temple meal – the establishing of table fellowship and communion among the participants and with God. Paul then moves into the cultural world of pagans, and although he denies the existence of other deities, he considers the existence of demons as real. Thus, the ritual practice at pagan temples is compared in terms of structure with the ritual practice at the temple in Jerusalem. Structurally they have the same function; the sacrifice offered at a pagan temple, although not offered to a deity according to Paul, involves nevertheless something – Paul calls them demons, which inherently renders such a demon the host of the public meal at the temple. Thus community between the 'demon' and the participants, and among the participants, is established and celebrated at the table of the demon. The understanding of the effects of the ritual of a temple meal is thus translatable between Jewish and non-Jewish culture and can establish understanding, even though the deity and possibly the diet involved are different. Participation in the table of demons is perceived to be challenging the exclusivity of participating in the table of the Lord. The logic seems clear. However, to designate the table of the Lord in terminology which resonates with temple worship, including sacrifice, is a bold move on Paul's part. (I will discuss this further below.)

The strange issue of participating in one cult only (from a gentile perspective) is complicated by the fact that the Jewish temple cult was only practised in Jerusalem. Although gentiles could participate in temple rituals up to a certain point (prayer in the outer court), full participation was not possible for them. It should be noted that such restrictive access against foreigners was not a Jewish peculiarity as some inscriptional evidence from Delos demonstrates. The six-foot long inscription from an Apollos temple in Delos reads, 'It is not lawful for a foreigner (ξένος) to enter.'[48] Thus, participating at the table of the God of Israel was not an option for the Corinthians for a number of reasons. This may have been

---

46.   Ciampa and Rosner refer to Mal. 1.7,12 (LXX), Ezek. 41.22, 44.16 as examples of references to the altar as the Lord's table: *1 Corinthians*, p. 482.

47.   Contra Thiselton, *1 Corinthians*, pp. 771–2. For a detailed discussion, see Ciampa and Rosner, *1 Corinthians*, pp. 477–8.

48.   Cf. P. Fredriksen, 'Dining with the Divine', *Bible Review* (Oct. 2002): 62.

an additional cause for confusion amongst these new Christ-followers. Since there was no Jewish ritual comparable to the pagan temple rituals in Corinth, and participation in temple worship in Jerusalem would have been very restricted for them as gentiles, it could be imagined that these Corinthians did not consider their participation in pagan temple meals as being in competition with any ritual involvement with the God of Israel. Participation in synagogue assemblies, and coming together for the Lord's supper, may not have been conceived by the Corinthians as comparable to participation in pagan temple rituals and at public meals at pagan temples.

This is possibly one instance where Paul's comparison of the temple tables and the table of the Lord is of decisive significance: in order to render comprehensible his demand that they all had to abstain from participating in pagan temple meals, whether they were 'full of knowledge' or 'weak in conscience', Paul had to formulate the reason for this in a way that made sense to them from within their cultural encyclopaedia and within their cultural coding system. The closest similarities between the Jewish and pagan coding system existed in terms of ritual practice. Other aspects, such as the narratives of their respective symbolic universes, certain ways of social interaction, and the cultural encyclopaedias associated with terms and narratives, may have been quite different.[49] In order for Paul to be able to communicate something, and expect to be understood, he had to refer to aspects of life where similarities were prevalent. It seems that the realm of ritual provided this dimension of sufficient similarity to enable potentially successful communication. Thus, I see Paul here arguing in the vein of ritual inter-cultural communication.

By requiring from these former pagan gentiles abstention completely from food offered to 'demons', and thus to dissociate themselves from the ritual, religious and social occasion of offering to, and receiving from, deities, Paul required of them to dissociate themselves from core aspects of their former self-understanding, which was intertwined with religious, social, civic and ethnic aspects. Not to have anything to do with offerings at a temple must have been very strange from a gentile perspective, even irrespective of its economic and social implications. The temple in Jerusalem, although it was at the centre of Paul's Jewish symbolic and social universe, could not move into the vacancy for these gentiles established by joining the Christ-movement. As mentioned above, although as gentiles they could participate in aspects of the temple cult to some extent, they could not be involved in the same way as Jews would

---

49.   Cf. my 'Lost in Translation – Paul a Broker/Go-Between in Inter-Cultural Communication?', paper presented at the SBL Annual Meeting 2010, Atlanta.

have been. This has nothing to do with a negative perception of the temple and its rituals; but the implications of this needs to be further explored, for example, whether the geographical distance of the Jerusalem temple added to the sense of vacancy of the sacred space for gentile Christ-followers or prevented difficult complications for them as non-Jewish worshippers of the God of Israel.

Paul seems to recognize the difficulty of the 'empty sacred space' to some extent, and argues that in sharing the cup and the bread at the Lord's supper they actually do participate in a table, in the Lord's table. This implies that they have fellowship with him and amongst each other in a similar vein as the participants at a temple meal, be it pagan or Jewish. Because the Jerusalem temple cult cannot substitute for these gentiles the space occupied formerly by the pagan temple ritual and temple meal, and because it seems to have been inconceivable to leave this space vacant, Paul argues that the Lord's supper be moved into this 'empty' space for these former pagan gentiles. Participation in Christ is established not by sharing food sacrificed to God, but by sharing in the cup and bread as the body of Christ. Thus Paul argues that the table of the Lord establishes fellowship for these gentiles in a similar vein as the table fellowship they had to give up in conjunction with pagan temple cults. Since a function is attributed to the Lord's table similar to that of the temple tables of demons, it is ruled out that Christ-following gentiles can take part in both. This is a clear argument against participation in pagan temple rituals but it is not a critique of the temple cult in Jerusalem.

In addition, the Lord's table here is not only seen as adopting the cultic function of the table of demons (or so-called deities) but also the function of providing actual nourishment for the participants as can be seen from the discussion in 11.17-34. The social and economic dimensions are central to the communal meal, and violating the need of the brother/sister is a threat for the community as a whole – again I would argue with relevance for its holiness. To humiliate the brother/sister is to hurt them; this 'profanes' the holy community (1 Cor. 11.27).

Paul here presents an argument for exclusive participation at only one table – the table of the Lord – by establishing a parallel between the Lord's supper and the temple tables of the respective contexts of Jews and gentiles. By creating this parallel he provides a clear argument for the exclusive fellowship with the host of this table – the Lord (whether this refers to Christ or God). The vacancy in the sacred space is filled; hence, there can be no doubt for Christ-followers where fellowship is established.

8.6. *Conclusion*

In the two passages I have chosen to discuss here, Paul's different ways of arguing were analysed in detail. Whereas in 1 Corinthians 8 the focus of Paul's argument against participation in public temple meals is the concern for the brother/sister who might draw wrong conclusions and be tempted to perceive him/herself as actually eating food offered to idols, Paul in 10.14-22 provides an additional argument, which this time clarifies that even though the 'knowledgeable' are correct in their perception that there are actually no idols, there is still no way that they can participate in pagan temple meals. Although there is agreement between the knowledgeable and Paul that there are no idols, and hence their participation in pagan temple meals cannot be classified as straightforward idolatry, Paul considers fellowship with demons, if not in the same category as idol worship, nevertheless as still an option which is ruled out when one participated in the table of the Lord.

The line of argument is different in both cases but the focus of the argument is identical in my view: Paul is concerned with the holiness of the community as the body of Christ. It is threatened by behaviour which endangers the brother/sister, in that such behaviour would convey moral impurity to the community, profane it, and thus contaminate their status as holy people.[50] In addition, Paul demands the knowledgeable to stay away completely from tables he considers as contaminated by paying tribute to second-tier spiritual beings. The honour of worshipping and cultic rituals is reserved exclusively for the One God and Lord, and those participating, although not being inherently impure, would have contracted impurity by such activities.[51]

The decisive aspect of the meals discussed in these Corinthian passages is not the food eaten but the fellowship at the table. The food is only relevant in relation to the table fellowship which is established through the context in which it is eaten. The identity of the κοινωνία at the table is decisively defined by the host; the exclusivist claim of worshipping only the One God of Israel is interpreted as being established at the table of the Lord Jesus Christ. This rules out any other κοινωνία at any table which is related to worshipping (even if it is only the worshipping of demons).

Paul has established that the Lord's supper moved into the vacancy left by the now forbidden pagan temple cult and thus is somewhat an activity with which holiness is associated. Christ-followers who participate in both

---

50.	The particular danger the siblings would face if they were to participate in both the Lord's table and the demons' table is destruction.

51.	Though Paul is careful not to call participation in the table of demons idolatry.

the table of demons and the table of the Lord contaminate the 'body of Christ'.[52] Holiness and impurity are incompatible and the result of them coming into contact with each other is disastrous. The implications of this interpretation of the Lord's table by Paul are far reaching: the exclusivist fellowship which is associated with it separates the Christ-followers from the ritual celebration of, and indebtedness to, the dominating ruling powers (λεγόμενοι θεοὶ ... θεοὶ πολλοὶ καὶ κύριοι πολλοί, 8.5); since the pagan temple meals also function as food provision for people who lived at subsistence level or below, a need for replacement of this provision might have arisen within the communities of Christ-followers which would support claims that the Lord's supper was a celebration which also served that purpose; and Paul's interpretation of the Lord's table as replacing the table of demons for gentiles (although not the altar in Jerusalem) attributed a cultic function to it which contributed to its development as the core ritual of emerging Christianity.

---

52. Hurting the brother/sister by not waiting for them at the Lord's supper has the same effect as tempting the weak to participate in the table of idols: the body of Christ, the Christ community which is called to be holy, is being 'profaned' by immoral behaviour against a brother/sister (11.27-34).

Chapter 9

THE POWER OF AN INVITATION:
EARLY CHRISTIAN MEALS IN THEIR CULTURAL CONTEXT[1]

Soham Al-Suadi

Special occasions – like the participation at a festive meal – are regarded
as having the ability to transform and challenge a person in his or her daily
life.[2] With regard to festive meals, scholars have studied the organization
of clubs and associations as well as the form and structure of those meals.
Socio-historical data, archaeological evidence and anthropological theories
have supported biblical scholars in deepening insights into the world in
which biblical and non-biblical sources are set. Such deepened knowledge
comprehends not just the social and political background of the groups but
also of the individuals. Based on the literary and archaeological record,
Dennis Smith observes that, 'Clubs and associations were organized in such
a way that individuals from a lower status in society could achieve a higher
status designation at the club banquets based on their rank within the club.'[3]
This recognition allows us to explore our understanding that communal

---

1.   Major parts of this contribution were presented at the conference 'Decisive Meals'
and at the Annual Meeting of the Society of Biblical Literature 2010 in Atlanta. I am grateful
to the participants of the conference 'Decisive Meals' and to the members of the SBL-Group
'Ritual in the Biblical World' for their comments. The paper deals with central aspects of my
published dissertation: S. Al-Suadi, *Essen als Christusgläubige*, TANZ 55 (Tübingen: Francke
Verlag, 2011).

2.   H. Taussig, *In the Beginning was the Meal: Social Experimentation and Early Christian
Identity* (Minneapolis, MN: Fortress Press, 2009), p. 54, notes 'Both as groups and as individuals,
many of those at the meal felt as if they were living in a different world. The ingestion of the
food and all its communal dynamics internalized the social values and vision. It is this obviously
simultaneous fantasy and transformation inside of the meal participants that made the meals
themselves spiritual and enhanced them as social experiments.' The challenge is therefore to
bridge the gap between the worlds experienced in daily life and during the meal. D. E. Smith,
From Symposium to Eucharist: The Banquet in the Early Christian World (Minneapolis, MN:
Fortress Press, 2003), p. 153, refers to the meal of the Essenes when he states that, 'Purity was so
closely associated with the boundaries of the community that purification rituals were required
for entrance into membership.'

3.   Smith, *From Symposium to Eucharist: The Banquet in the Early Christian World*, p. 11.

meal gatherings are contexts for highly developed social skills that allow a person's religious, social or cultural transformation.

There is common agreement that 'the meal represents a "social code", which expresses patterns of social relations'.[4] But so far the discussion has focused upon behaviour during the meal or just before and after the meal only. Recent scholarship has concentrated on the rituals of the meal itself and sometimes the baths before the meal and the symposium after.[5] In this paper I will point out that a wider chronological perspective is needed to ask whether patterns of social relations prepared for or even allowed transformation to happen prior to the actual meal itself. In order to ask whether transformation happens at places other than the actual meal, it is central to discuss the most obvious event that precedes the festive meal – the invitation.

Although the invitation is an important factor for the occasion, the meal itself, and the group and functions as an initiator for a specific gathering it has not yet received sufficient scholarly attention.[6] The undervaluation of previous scholarship relates to both the literary invitation and its cultural context. An early attempt to study meal-invitations was made by Chan Hie Kim in 1975. He has done some textual comparison without exploring the context of the literary and archaeological sources thoroughly. Instead, his description of the context remained under the umbrella-term Hellenism.[7]

This study will argue that the invitation is part of the system of highly developed social skills and precedes not only the meal but also the transformative process of individuals and groups participating at the meal. It will examine relevant New Testament texts that mention the invitation to a meal to explore the importance of the invitation for the whole meal practice. This leads to the question of the sociological embeddings of the invitation. This paper shows that Hellenism is a valid basis for the understanding

---

4.   D. E. Smith and H. Taussig, *Many Tables: The Eucharist in the New Testament and Liturgy Today* (London, Philadelphia: SCM Press, Trinity Press International, 1990), pp. 30–1.

5.   M. Klinghardt, *Gemeinschaftsmahl und Mahlgemeinschaft: Soziologie und Liturgie Frühchristlicher Mahlfeiern*, TANZ 13 (Tübingen: Francke Verlag, 1996), pp. 47–9. Klinghardt describes how baths before the meal became part of the meal. This is not only because appetizers and drinks were already served, but also because cleaning safeguarded against the invitation of unknown people and marked the social standard when expensive oils or massages were included.

6.   Invitations have been part of the discussion from the very start of socio-historical studies, but unfortunately they have been regarded as only a technical necessity. Smith and Taussig, *Many Tables: The Eucharist in the New Testament and Liturgy Today*, pp. 23ff. distinguish between oral and written invitations. In 2003 Dennis Smith focuses on invitations as necessities and elaborates their significance for the meal gathering (Smith, *From Symposium to Eucharist: The Banquet in the Early Christian World*, pp. 22–5).

7.   C.-H. Kim, 'The Papyrus Invitation', *JBL* 94 (1975): 391ff. n. 1, says that he is well aware of the difference in historical circumstances in Egypt and Palestine. Despite that he is interested in a form that was common to both contexts.

of the general meal practice, but not adequate enough to describe the relevant contextual details of transformative processes. To examine these theses, this paper will focus on a letter from a young Sarapis follower to his parents (*P.Mich.inv. 4686*) and on Paul's letters to the communities in Galatia, Rome and Corinth. The comparison of the two Hellenistic texts leads to some suggestions for future comparisons of Hellenistic Egyptian and Pauline texts.

9.1. *Meal Invitations*

The Hellenistic meal was composed of several elements, which were more or less part of every festive and daily meal occasion. Matthias Klinghardt and Dennis Smith examined the structure of Hellenistic meals and showed that the meals described in New Testament Scriptures match this overall social practice.[8] Hal Taussig identifies a clear typology of five points that characterize the Hellenistic meal:

- 'the reclining of (more or less) all participants while eating and drinking together for several hours in the evening
- the order of a supper (*deipnon*) of eating, followed by an extended time (*symposion*) of drinking, conversation, and performance
- marking the transition from *deipnon* to *symposion* with a ceremonial libation, almost always of wine
- leadership by a "president" (*symposiarch*) of the meal – a person not always the same, and sometimes a role that was contingent or disputed
- a variety of marginal personages, often including servants, uninvited guests, "entertainers," and dogs'.[9]

Each point stands for different social skills that allowed members of the community to interact with one another and to develop a specific cultural practice which was the basis for communal and individual transformation. It is important to note that the distinctive feature of a group's meal practice is dependent upon the varied interpretations of the Greco-Roman banquet, which provided the basis for special forms of social relations and identity markers.[10]

---

8.   Klinghardt, *Gemeinschaftsmahl und Mahlgemeinschaft: Soziologie und Liturgie Frühchristlicher Mahlfeiern*, chapter I; Smith, *From Symposium to Eucharist: The Banquet in the Early Christian World*, pp. 13–46.

9.   Taussig, *In the Beginning was the Meal: Social Experimentation and Early Christian Identity*, p. 26 (italic in original). Invitations are not included in this typology.

10.   Smith and Taussig, *Many Tables: The Eucharist in the New Testament and Liturgy Today*, p. 35. This monograph shows the beginnings of Taussig's and Smith's discussion. Their argument is based on the identification of a Greco-Roman banqueting practice, which allowed social bonding, social obligation, social stratification and social equality within the banquet's ideology (pp. 30–4).

Invitations found on inscriptions, papyri or ostraca are evidence that certain groups came together for specific purposes.[11] These groups included religious and non-religious, private and non-private[12] associations and clubs.[13] Whether the invitation was given formally or informally, it literally opened the door to another person's house or to another god's temple. Chan Hie Kim studied written invitations from the Hellenistic period in Egypt in order to identify their common structure and form. Out of 30 invitations, 25 had a common structure.[14] The basic invitation is composed of: 1) a verb of invitation; 2) a reference to the invited guest; 3) the naming of the host; 4) the purpose of the invitation; 5) the occasion; 6) the place; 7) the date; and 8) the time.[15] At the same time it sets the rules for the entrance. In addition to the information regarding place and time, it gives the invitee a taste of what to expect and allows the invitee to picture the occasion to come. Additionally, it activates other social networks so as to realize a person's participation.

11. Smith, *From Symposium to Eucharist: The Banquet in the Early Christian World*, pp. 22–5.

12. Klinghardt's notion to resolve the difference between private and public meals, based on the observation that 'private' meals could have happened in non-private places provided that they were paid for privately. This means that meals of associations and clubs can also be considered 'private' (Klinghardt, *Gemeinschaftsmahl und Mahlgemeinschaft: Soziologie und Liturgie Frühchristlicher Mahlfeiern*, p. 29).

13. E. Ebel argues in *Die Attraktivität früher Christlicher Gemeinden. Die Gemeinde von Korinth im Spiegel Griechisch-Römischer Vereine*, WUNT 2 (Tübingen: Mohr Siebeck, 2004), that meals played a central role in early Christian society. She analyses the *cultores Dianae et Antinoi* and the Athenian Iobakchen to compare and contrast the features of the communities and their members. Knowing that associations functioned as burial insurance for members with lower social status (*cultores Dianae et Antinoi* were in need of this social security) helps one to realize that there was no strict line between religious and non-religious gatherings, because the worship of Dianae and Antinoi was as much part of the association as the social security (pp. 66–8). In addition, P. Harland, *Associations, Synagogues, and Congregations: Claiming a Place in Ancient Mediterranean Society* (Minneapolis, MN: Fortress Press, 2003), p. 61, draws attention to embedded religious systems that could not be regarded as 'religious' in modern terms.

Papyri studied by Kim: *POxy 2592, POxy 110, POxy 523, POxy 524, POxy 2791, POsl 157, SB 7745, PFouad I Univ 7, PFouad 76, PYale 85, POxy 747, POxy 1484, POxy 1485, POxy 1755, POxy 2147, POxy 111, POxy 926, POxy 927, POxy 1579, POxy 1580, POxy 2678, POxy 2792, PFay 132, POxy 1486, POxy 1487, BGU 596, BGU 333, POxy 112, POxy 1214, PApoll 72.*

Smith knows of a total of 32 papyrus invitations including the collection at Columbia University (Smith, *From Symposium to Eucharist: The Banquet in the Early Christian World*, p. 23). The number indicates either that clubs and associations, which met on a regular basis, must have come to an agreement regarding standing invitations or that invitations were not preserved over a long period of time.

15. Kim, 'The Papyrus Invitation', p. 392.

9.2. *Meal Invitations in the New Testament*

Meal invitations, of course, are also mentioned in the New Testament. The New Testament tells us about a variety of meal practices including their invitations. We know about formal and informal occasions. We also learn that for Jesus, his followers and the early Christian communities, eating together was decisive for the group and the place of the group in society.

Matthew 22.1-14 and Lk. 14.15-24 tell us about the parable of the great supper.[16] Jesus compares the kingdom of heaven to a king who gave a wedding banquet for his son and who had to extend the invitation to guests he normally would not invite. Although Mt. and Lk. differ in their presentation of the parable, they agree in the extended invitation to good and bad, or the poor, the crippled, the blind and the lame because the invitees were not worthy of the invitation. Invitations to weddings are also mentioned in Lk. 14.8 where Jesus advises his disciples to go and sit down at the lowest place. In addition, Jn 2.1-11 speaks about how Jesus and his disciples were invited to a wedding in Cana. Revelation 19.9 speaks about the marriage supper of the lamb and connects the invitation with the 'true words of God'. The New Testament also gives us information about informal invitations. In Lk. 11.37 it says that Jesus was invited to dine with a Pharisee while he was speaking.[17] Jesus turns out as a troublesome guest because he does not wash his hands and accuses the Pharisee of being a fool. But our texts are not only about invitees. Acts 10.23 tells us that Peter invited Cornelius' men who had been sent to invite Peter over to Cornelius' house. Peter, who was hungry when the men came and had had his dinner prepared, invited the men in and gave them lodging before they left the next day. In between the formal invitations to wedding banquets and the rather spontaneous invitations, we find Paul's advice to the community in Corinth. In his first letter to the Corinthians he writes in 1 Cor. 10.27: 'If an unbeliever invites you to a meal and you are disposed to go, eat whatever is set before you without raising any question on the ground of conscience.'

This corresponds with his advice in 1 Cor. 10.25 where he says that the Corinthians can eat what is sold in the meat market but it conditions the latter verse where he says that if someone says to them, 'This has been offered in sacrifice,' they should not eat it.

We can notice from the table below that the invitations described in the New Testament match the generic content Kim discerned in the Egyptian invitations.

---

16.   Mt. 22.3–4.8-9 uses the verb καλέω. Lk. 14.12-13; 16-17.24 uses καλέω (parallel to *Gos Thom § 64*), too, but Lk. 14.12 differs in using φωνέω and ἀντικαλέω. Kim, 'The Papyrus Invitation', p. 393ff., states that both verbs are equally used for wedding invitations although 16 against 9 Egyptian invitations use φωνέω.

17.   Lk. 11.37 uses ἐρωτάω to describe the invitation – the same as Lk. 7.36.

Table 1: Kim's generic content of the invitation fits with the New Testament texts.

	Mt. 22.1-14	Lk. 14.15-24	Lk. 14.8-10.12-14	Jn 2.2-11	Rev. 19.9	Lk. 11.37-38	Acts 10.23	1 Cor. 10.27
invitation verb	Mt. 22.1 καλέω	Lk. 14.16 καλέω	Lk. 14.10 καλέω Lk. 14.12 φωνέω ἀντικαλέω	Jn 2.2 καλέω	καλέω	Lk. 11.37 ἐρωτάω	Acts 10.23 εἰσκαλέομαι	καλέω
invited guest	Mt. 22.3 τοὺς κεκλημένους Mt. 22.9 ὅσος	Lk. 14.15 πολύς Lk. 14.21 ὁ πτωχὸς καὶ ἀνάπειρος καὶ τυφλός καὶ χωλός	Lk. 14.13 πτωχός ἀνάπειρος χωλός τυφλός	Jn 2.1 ἡ μήτηρ τοῦ Ἰησοῦ Jn 2.2 Ἰησοῦς μαθητής		Lk. 11.37 [Ἰησοῦς]	Acts 10.17 οἱ ἄνδρες οἱ ἀπεσταλμένοι ὑπὸ τοῦ Κορνηλίου	τῶν ἀπίστων
naming of the host	Mt. 22.2 βασιλεύς	Lk. 14.16 ἄνθρωπος Lk. 14.21 οἰκοδεσπότης	Lk. 14.10 ὁ κεκληκώς	Jn 2.11 νυμφίος		Lk. 11.37 Φαρισαῖος	Acts 10.23 Πέτρος	
purpose of the invitation	Mt. 22.4 ἄριστον	Lk. 14.16 δεῖπνον	Lk. 14.12 ἄριστον		ἀρνίον	Lk. 11.38 ἄριστον	Acts 10.23 ξενίζω	
occasion	Mt. 22.3 γάμος			Jn 2.1 γάμος	γάμος		Acts 10.10 πεῖνα	
place		Lk. 14.23 οἶκος		Jn 2.1 Κανά			Acts 10.17 τὴν οἰκίαν τοῦ Σίμωνος	
date				Jn 2.1 τῇ ἡμέρᾳ τῇ τρίτῃ			Acts 10.9 ἐπαύριον	
time		Lk. 14.16 ὥρα					Acts 10.9 περὶ ὥραν ἕκτην	

Although the texts in the New Testament are not composed as invitations, they give the reader enough information to understand the setting of the meal gathering. This fundamental information forms the basic understanding of the story and prepares for the theological remarks in the text. Consequently the invitation (that is, the information given by an invitation) is the starting point for a decision-making process that can result in initiations, marriage, fellowship, and much more. The New Testament texts show us that this process might turn out to be very complicated. Invitations can be declined, they can be extended to other people, they can mark the beginning of a fellowship, and they can provoke thoughts about eating sacrificed meat. Knowing that the starting point of the decision-making process is fragile and complicated makes us aware of the difficulties that come up with social, cultural or religious transformations.

With these images in mind, we can focus on the decisions that are made by extending an invitation or being invited to a festive meal. We will see that the invitation sets out the grounds for the cultural and religious processes of transformation and should not be underestimated.[18]

9.3. *Ptolemaios to his Father* (P.Mich.inv. 4686)

Knowing that political, social and religious interactions were also expressed by the use of the body, the choice of food, the singing of hymns, and many more things, encourages one to examine the changed social and religious identity of participants of festive meals.[19] To elaborate the circumstances and social, political and religious variables of the Hellenistic meal practice, scholars like Matthias Klinghardt, Dennis Smith, Philipp Harland and others, include knowledge about pagan cults. As elaborated earlier, Hellenistic culture of the first centuries AD is used as an umbrella-term to discuss common social, cultural and religious behaviour. Papyri from Oxyrhynchos give specific information regarding the Sarapis cult and the invitation to the *kline* of Sarapis.[20] Another interesting papyrus text is *P.Mich.inv. 4686*, a private letter from Ptolemaios to his father, in which Ptolemaios informs his

---

18.   U. Egelhaaf-Gaiser, *Kulträume im Römischen Alltag: Das Isisbuch des Apuleius und der Ort von Religion im Kaiserzeitlichen Rom* (Stuttgart: F. Steiner, 2000), p. 272, relates initiation and festive meal, and discusses Hellenistic meal invitations.

19.   Taussig, *In the Beginning was the Meal: Social Experimentation and Early Christian Identity*, pp. 78–9, elaborates the choices relating to the libation. Choosing out of the multiplicity of gods for the libation maps the choices that keep coming up in real life.

20.   Cf.: M. Vandoni, *Feste Pubbliche e Private nei Documenti Greci*, Testi E Documenti Per Lo Studio Dell'antichità; 8. Serie Papirologica. 1 (Milano, Varese: Cisalpino, 1st edn, 1964), pp. 138 (*POxy 1484*), 140 (*POxy 110*), 142f. (*POxy 523; POsl. III. 157*), and 145 (*POxy 1755*). Vandoni provides an excellent collection of papyri relating to public and private meals. Cf. *POxy 2592, PYale 85*.

parents that he has chosen to act as *agoranomos* for a cult banquet in honour of Sarapis. Ptolemaios asks for help in providing five loads of wood for the banquet.[21] The papyrus was found with the archive of the officer (*praktor*) Sokrates son of Sarapion and was nearly complete, though only a few traces of ink remained of the address on the verso.[22] The letter was recovered at Karanis, a province on the north-east rim of the Fayyum basin – today's Kom Aushim – 35 miles west of Memphis.[23] It was written in Memphis or Arsinoe in the early part of the third century.[24] Ptolemaios writes to his father:

> Ptolemaios to his father, greeting. I want you and my mother to know that the novices' fee (*siopetikon*)[25] for the banquet is 24 drachmai and for a place another 22 drachmai. After consideration, therefore, I have taken up the post of *agoranomos*[26] so that I need not pay the novices' fee nor for a place; but also I receive double portions, and I provide them with wood. For this reason, then, give the matter thought, and if you come up you will receive the freightage for the donkeys. For there is a need of 5 loads. If you need me, send me word and I will come down with two friends as well in order that you may not tire yourself. For a man cannot refuse our lord Sarapis. It is another two months until the banquet. If you are able to bring up the wood with your donkey, bring it up, and you will get the money to cover your expense.
> (2nd hand) Farewell.[27]

The letter written at a place of Sarapis worship gives us a lot of insight into the organization of the banquet. Obviously the invitation of Sarapis was

---

21. http://quod.lib.umich.edu/cgi/i/image/image-idx?id=S-APIS-X-2260%5D1 (07.03.2011).

22. http://quod.lib.umich.edu/cgi/i/image/image-idx?id=S-APIS-X-2260%5D1 (07.03.2011).

23. H. C. Youtie, 'The Kline of Sarapis', *HThR* 41.1 (1948): 15.

24. Youtie argues for Memphis or Arsinoe because the distance from Karanis to Oxyrhynchus would be too great for a donkey (it would exceed 35 miles). Youtie, 'The Kline of Sarapis', 15ff. n. 36.

25. *Siopetikos* (σιωπητικός) can be derived from σιωπάω or σιωπῆ meaning 'silence'. Youtie argues that Ptolemaios uses the same word as a stone inscription from the second century AD. This inscription lists 400 initiates of a society devoted to the cult of Bacchus in order of their importance. Twenty-three individuals are named as σιγηταί. The singularity of both terms during that time supports his understanding of Ptolemaios as a novice. Youtie, 'The Kline of Sarapis', 17–20. Cf. M. P. Nilsson, 'En Marge De La Grande Inscription Bacchique Du Metropolitan Museum', *Studi e materiali di storia delle religioni* X (1934): 1–18.

26. The word *agoranomos* is known from Greek cities in Egypt and refers to municipal officials serving a liturgy. They were in charge of the supervision of markets, licensed merchants, watched for violations of the price scale, and examined weights and measures. Youtie compares Ptolemaios' duties with a *agoranomos* from Messenia (92 BC), who had to keep an eye on the water supply and regulate the baths during the celebration of the mysteries too. The only difference is that Ptolemaios' position is temporary (Youtie, 'The Kline of Sarapis', 23–6).

27. *P.Mich.inv. 4686*: cf. Youtie, 'The Kline of Sarapis', 17, and M. Totti, *Ausgewählte Texte der Isis- und Sarapis-Religion*, Subsidia Epigraphica (Hildesheim, Zürich; New York: Georg Olms, 1985), p. 129.

unavoidable for Ptolemaios and his parents, 'because a man cannot refuse the lord Sarapis'. Ptolemaios writes to his parents about an invitation to the *kline* and informs them that he could save 46 drachme if he would serve as the *agoranomos* and contribute the wood needed.[28] He describes himself as a *siopetikos*, that is, someone who is a silent member of the banquet, a neophyte of the society. He also writes about the privilege of receiving double portions. This gives us a clear idea of the importance attached to his duties and points to the resources that were needed to live up to his duties. First, he had to contribute five loads of wood, which was needed for the festival ritual of the temple, the sacrifice preceding the dinner, the dinner itself, and the construction of ceremonial furniture.[29] Knowing that wood was rare in Egypt increases the importance of that supply and indicates that Ptolemaios' family was needed to provide for a crucial part of the meal.[30] The letter indicates that the father is not strong enough to carry the wood. Significant to that discussion is that Ptomelaios not only offers to carry the wood himself but also to ask two friends to help him. It is obvious that Ptolemaios can fall back on a social network that extends beyond his family. In addition, Ptolemaios writes that he will be the *agoranomos*. This term, derived from municipal officials that are in charge of the supervision of markets and took responsibility for smooth proceedings, highlights that Ptolemaios' duty expanded to include a corporate responsibility. Although Ptolemaios held only a temporary mandate, an entrance into the social, political and religious support-system had been offered. Much more can be said about the responsibilities with which Ptolemaios is faced. Central to the situation is that the invitation to the feast unleashed a cascade of further involvements. Ptolemaios expected his father to support him, intended to recruit friends, take up corporate responsibilities and begin his novitiate.[31]

The letter makes clear that the decision-making process involved several people and combined financial and personal aid in order to achieve a higher social and religious status for an individual and indirectly for his team of supporters too.[32] It illustrates that the invitation to a meal provides the basis

28. Although Ptolemaios cannot refuse the Lord Sarapis the letter does not indicate that Ptolemaios was forced to supply the wood or serve as *agoranomos*.

29. Youtie, 'The Kline of Sarapis', 23.

30. For other integral supplies cf. *P.Mich.inv. 6877* (dating c. 184–6 AD, origin probably either Karanis or Ptolemais Hormou, Herakleidou meris, Arsinoite nome, province of Egypt). This is a list of animals, offered as forced contributions by each village of the division of Herakleides for the feast of Sarapis (http://quod.lib.umich.edu/cgi/i/image/image-idx?id=S-APIS-X-2982]6877R.TIF).

31. The letter not only shows that Sarapis sponsored rites of initiation, but also indicates the grades of initiation that needed financial and personal contributions (Youtie, 'The Kline of Sarapis', 21).

32. A far less voluntary supply-system is shown by *P.Mich.inv. 6877* (origin probably Ptolemais Hormou, Herakleidou meris, Arsinoite nome, province of Egypt; c. 184–6 AD). It is a

for a social, cultural or religious transformation. Although written in third-century Egypt and not in the first- or second-century Mediterranean, it is as Hellenized as the Jewish texts of the New Testament and fosters the general understanding of a common Hellenistic cultural code. Therefore, it helps with the understanding of meal invitations where Pauline and other New Testament texts do not give us enough background information.

9.4. *Difficulties with Invitations for Paul*

Where Ptolemaios expresses his ambitions to his family, Paul makes the reader aware of the difficulties that are connected with the meal because of different social and religious influences on the meal. With the exception of 1 Cor. 10.27, he does not mention invitations nor cite them.

In Gal. 2.11-14 the reader is not much informed about the terms and conditions of the meal; the concern is the common reclining of Jews and gentiles during the meal. By separating himself from the table in Antioch, Cephas is separating himself from the table of the new creation. Romans 14 illustrates the consequences when the relationship of the Christ-believers is disturbed. The brother or sister in Rom. 14 can be judged and despised (10); a stumbling block or hindrance can be put in the way of another (13); and he or she can be injured by what one eats (15). First Corinthians 11.17-34 illustrates clearly that the different social backgrounds of the participants are conflicting within the aim of the Lord's supper. And last, but not least, in 1 Cor. 10 the reader is advised to eat meat unless he asks or is told that the meat was sacrificed to another god. Reading these warnings make us conscious of the community, which understands itself as the body of Christ, and the perceived dangers of interaction being transformed into participation.

Consequently, invitations to a meal do not only establish a basis for communal eating, but also raise questions and difficulties for the invitees. Therefore, the invitation provokes the participant to live up to the chance of being part of a mutual transformation.

So far we have seen that 'Clubs and associations were organized in such a way that individuals from a lower status in society could achieve a higher status designation at the club banquets based on their rank within the club.'[33] But we have to add that the participation itself was not enough

---

list of animals, offered as forced contributions by each village of the division of Herakleides for the feast of Sarapis. It lists 20 young pigs and at least ten calves (http://quod.lib.umich.edu/cgi/i/image/image-idx?id=S-APIS-X-2982]6877R.TIF).

33.   Smith, *From Symposium to Eucharist: The Banquet in the Early Christian World*, p. 11.

to start the process. It needed thorough preparation and the utilization of several people's help and resources to enter the meal setting.

9.5. *Hellenism in Context*

The discussion could end at that point: the *tertium comparationis* between Ptolemaios or a Christ-believer in Corinth is the common experiences they had, leading to the communal meal, which was motivated by official calendars or personal reasons.[34] Thinking of them as two sides of a coin identifies one as the ambitious neophyte and the other as the failed and confused participant. We could end with the observation that over its long cultural influence, Hellenism allowed people with different social or religious backgrounds to experience a similar ritual which only varied in its local characteristics. In this case the common cultural code would soften the age difference of the sources and would minimize the differences in place. It would even out the differences and allow the focus on the highly developed identity formations that we can observe: on the one side, Ptolemaios who becomes a Sarapis-follower, and on the other side, Jews or Pagans who identified as followers of Christ.

As we have seen, Hellenism is a legitimate category to describe the cultural setting and assess the socio-historical background of a person's expectations. But is the common Hellenistic culture reason enough to argue for challenged social identities and the beginnings of new religious identification at the same time? In other words, is the transformation of Ptolemaios, who becomes a Sarapis-follower, the same social and religious transformation as that of a believer in Christ? On an individual level the parallel experience with Hellenized social realities is valid and is worthy of scholarly attention, but the question does not only relate to the study of individual social settings. The wider context behind the individual transformation is the establishment of modified religious communities. Hence we have to ask whether the formation of the Hellenized Egyptian god Sarapis in Egypt was rooted in the same social and religious experimentation as the beginnings of Christianity.

Because the formation of religious groups and identities is not a stable development it is important to compare and contrast the interests in the Hellenistic meal for the Serapis cult and the believers in Christ.

---

34.   Egelhaaf-Gaiser, *Kulträume im Römischen Alltag: Das Isisbuch des Apuleius und der Ort von Religion im Kaiserzeitlichen Rom*, p. 273, describes personal and official motivations for festive meals.

9.6. *Hellenism Reconsidered*

In its scholarly use, the term Hellenization can be discussed with reference to Johann Gustav Droysen who stretched the meaning of the word to signify the period of transition from the pagan to the Christian world which started with Alexander the Great. It became consolidated to interpret Hellenism as a special period of history in antiquity characterized by a mixture of Greek and oriental elements after Droysen's second edition of *Geschichte des Hellenismus*.[35] The Greek language, the adoption of Greek names, educational institutions, the growth of literature and philosophy influenced by Hellenistic features and the religious deviation and syncretism, as seen in legal institutions and in art, indicate the widespread cultural influence. Jean Bingen and Roger S. Bagnall illustrate clearly that the discourse of Hellenism focused especially on 'Greeks' and 'Egyptians', though 'other types of investigations have established the heterogeneous character of both of these groups'.[36] In addition, Lee Levine notes that the discussion of Hellenism and Hellenization over the last several generations has been based on two assumptions. The first is that Hellenism involved Greek ideas and practices that reached the East either directly from Greece itself or, more likely, via one of several major Hellenistic urban centres, such as Alexandria or Antioch.[37] The second assumption is that Hellenism was a given phenomenon, to be either affirmed or denied: 'Judea is considered either Hellenized or not.'[38]

These assumptions suggest a phenomemon that is simpler than in fact it was. Of course, Hellenism and Hellenization do not necessarily mean the import of 'classical' Greek culture. The particular 'Greekness' of economic, social, political, material, religious or cultural behaviour was influenced by local factors as well. And, of course, the measure of 'Greekness' is not measurable by the extent people and cultures were drawn to this one regnant culture. It is fair to say that we should talk rather about a process of selection, adoption and imitation. Influences should be described as uneven and indirect rather than talking about the Greek influence on a non-Greek culture.

Following this alternative paradigm we can expect a great extent of contextualization, which leads us to the investigation of individual and communal experiences of an impressive cultural product that was adapted

35. Cf. J. G. Droysen, *Geschichte des Hellenismus*, 2nd edn (Gotha: Perthes, 1877).

36. J. Bingen and R. S. Bagnall, *Hellenistic Egypt: Monarchy, Society, Economy, Culture* (Edinburgh: Edinburgh University Press, 2007), p. 216.

37. L. I. Levine, *Judaism and Hellenism in Antiquity: Conflict or Confluence* (Seattle: University of Washington Press, 1998), p. 17.

38. Levine, *Judaism and Hellenism in Antiquity: Conflict or Confluence*, p. 17.

and modified. When we focus on the festive meal practices, which conveyed a particular way of 'Greekness' throughout the ancient Mediterranean, we return to the Hellenized Sarapis in the Greco-Roman and the Egyptian world.

9.7. *The Hellenized Sarapis*

The Hellenization of the Serapis cult is obviously disputed and difficult to outline precisely because Egyptian, Greek and Roman influences were continuously in flux. Thomas Allan Brady discussed the Egyptian influence upon the Greco-Roman Mediterranean cultures and argues for Egyptian success in Hellenism because of the human appearance of Sarapis, his ability to cure, and his 'support' for imperial leadership.[39] Brady correlates the successful spread of the cult with shared political interests between Athens and Egypt. His assumption includes the general tendency of the Egyptian cult to be accessible to Hellenistic societies and their culture. Ladislav Vidman expresses this tendency when he observes that even in pre-Hellenistic times the Isis and Osiris cult had a character that matched the conception of Hellenism.[40] The accessibility of the cult for larger groups of societies, as John Stambaugh argues, is the result of an important factor.[41] '[K]ings and commoners, merchants and slaves, Greeks and orientals, men and women, cities and individuals all venerated Sarapis and prayed to him from the earliest years of the Hellenistic period, and we know that he answered those prayers with satisfying frequency.'[42] Archaeological evidence provides a basis for estimating the popularity of rendering homage to Sarapis. We have verification of Sarapis' presence in Athens, Delos and Corinth.[43] For Corinth in particular the material evidence of the Hellenistic period alone appears rather insignificant. One should not underestimate, however, the literary evidence given by Pausanias and Apuleius.[44] The evidence is more substantial in the Roman period and allows a collection of data about sanctuaries, inscriptions, statuary art, coins, lamps, terracottas, festivals, prosopography, and decorative art of

39. T. A. Brady and C. F. Mullett, *Sarapis and Isis: Collected Essays* (Chicago: Ares, 1978), p. 12.

40. L. Vidman, *Isis und Sarapis bei den Griechen und Römern: Epigraphische Studien Zur Verbreitung und zu den Trägern des Ägyptischen Kultes* (Berlin: De Gruyter, 1970), p. 12.

41. J. E. Stambaugh, *Sarapis under the Early Ptolemies* (Leiden: Brill, 1972), p. 98.

42. Stambaugh, *Sarapis under the Early Ptolemies*, p. 98.

43. Cf.: P. Roussel, *Les Cultes Égyptiens à Délos du Iiie au Ier Siècle Av. J.-C* (Nancy: Berger-Levrault, 1916), and S. Dow, 'The Egyptian Cults in Athens', *HTR* 30 (1937).

44. D. E. Smith, 'The Egyptian Cults at Corinth', *HTR* 70 (1977): 226.

Sarapis in Corinth.[45] Tessa Rajak illustrates the conjunction of pagan cults and festivals in Hellenistic societies in her essay 'Jews and Christians as Groups in a Pagan World'. She concludes that not only temples, theatres and stadia but also town squares would be taken over by festive celebrations which included sacrifice.[46] The political importance and the publicity of the cult clearly represent pagan festival occasions, which were woven thickly into the social fabric of the Greek city. Festivals and meals in the temple visibly dominated the Greek city.

The pounding of the Hellenistic wave, which influences the originally Egyptian cult, reaches back to the country of origin. Youtie observes this interdependence between the Greek and the Egyptian cities with reference to Ptolemaios.

The search for parallels has taken us to the Greek cities of Egypt or led us out of Egypt into the Greek mainland, the Greek islands, Greek Asia Minor, and into the Campagna, where an important Bacchic society with Greek antecedents left a record of itself on a stone. When Ptolemaios identifies himself as a novice in religious mysteries, assumes the office of agoranomus, supplies wood, and receives double portions at a cult banquet, he is following precedents that reach far back into the life of the Greeks before Alexander.[47]

In 1948, Youtie concluded that the pattern of the festival and the banquet were 'not specifically Egyptian'.[48] At the same time he moderates his statement by observing that, 'The cult of Sarapis at Memphis, hence all the more at Alexandria, was Greek; it exhibited that proper mark of Hellenistic civilization, a peculiar, variable mixture of Greek and native elements.'[49] And he gives more credit to the cultural fusion in his footnotes: 'Hellenistic civilization in Egypt was a more or less unstable fusion of things Greek and non-Greek.'[50]

Ptolemaios' letter to his parents exemplifies this heterogeneity. Ptolemaios was interested in being part of the Greco-Roman world that was attainable for him through the Sarapis cult societies. Sarapis provided a powerful impulse for many Egyptian as well as Greek devotees toward the Hellenization of

45.   Smith, 'The Egyptian Cults at Corinth', pp. 210–26. Smith outlines three locations of Sarapis-worship: 'A shrine of Sarapis was located in the Forum, not far from the two sanctuaries of the god' (p. 228).

46.   T. Rajak, 'Jews and Christians as Groups in a Pagan World', in *The Jewish Dialogue with Greece and Rome: Studies in Cultural and Social Interaction*, ed. T. Rajak (Boston, Leiden: Brill Academic Publishers, 2002), p. 359.

47.   Youtie, 'The Kline of Sarapis', 27, refers to the Bacchic stone inscription from the seconnd century AD.

48.   Youtie, 'The Kline of Sarapis', 27.

49.   Youtie, 'The Kline of Sarapis', 28.

50.   Youtie, 'The Kline of Sarapis', 28, n. 91.

Egypt. This life represented by the temple was accessible for Ptolemaios by buying himself in and by activating his social network. Ptolemaios was invited by Sarapis to take part in the festive meal, which was a symbol of a Hellenistic-Egyptian identity marker.

The Pauline interest differs from the identity experienced at the Sarapis cult. Considering the public presence of festive meals in the temple, Paul reduces his critique regarding the communal experience to the recently-established communities in private houses. Especially in Gal 2.11-14 and 1 Cor. 11.17-34, Paul draws the boundaries sharper and more complete between temple meals and meals in private houses (although he does not deny that the strong might be able to take part in other festive meals in Romans 14). His language, his value-system and the tight structure of his argumentation focus upon the community as the body of Christ seeking the glory of God. By locating the Lord's supper within private houses, Paul is writing to the communities to raise consciousness of them and to avoid the integration of them into a bigger public movement of temple meals. Quite the contrary, Paul's imagined 'body of Christ' represents the group and the local communities represent the subgroups, which ought to behave as he wishes. Therefore Paul is dealing with the identity of a subgroup, which lives out its identity through ritual experimentation. He is confronted with different approaches to meal invitations and has to deal with the multiplicity of ritual performances. Smith and Taussig contextualized that form of ritual action as follows:

> Rather than try to come up with a common and final solution to the differences, the multivalent symbols of ritual keep allowing for indirect recognition of those differences. This allows each different sub-group to be recognized and for the group as a whole to work regularly on non-final, adaptive and constantly revised compromises.[51]

Reading Paul's letters shows how much effort Paul put into the negotiation between his imagined group, 'the body of Christ', and the local subgroups, which came together for a festive meal. Inevitably this does not mean that the establishment of the subgroup did not serve the society. Even though Paul did not express the sociological significance of the Christ-believing subgroups, their importance for the Greco-Roman society should not be underestimated. We can observe that the formation of guilds and associations contribute to the function of a whole, as a system of wheels-within-wheels, because the code within the small group endorses and validates that within the larger. Having the spread of Christianity in mind, one can say that small groups offer a training ground and practice in the operation of the larger

---

51.   Smith and Taussig, *Many Tables: The Eucharist in the New Testament and Liturgy Today*, p. 102.

group.[52] As distinguished from Ptomelaios, who utilized the Hellenistic meal for his integration into the Greco-Roman society, one can conclude that the social identity of being a small subgroup, especially as individual households or families, constituted the Pauline use of the Hellenistic meal. Paul is promoting a behaviour that incorporates the performance of the temple in private houses and vice versa.

From this perspective we have seen that the identification of Hellenized practices itself is not enough to examine the underlying forces of identity formation. Political, social and religious transformations happen in both examples we have examined, but if Paul's writings to the communities give us an insight into the beginnings of Christianity one can recognize that his use of the Hellenistic meal practice was not leading to public social performances in a temple. The meal practice of the Sarapis cult on the other hand was oriented toward the public temple cult. Although meals were held in private houses too, the social identification was aligned with the temple and not with a new identity created in a subgroup.

9.8. *Conclusion*

As we have seen, invitations set the grounds for a cultural process of transformation and should not be underestimated because transformation does not happen at the meal gatherings only. Ptolemaios, as well as a Christ-believer, engaged in the realization of the invitation as part of a system of highly-developed social skills and social networks. Whether the meals guaranteed the chance of achieving a higher status and/or bared the risk of ritual failure, as interpreted by Paul, the invitation started a multi-level decision-making process. Of course this process was embedded into a common culture that was generically regarded as Hellenistic. Knowing that cultural codes are processes of selection, adoption and imitation, leads to the appreciation of uneven and indirect influences of 'Greekness' that were present for the participants of the meal as well as their social backgrounds. In comparison to the Sarapis cult, which became a challenge as a public identity marker at least for Ptolemaios but also for his family and friends, the Pauline interests raised cautiousness and a behaviour that incorporates the public into the private to gain a common identification as the body of Christ.

We have seen that the Hellenistic cultural code gave room for a decision-making process including the transformation of political, social and religious

52. T. Rajak, *The Jewish Dialogue with Greece and Rome: Studies in Cultural and Social Interaction* (Leiden: Brill, 2002), p. 468.

collective identities. But the shared features of Hellenistic culture do not provide sufficient explanation for the fact that social and religious identities were challenged and new religious identification emerged simultaneously. Taking the differences regarding the Hellenistic significance of individual cult participation seriously is a useful starting point for further investigations relating to the beginnings of Christianity and its cultural context.

Chapter 10

MEALS AS ACTS OF RESISTANCE AND EXPERIMENTATION:
THE CASE OF THE REVELATION TO JOHN

Hal Taussig

In this essay I read portions of the Revelation to John at early Christian meals. I take seriously the dynamics of the meal as ways to hear the text of the Revelation to John. This reading belongs to two larger projects of mine: 1) to learn to think about early Christianity primarily through a social lens (and in this vein to think of meals as a primary social practice of early Christianity); and 2) to destabilize text through its marriage to performance (and here, too, seeing early Christian meals as a central performancial dynamic of early Christianity). To this end, imagining and rationalizing the performance of specific texts from the Revelation to John at early Christian meals is meant to be the primary product of this paper.[1]

Before the specifics of the Revelation to John, I want to lay out some assumptions at the beginning in order to identify ways that approaches of this essay overlap, coincide and/or collide with the approaches in the other essays of this volume.

The first assumption has been the guiding insight of the Society of Biblical Literature's Seminar on Meals in the Greco-Roman World over the past ten years. It is based on the mutually corroborating work of Matthias Klinghardt of the University of Dresden and of Dennis Smith of Phillips Theological Seminary.[2] Independently of one another – indeed in quite different academic worlds – Klinghardt and Smith produced two extensive studies of meals in the Greco-Roman world with specific reference to their relationship to early Christianity. Astonishingly both Smith and Klinghardt

---

1.   Cf. my *In the Beginning Was the Meal: Social Experimentation and Early Christian Identity* (Minneapolis: Fortress Press, 2009).

2.   Matthias Klinghardt, *Gemeinschaftsmahl und Mahlgemeinschaft: Soziologie und Liturgie frühchristlicher Mahlfeiern* (Basel: Francke Verlag, 1996); and Dennis Smith, *From Symposium to Eucharist: The Banquet in the Early Christian World* (Minneapolis: Fortress Press, 2003).

came up with almost exactly the same hypothesis. This hypothesis has been tested in a range of ways by the SBL Seminar during its ten years of work. The Klinghardt–Smith hypothesis is this: what might be referred to as the Greco-Roman banquet forms a firm overarching typology for festive meals of the Hellenistic and Greco-Roman periods, and as such dismisses all the various earlier projects that saw a broad range of types of meals in these periods. This striking agreement from two very different scholars and the subsequent testing of their intuitively joint hypothesis further situated the character of early Christian meals. After Smith and Klinghardt, it is no longer necessary to seek one or another meal type ('Eranos', 'Jewish', 'sacrificial', 'mystery cult', 'Dionysian god-consuming', 'Mythraic dying and rising', 'Qumran') to correspond to particular parts of early Christian literature or practice. Rather, we can assume that more or less all references to meals in the first two centuries of proto-Christianity can be understood as belonging to the common Greco-Roman paradigm established by Klinghardt and Smith. (Of course, it is not that Smith and Klinghardt think that all banquet meals were exactly the same, but their typology undermines previous notions of very different kinds of banquet meals.) What is equally convincing to me about Klinghardt and Smith's work is how their close attention to New Testament and other early Christian texts supports the idea of a common banquet type. Perhaps even more to the larger point of this volume is the way the Jewish scholars in the SBL Seminar also have concurred that Jewish meals of the first two centuries CE need to be considered as belonging to Klinghardt and Smith's Greco-Roman paradigm.[3]

The second assumption I make also comes out of the recent years of the SBL Seminar, but is more directly related to my own work in my recent book, *In the Beginning Was the Meal: Social Experimentation and Early Christian Identity.* This assumption is that ritual theory can be applied to understanding early Christian meals. I do think that my work is too new to assume broad acceptance in this regard. And, although the SBL Seminar has strongly endorsed my approach,[4] there is clearly not yet a scholarly

---

3.   Cf. the papers of the Third Session of the concluding meeting of the Seminar in Atlanta, 20–21 November 2010. Perhaps the most dramatic dimension of this session were the ten theses entitled, 'Table as Generative Locus for Social Formation in Early Judaism', prepared by Jonathan Brumberg-Kraus, Susan Marks and Jordan D. Rosenblum. Cf. in the same session, the three papers, Jonathan Brumberg-Kraus, 'The Table and Early Judaism I'; Susan Marks, 'The Table and Early Judaism II'; Jordan Rosenblum, 'The Table and Early Judaism III'; followed by the extensive response by Judith Hauptman. All of these materials are available on the Seminar website at http://www.philipharland.com/meals/GrecoRomanMealsSeminar. htm#Seminar_Papers_Online_(for_2005).

4.   Cf. my paper at the 17 November 2007 First Session of the SBL Seminar, 'Greco-Roman Meals and Performance of Identity: A Ritual Analysis', along with the responses from Dennis Smith and Matthias Klinghardt on the Seminar website: http://www.philipharland.

consensus on whether my proposal that ritual theory of the twentieth and twenty-first century can really be applied to first and second century early Christian meals. Nor is it theoretically unproblematic methodologically to apply ritual theory to texts about meals, as I do. Two issues must be raised about this use of ritual theory in the study of Greco-Roman meals: 1) how applicable are twentieth and twenty-first century ritual theories to first and second century meals; and, 2) how is the use of ritual theory in relationship to events known only through ancient texts and archeological studies?[5] So, although I assume ritual theory's applicability to the study of Greco-Roman and early Christian meals, there is not enough space in this essay to make that point. Nor do I expect everyone to accept this assumption. As noted above, this larger proposal must first weather or be amended by a season of scholarly response to my larger proposal as presented in detail in *In the Beginning Was the Meal*.

10.1. *Explicit Meal References in The Revelation to John*

I want to consider how the text of the Revelation may have acted performancially within early community meals as a way of experimenting with social identity and enacting a range of resistance modalities to Roman imperial rule. On what textual basis may this be considered?

The Revelation to John does have a set of references to the practice of early Christian meals. Perhaps most well known are:

1. the invitation of the Christ to the church of Laodicea in 3.20 ('Here I stand knocking at the door. If anyone hears my voice and opens the door, I will come in and recline with him and he with me');
2. the invitation to the wedding supper of the lamb in Rev. 19.9; and
3. the explicit positioning of the whole revelation on 'the Lord's day' (1:10), the day in which many Christian groups did gather for a meal.

Less attended to in scholarship is the strong interest in eating in the seven letters to the churches. In addition to the invitation to supper in the letter to Laodicea, the letter to Ephesus promises 'eating from the tree of life' (2:7). The letter to Pergamum likewise concludes with a promise of 'hidden manna' (2.17). Pergamum is accused of 'having committed

com/meals/GrecoRomanMealsSeminar.htm#Seminar_Papers_Online_(for_2005). Cf. also the responses to my *In the Beginning Was the Meal* at the 22 November 2009 First Session of the SBL Seminar by Dennis Smith, Angela Standhartinger and Matthias Klinghardt on the Seminar website (address above).

    5.   Cf. my responses to these issues in *In the Beginning Was the Meal*, pp. 55–7.

adultery through the eating of food sacrificed to idols' (2.14), similar to the letter to Thyatira's accusation against 'Jezebel' that she had 'committed the adultery of eating food sacrificed to idols' (2.20).

I do not think that it can be overlooked that these meal references in the seven letters are a part of a fabric of traumatization that involves 'suffering for my name' (2.3), 'hardships' (2.9), 'being thrown into prison' by the Devil (2.10), 'living in the place where Satan is enthroned' (2.13), the 'faithful witness Antipas being killed' (2.13), 'perseverance' (2.19), 'not disowning my name' (3.8), and 'the time of trial which is coming' (3.10). It does not seem accidental that meal disputes themselves about food sacrificed to idols are located in the same letters, reflecting political and religious pressure on the communities.

Without accounting for all the other dimensions of the letters and without wanting to reduce all these dimensions to either issues of meals or imperial persecution, I would suggest the following meal-specific sketch of the seven communities. At least in the eyes of the author(s) of the Revelation to John, these communities gather on the Lord's day for meals together. The centrality of these meals together is indicated by the way the texts lean into mythic, cosmic and eschatological qualities of meals (e.g., eating the tree of life, receiving hidden manna and celebrating the wedding feast of the lamb). But the meals are not at all unproblematic as events, and seem entangled in the complex of issues on how to resist and accommodate imperial power and presumption, especially around the buying of meat sacrificed at local temples, which were probably imperially inclined. It seems likely then that the highly charged meals of different early Christian groups in the Asia Minor of the Revelation to John each may have had relatively different practice relative to whether they ate meat sacrificed to other gods.

10.2. *Meal Structure and Ritual Theory*

It is at this point that both the Klinghardt–Smith typology and ritual theory help me think about the relationships between the Revelation text and early Christian meals. I have suggested elsewhere that the combination of stability and flexibility in the Greco-Roman banquet (per Klinghardt–Smith) provided, on the one hand, a structure through which meal participants could both rely on the meal framework for safety, and, on the other hand, as an opportunity to address unprocessed parts of their lives.[6] Several examples of this combination of structure and improvisation in the Greco-Roman meal typology may be helpful here.

6. Cf. *In the Beginning Was the Meal*, pp. 21–54, 67–86, 145–72.

For our purposes here, every such banquet entailed a several-hour long *symposion* in which debate, performance, drinking, singing, teaching and game-playing could happen, providing both a structure for these kinds of activities and an invitation to bring not altogether anticipated parts of people's lives – such as inter-familial quarrels, problems with political bribery or intrigue, or economic fortune – to this *symposion*.

Or, similarly, every meal had a libation marking the transition from the supper/*deipnon* to the *symposion* structured into the meal, both a regularized transition and an occasion for saluting important deities and persona at the meal.

Or, as a third example of such combination of structure and openness, the taking of food during the supper was accompanied by the socially prestigious activity of reclining, giving social importance to the foodstuffs themselves and eating itself, and thereby prompting – in both early Christian and non-Christian literature – endless debates about what to eat and who could eat what on these occasions.

These examples of the structured, yet open-ended, character of the Greco-Roman banquet fit quite well with a number of theories of ritual. Victor Turner, for instance, asserts that ritual is done with the dynamics of *communitas,* which – when related to ritual – occasion a certain liminality.[7] Pierre Bourdieu understands ritual within the larger stability of cultural *habitus,* yet gives ritual itself the character of being able to disguise and sanction collision of contradictory principles.[8] Similarly, Catherine Bell portrays ritual as a specifically modulated pattern of human actions within a special and highly constructed environment (in this case, the Greco-Roman banquet) that aids in sorting through basic social schemes (in this case the various options for social behavior in the unstable colonized setting of Asia Minor).[9] And, Jonathan Z. Smith points out the ritual as a constructed environment that allows a group of people to think about irreconcilable differences.[10]

7.   Cf. Victor Turner's *The Forest of Symbols: Aspects of Ndembu Ritual* (Ithaca, NY: Cornell University Press); *Ritual Process: Structure and Anti-Structure* (Chicago: Aldine, 1969); and *Revelation and Divination in Ndembu Society* (Ithaca, NY: Cornell University Press, 1985). See also Jonathan Z. Smith's critique in 'The Domestication of Sacrifice', in Robert G. Hamerton-Kelly, ed., *Violent Origins: Walter Burkert, Rene Girard, and Jonathan Z. Smith on Ritual Killing and Cultural Formation* (Stanford: Stanford University Press, 1987); and the critique of Catherine Bell, *Ritual: Perspectives and Dimensions* (New York: Oxford University Press, 1997).

8.   Pierre Bourdieu, *Outline of a Theory of Practice,* p. 133.

9.   Catherine Bell in *Ritual: Perspectives and Dimensions*; and *Ritual Theory, Ritual Practice* (New York: Oxford University Press, 1992).

10.   Jonathan Z. Smith, *Imagining Religion: From Babylon to Jonestown* (Chicago: University of Chicago Press, 1982); and *To Take Place: Toward Theory in Ritual* (Chicago: University of Chicago Press, 1987).

10.3. *Social Negotiations of Meat Sacrificed*

From these perspectives of the Greco-Roman meal paradigm and ritual theory, one of the most interesting parts of the seven letters in Revelation becomes the range of positions represented on the issue of eating meat sacrificed to other gods. That is, it seems likely that the targeted early Christian meal communities in Asia Minor had different practices in this regard. Clearly, there was a difference between the author(s) of Revelation and the communities of Pergamum and Thyatira. And clearly within Pergamum and especially Thyatira, there were elements (I assume different meal groupings in these settings) who had different practices about meat sacrificed to other gods.

Rather than simply make the judgement of Revelation's author(s) the only perspective on eating meats sacrificed to other gods, a ritual theory perspective on these early Christian meals would note that the stability of the structure of the meal practice allowed the various communities to experiment around the issue of what meats to eat. For all these groups, eating together was an expression of community and solidarity. And, for all these communities, some tension between themselves and Roman rule needs to be assumed, if only to the degree that Roman rule was in some tension with much of the longer history and consciousness of life in Asia Minor.

But there was not necessarily an obvious way to handle these tensions around meat in the marketplace, emerging early Christian identity and Roman rule.[11] The question of what meat to eat was probably also heightened by the importance of the banquet itself for emerging identities and the fact that eating the meat or not was one of a few places where the communities could actually choose what relationship they had to imperial-related deities without being subject to immediate punishment or threat. So the relative safety of the meal and the lack of prescriptions about meat from the imperium itself opened up what Catherine Bell calls the dynamics of 'deployment' and 'negotiation' around a larger complex of issues about the alleged divine rule of Rome.[12] It seems quite possible that, in the spectrum of meal practice among the seven churches in Revelation, there may have been even more difference than just that between the Revelation

---

11.   On the relationship between sacrificed meat and Roman imperial domination, cf. Brigitte Kahl, *Galatians Re-Imagined: Reading with the Eyes of the Vanquished* (Minneapolis: Fortress Press, 2010); and Paul Plass, *The Game of Death in Ancient Rome: Sport and Political Suicide* (Madison: University of Wisconsin Press, 1995), pp. 39–47.

12.   Catherine Bell, *Ritual Theory, Ritual Practice*, p. 221.

author(s), Pergamum and Thyatira. And, indeed, the drama of the exile of the John of Patmos in Revelation itself serves as a dramatic reminder that there was not an obvious choice of how to relate to Roman rule without being punished.

That there was no obvious way of relating to the consumption of meat sacrificed to other gods is strongly corroborated intertextually within the New Testament. On this very issue, it seems even in 1 Corinthians that Paul takes more than one position. Although some have proposed ways of unifying Paul's perspective on eating meat sacrificed to other gods, at least on the surface, one can identify four different positions:

1. In 1 Corinthians 8, Paul seems to state clearly that it does not matter whether one eats meat sacrificed to other gods. 'But, of course, food cannot make us acceptable to God. We lose nothing by eating it. We gain nothing by eating it' (8.8). This seems quite similar to what Paul also says in 10.25: 'Eat anything that is sold in butchers' shops. There is no need to ask questions for conscience's sake.'
2. Later in chapter 8, however, this position seems to be amended to include another position: 'If food can be the cause of a brother's downfall, then I will never eat meat anymore' (8.13).
3. In chapter 10 he at first takes a hard categorical line against any eating of such sacrifices. 'When gentiles sacrifice, what is sacrificed by them is sacrificed to demons, who are not God. I do not want you to share with demons' (10.20).
4. Later in chapter 10, this categorical rejection of never eating meat sacrificed to other gods is clearly changed in specific instructions for certain cases. 'Eat whatever is put before you. You need not ask questions of conscience first. But if someone says to you, "this food has been offered in sacrifice;" do not eat it, out of consideration for the person that told you' (10.27, 28).

Given that there are some 40 years between Paul and Revelation, one might object that these two approaches to meat sacrificed to other gods cannot be compared. But this objection cannot stand, since it is exactly differences about whether to eat this meat among early Christian communities addressed by Revelation that the author(s) condemn. Indeed, that the questions remained for 40 years seems to indicate the intractable character of the issue for early Christians.

My purpose here is not to decide what was the correct early Christian position on eating meats sacrificed to other gods. Rather, it is to highlight that the meals themselves provided opportunities to try out different positions on very difficult issues for early Christian identity. The solidarity and structure of the meal itself provided safety for trying out a range of identities of early Christians relative to Roman domination.[13]

Nor do I mean to avoid important questions about whether and how early Christians resisted Roman power and social pressure. Indeed, I think that the frequent Roman opposition to any associations gathering for meals indicates that these meals themselves were experienced by the Romans, early Christian groups and other associations as a kind of resistance. That is, in the case of eating meat sacrificed to imperial gods at early Christian meals, the question was not whether their meals were resistant, but how they were resistant, how strongly they were resistant, and what were the consequences for the meal assemblies themselves, both in their own internal processes and in their fate as groups relative to outside power. The work of James C. Scott is helpful in this regard. Scott notes:

> Subordinate groups manage to assert their resistance, in disguised form, into the public transcript ... The realities of power for subordinate groups mean that much of their political action requires interpretation precisely because it is intended to be cryptic and opaque ... These ambiguous, polysemic elements of folk culture mark off a relatively autonomous realm of discursive freedom on the condition that they declare no *direct* opposition to the public transcript authorized by the dominant ... The subordinate group must carve out for itself social spaces insulated from control and surveillance from above. If we are to understand the process by which resistance is developed ... the analysis of the creation of these offstage spaces becomes a vital task ... As domains of power relations in their own right, they serve to discipline as well as to formulate patters of resistance.[14]

This is not meant to idealize or ideologize early Christian relationships to Roman domination. Even cursory examination of early Christian literature demonstrates sloppiness and inconsistency in finding a way to respond to Roman power and prerogatives. Early Christians compromised with Roman rule, explicitly and implicitly supported it, resisted it, and claimed freedom from it. My major focus here is to understand early Christian meals as a site of negotiation of social identity relative to Roman power.

In Scott's terms these meals were the ambiguous, polysemic social spaces insulated from control. The relative isolation and strong indigenously created structure of the meals then allowed for a creative and rigorous processing of the almost impossible social choices facing early Christians. More often than not, this processing of these difficult issues occurred in the coded and only semi-conscious modalities of ritual gesture. In the case of meats sacrificed to other, often imperial, gods, early Christian groups

---

13.   The relationship between emperors, gods and food is explored in Bruce Winter, *Seek the Welfare of the City: Christians as Benefactors and Citizen* (Grand Rapids: Eerdmans, 1994), p. 132.

14.   James C. Scott, *Domination and the Arts of Resistance* (New Haven: Yale University Press 1990), pp. 118, 119.

eating, not-eating, eating-without-knowing, or eating-while-proclaiming-Jesus-as-Lord, became a hidden transcript of negotiating their emerging early Christian identities in a range of specific circumstances. I would suggest that all options around eating/not-eating this meat were crucial and partial elements of the identities-in-the-making.

10.4. *Performance*

Crucial for me in this analysis is the term 'performance'.[15] I use the term in two ways, and in this case both apply. In identity studies like those of Judith Butler,[16] performance is a term used to help analyze the character of identity. Used in this way, performance is an anti-ontic and anti-essentialist dimension of identity. That is, 'performance' is used to show how identity is a series of performances, none of which are core or definitional to identity and all of which are germane. The second way I use performance is to connote actual dramatic expression within a group. Here performance is meant as something that is produced like theatre, dance or poetic reading.

For me, the eating, occasional eating, eating without knowing, or never eating meat sacrificed to other gods by early Christians is a performance in both senses. In terms of identity, all actions by early Christians with/without meat sacrificed to other gods perform an ongoing, inconsistent and complex identity of the particular groups. What they do in relationship to this meat becomes a way for them to actively work on who they are/what their identity is. By the same token, their eating or non-eating of this meat is indeed a dramatic performance. That is, the presentation and consumption of foodstuffs at these banquets always means more than just eating. The banquet event knows that what is eaten deserves dramatic display and enactment. Meat is always a central moment in the Greco-Roman meal, and carries multiple significations, in this case as signifier of relationships to other (often imperial) gods.

In this case, the performance dimension of the Revelation text need not necessarily be considered as some kind of recitation or dramatization of the text itself. Rather, the performance – in terms of both identity and drama – is in the action within the meal relative to meat sacrificed to other gods. As we noted earlier, the seven letters intertwine the issues of food and the experiences of persecution and suffering. Given the choices available to

---

15. Catherine Bell's essay, 'Performance and Other Analogies', in *The Performance Studies Reader*, ed. Henry Bial (New York: Routledge, 2004), discusses the close connection between ritual studies and performance studies in this regard.

16. Cf. Judith Butler, *Gender Trouble: Feminism and the Subversion of Identity* (New York: Routledge, 1990).

these communities around meat offered to other gods at the meal, it seems clear that these choices provide the possibility of subliminal performancial processing and positioning relative to the larger and less controllable realities of persecution itself.

10.5. *Complex Identity Construction*

I submit one other text from Revelation deeply connected to performance of drama and performance of identity. The text of Revelation 18.1-3 reads:

> After this, I saw another angel come down from heaven, with great authority given to him. The earth was shining with his glory. At the top of his voice he shouted, 'Babylon has fallen. Babylon the Great has fallen, and has become the haunt of devils and lodging for every foul spirit and dirty loathsome bird. All the nations have drunk of the wine of her prostitution. Every king on earth has prostituted himself with her, and every merchant grown rich through her debauchery.'

Then in three successive sections of chapter 18 another voice predicts the destruction of Babylon, and three different verses present a dirge that people will say/sing:

> 'Mourn, mourn for this great city. Babylon so powerful a city. In one short hour your doom will be upon you.' (18.10)
> 'Mourn, mourn for this great city; for all the linen and purple and scarlet that you wore, for all your finery of gold and jewels and pearls. Your huge riches are all destroyed in a single hour.' (18.16)
> 'Mourn, mourn for this great city whose lavish living has made a fortune for every owner of a sea-going ship, ruined in a single hour.' (18.19)

I would suggest that it is almost impossible to conceive of this text as anything other than a dramatic presentation. And, I assume that the primary location for such dramatic presentation for early Christian groups was consistently the *symposium* part of their meal together. Both the words of the angel and the dirge demand dramatic expression and display, whether the dining room is a rented space with straw for couches or in an aristocratic dining room with pictures of epic battles on the wall. This text was performed dramatically.

Of course, the overt coding of Babylon for Rome reminds one of James C. Scott, but the meaning of such a performed text is really not hidden from anyone. This is a clear declaration of freedom from and resistance to Roman domination and greed. Almost as obvious is the multi-dimensional effect of the text. Anger at Roman exploitation stands out. But at the same time humour is almost as strong. That the 'mourn, mourn, mourn' is followed in each case by a declaration that the destruction of Rome has already happened must have been performancially accompanied by smiles and laughter. Just the vision of Rome having been destroyed brings forth delightful irony. And, this ironic humour obtains another edge in the repetition of the 'mourn, mourn, mourn'. This destruction is obviously not an indication of sadness for those performing it in the early Christian meals of Asia Minor. Rather, the repeated call to mourning drips with sarcasm.

The obvious performancial character of this text and its not-so-subtle meaning for early Christians under Roman rule also has ready application as a performance of emerging early Christian identity. And here, both the merit of performed identity theory and James C. Scott's work emerges. That is, the performance of Revelation 18 does not function as a straightforward manifesto of freedom from Rome. The intractable character of early Christian life under Rome in this era makes such manifestos insane or immediate cause for execution or exile. The 'freedom' this text performs has mostly to do with the identity constructed in the performance of the text at the meal. But this performance and the ensuing identity emerging from it is complex, and in stark contrast to direct assertions of unmitigated freedom. That is, the performance of identity here is a subtle combination of the expression of anger within the safety of the meal setting, the healing and deflection of drawing humorous pictures of Rome's downfall, the development of irony as a way of safeguarding hope and realism, and group appropriation of sarcasm. The safely expressed anger, humour, irony and sarcasm construct a complex sense of freedom that keeps twisting and adjusting itself in the middle of very difficult situations. So the actual dramatic performance of Revelation 18 becomes complexly resistance to Roman influence.[17] It deflects conflict from real life into the imaginary. The performance renews the group and individual through laughter. It compensates for the relative powerlessness of the early Christians through sarcasm. Through the performance of the text, the social experimentation at the meal generates a complex, resistant and somewhat free identity, which needs further performance of the same and other texts in order to continue the complex construction of Christian identity under pressure.

17. Cf. the fascinating study of resistance in the Revelation to John and the barrio of East Los Angeles by David A. Sanchez, *From Patmos to the Barrio: Subverting Imperial Myths* (Minneapolis: Fortress Press, 2008).

BIBLIOGRAPHY

Achelis, H., *Das Christentum in den ersten drei Jahrhunderten* (Leipzig: Quell & Meyer, 1912).

Achtemeier, P., 'The Origin and Function of the Pre-Marcan Miracle Catenae', *JBL* 91 (1972): 198–221.

Al-Suadi, S., *Essen als Christusgläubige* (Tübingen: Francke Verlag, 2011).

Altmann, P., *Festive Meals in Ancient Israel: Deuteronomy's Identity Politics in Relation to Their Ancient Near Eastern Context* (BZAW, 424; Berlin: de Gruyter, 2011).

Andrews, A.C., 'Ernährung A', *RAC* 6 (1966): 222–3.

Bauer, J. B., '"Kein Leben ohne Wein" (Jesus Sirach 31,27). Das Urteil der Hl. Schrift', *BiLi* 23 (1955–6): 55–9.

Beentjes, P. C., *The Book of Ben Sira in Hebrew. A Text Edition of All Extant Hebrew Manuscripts and a Synopsis of All Parallel Hebrew Ben Sira Texts* (VT.S 68; Leiden: Brill, 1997).

Behnk, J., *Dionysos und seine Gefolgschaft. Weibliche Besessenheitskulte in der griechischen Antike* (Hamburg: Diplomiva-Verlag, 2009).

Bell, C., 'Performance and Other Analogies', in Henry Bial (ed.), *The Performance Studies Reader* (New York: Routledge, 2004).

—— *Ritual: Perspectives and Dimensions* (New York: Oxford University Press, 1997).

—— *Ritual Theory, Ritual Practice* (New York: Oxford University Press, 1992).

Benko, S., *Pagan Rome and the Early Christians* (Bloomington: Indiana University Press, 1984).

Ben-Porat, Z., 'The Poetics of Literary Allusion', *PTL* 1 (1976): 105–28 (107–08, n. 5).

Berger, K., *Formgeschichte des Neuen Testaments* (Heidelberg: Quelle und Meyer, 1984).

Berlin, A., *Esther, The JPS Bible Commentary* (Philadelphia: Jewish Publication Society, 2001).

Bettenworth, A., *Gastmahlszenen in der antiken Epik von Homer bis Claudian. Diachronische Untersuchungen zur Szenentypik* (Göttingen: Vandenhoeck & Ruprecht, 2004).

Bickermann, E., 'Ritualmord und Eselskult', *MGWJ.NF* 35 (1927): 171–87, 255–64.

Bieler, A. and L. Schottroff, *The Eucharist. Bodies, Bread and Resurrection* (Minneapolis: Fortress Press, 2007).

Billings, B. S., 'The Disputed Words in the Lukan Institution Narrative (Luke 22:19b–20). A Sociological Answer to a Textual Problem', *JBL* 125 (2006): 507–26.

Bingen, J., and R. S. Bagnall, *Hellenistic Egypt: Monarchy, Society, Economy, Culture* (Edinburgh: Edinburgh University Press, 2007).

Bock, D. L., *Acts* (Grand Rapids: Baker Academic, 2007).

Bolkestein, H., *Wohltätigkeit und Armenpflege im vorchristlichen Altertum* (Utrecht: Oosthoek, 1939).

Böll, H., *Billards at Half Past Nine* (London: Penguin Books, 1959).

Boobyer, G. H., 'The Eucharistic Interpretation of the Miracles of the Loaves in St. Mark's Gospel', *JTS* 3 (1952): 161–71.

Borgen, P., *Bread from Heaven: An Exegetical Study of the Concept of Manna in the Gospel of John and the Writings of Philo* (Leiden: Brill, 1965).

—— 'The Unity of Discourse in John 6', *ZNW* 50 (1959): 277–78.

Börner-Klein, D. and E. Hollender, *Rabbinische Kommentare zum Buch Ester: Die Midraschim zu Ester,* Vol. 2 (Leiden: Brill, 2000).

Börner-Klein, D. and B. Zuber (eds), *Jossipon. Jüdische Geschichte vom Anfang der Welt bis zum Ende des ersten Aufstands gegen Rom* (Wiesbaden: Marixverlag, 2010).

Bornkamm, G., 'Die eucharistische Rede im Johannes-Evangelium', *ZNW* 47 (1956): 161–69.

Bourdieu, P., *Outline of a Theory of Practice* (trans. R. Nice; Cambridge Studies in Social and Cultural Anthropology; Cambridge: Cambridge University Press, 1977, trans. of *Esquisse d'une théorie de la pratique, précédé de trois études d'ethnologie kabyle* (Travaux de droit d'économie, de sociologie et de sciences politiques 92; Geneva: Droz, 1972).

Bovon, F., *Das Evangelium nach Lukas I* (EKK 3, 1; Zurich et al.: Benziger Verlag, 1989).

Boyarin, D., *Border Lines. The Partition of Judaeo-Christianity* (Philadelphia: University of Pennsylvania Press, 2004).

Brady, T. A., and C. F. Mullett, *Sarapis and Isis: Collected Essays* (Chicago: Ares, 1978).

Briant, P., *From Cyrus to Alexander: A History of the Persian Empire* (Winona Lake, IN: Eisenbrauns, 2002).

Brown, R. E., 'The Eucharist and Baptism in John', in R. E. Brown (ed.), *New Testament Essays* (Garden City, NY: Image Books, 1965), pp. 77–95.

—— *The Gospel According to John* (Garden City, NY: Doubleday, 1966–70).

Brumberg-Kraus J., 'The Table and Early Judaism I', paper presented at SBL 2010, Atlanta, now available under Susan Marks, 'The Table and Early Judaism II'; Jordan Rosenblum, 'The Table and Early Judaism III'; followed by the extensive response by Judith Hauptman. http://www.philipharland.com/meals/GrecoRomanMealsSeminar.htm.

Brumberg-Kraus J., S. Marks and J. D. Rosenblum, 'Table as Generative Locus for Social Formation in Early Judaism', paper presented at SBL 2010, Atlanta, now available at: http://www.philipharland.com/meals/GrecoRomanMealsSeminar.htm.

Bultmann, R. K., *Das Evangelium des Johannes* (Göttingen: Vandenhoeck & Ruprecht, 1986).

Burge, G. M., *The Anointed Community: The Holy Spirit in the Johannine Tradition* (Grand Rapids: Eerdmans, 1987).

Burkert, W., *Ancient Mystery Cults* (Cambridge, MA: Harvard University Press, 1987).

—— *Homo necans: Interpretationen altgriechischer Opferriten und Mythen* (Berlin: Walter de Gruyter, 1997).

Burkett, D. R., *The Son of the Man in the Gospel of John* (Sheffield: JSOT Press, 1991).

Butler, J., *Gender Trouble: Feminism and the Subversion of Identity* (New York: Routledge, 1990).

Campbell, E. F., *Ruth* (AB, 7; Garden City, NY: Doubleday, 1978).

Campbell W. S., 'Covenantal Theology and Participation in Christ: Pauline Perspectives on Transformation', in R. Bieringer and D. Pollefet (eds), *Paul and Judaism: Crosscurrents in Pauline Exegesis and the Study of Jewish-Christian Relations* (London, New York: T&T Clark, 2011).

—— *Paul and the Creation of Christian Identity* (London, New York: T&T Clark, 2008).

Cheung, A.T., *Idol Food in Corinth: Jewish Background and Pauline Legacy* (Sheffield: Sheffield Academic Press, 1999).

Chilton, B., *A Feast of Meanings: Eucharistic Theologies from Jesus Through Johannine Circles* (Leiden: Brill, 1994).

Ciampa, R. E. and B. S. Rosner, *The First Letter to the Corinthians* (Grand Rapids, MI: Eerdmans, 2010).

—— 'The Structure and Argument of 1 Corinthians: A Biblical/Jewish Approach', *NTS* 52 (2006): 205–18.

Cohen, S. J. D., *The Beginnings of Jewishness. Boundaries, Varieties, Uncertainties* (Berkeley: University of California Press, 1999).

Collins, A. Y., *Mark. A Commentary* (Minneapolis: Fortress Press, 2007).

Corley, J., 'Searching for Structure and Redaction in Ben Sira. An investigation of Beginnings and Endings', in A. Passaro and G. Bellia (eds), *The Wisdom of Ben Sira. Studies on Tradition, Redaction, and Theology* (Deuterocanonical and Cognate Literature Studies, 1; Berlin: de Gruyter, 2008), pp. 21–47.

Culler, J., *The Pursuit of Signs: Semiotics, Literature, Deconstruction* (London: Routledge, 1981).

Danker, F. W., W. Bauer and W. F. Arndt, *A Greek-English Lexicon of the New Testament and Other Early Christian Literature* (Chicago: University of Chicago Press, 2000).

D'Arms, J. H., 'Between Public and Private: The Epulum Publicum and Caesar's Horti trans Tiberim', in Eugenio La Rocca (ed.), *Horti Romani* (Rome: L'Erma di Bretschneider, 1998), pp. 33–43.

—— 'P. Lucilius Gamala's feasts for the Ostians and their Roman Models', *Journal of Roman Archeology* 13 (2000): 192–200.

—— 'The Roman *Convivium* and the Idea of Equality', in *Sympotica. A Symposium on the Symposion* (Oxford: Clarendon Press, 1990).

Dölger, F. J., 'Sacramentum Infanticidii. Die Schlachtung eines Kindes und der Genuß seines Fleisches und Blutes als vermeintlicher Einweihungsakt im ältesten Christentum', *AuC* 4 (1934): 188–228.

Donahue, J. F., 'Euergetic Self-Representation and the Inscription at Satyricon 71.10', *Classical Philology* 94 (1999): 69–74.

—— *The Roman Community at Table during the Principate* (Ann Arbor: University of Michigan Press, 2004).

—— 'Toward a Typology of Roman Public Feasting', *American Journal of Philology* 124 (2003): 423–41.

Douglas, M., 'Deciphering the Meal', in C. Geertz (ed.), *Myth, Symbol and Culture* (New York: Norton, 1971), pp. 61–81.

Dow, S., 'The Egyptian Cults in Athens', *HTR* 30 (1937): 183–232.

Downing, F. G., 'Cynics and Christians, Oedipus and Thyestes', *JEH* 44 (1993): 1–10.

Droysen, J. G., *Geschichte des Hellenismus* (Gotha: Perthes, 1877).

Dunbabin, K. M. D., *The Roman Banquet. Images of Conviviality* (Cambridge: Cambridge University Press, 2003).

Dunn, J. D., 'John 6. A Eucharistic Discourse?', *NTS* 17 (1971): 328–38.

Ebel, E., '"... damit wir ungestört und heiter an den Festtagen speisen können". Die gemeinsamen Mähler in griechisch-römischen Vereinen', in J. Hartenstein, S. Petersen and A. Standhartinger (eds), *Eine gewöhnliche und harmlose Speise? Von den Entwicklungen frühchristlicher Abendmahlstraditionen* (Gütersloh: Gütersloher Verlagshaus, 2008) pp. 34–56.

—— *Die Attraktivität früher christlicher Gemeinden. Die Gemeinde von Korinth im Spiegel griechisch-römischer Vereine* (Tübingen: Mohr Siebeck, 2004).

Ebner, M., 'Mahl und Gruppenidentität. Philos Schrift *De Vita Contemplativa* als Paradigma', in M. Ebner (ed.), *Herrenmahl und Gruppenidentität* (QD 221; Freiburg et al.: Herder, 2007), pp. 65–90.

Eckey, W., *Die Apostelgeschichte. Der Weg des Evangeliums von Jerusalem nach Rom*, Part I (Neukirchen-Vluyn: Neukirchener Verlag, 2000).

Edwards, M. J., 'Some Early Christian Immoralities', *AnSoc* 23 (1992): 71–82.

Egelhaaf-Gaiser, U., *Kulträume im römischen Alltag: Das Isisbuch des Apuleius und der Ort von Religion im Kaiserzeitlichen Rom* (Stuttgart: F. Steiner, 2000).

Ehling, K., 'Die Speisung der Fünftausend und die Reisekasse der Jünger. Anmerkungen zu Mk 6.35-57', *Münsterische Beiträge zur antiken Handelsgeschichte* 23 (2005): 47–58.

Ehrensperger, K., '"Called to Be Saints" – the Identity Shaping Dimension of Paul's Priestly Discourse in Romans', in K. Ehrensperger and J. B. Tucker (eds), *Reading Paul in Context: Explorations in Identity Formation* (London, New York: T&T Clark, 2010), pp. 90–109.

—— 'Lost in Translation – Paul a Broker/ Go-Between in Inter-Cultural Communication?', paper presented at the SBL Annual Meeting 2010, Atlanta.

—— *Paul at the Crossroads of Cultures – Theologizing in the Space-Between* (London, New York: T&T Clark, forthcoming).

Ellington, D. W., 'Imitating Paul's Relationship to the Gospel: 1 Corinthians 8.1– 11.1', *JSNT* 33 (2011): 303–15.

Fischer, I., *Rut* (Freiburg i. B.: Herder, 2001).

Fleming, D. E., *Time at Emar: The Cultic Calendar and the Rituals from the Diviner's Archive* (Mesopotamian Civilizations, 11; Winona Lake, IN: Eisenbrauns, 2000).

Fotopoulos, J., *Food Offered to Idols in Roman Corinth: A Social-Rhetorical Reconsideration of 1 Corinthians 8:1–11:1* (Tübingen: Mohr Siebeck, 2003).

Fox, M. V., *Character and Ideology in the Book of Esther* (Grand Rapids, MI: Eerdmans, 2nd edn, 2001).

Frayne, D., *Sargonic and Gutian Periods (2334–2113 BC)* (The Royal Inscriptions of Mesopotamia, 2; Toronto: University of Toronto Press, 1993).

Fredriksen, P., 'Dining with the Divine', *Bible Review* (October 2002): 62.
—— 'Gods and the One God', *Bible Review* (February 2003: 12–14.
—— '"Judaizing the Nations": The Ritual Demands of Paul's Gospel', *NTS* 56 (2010): 232–52.
—— 'Paul, Purity and the Ekklesia of the Gentiles', in R. Pastor and M. Mor (eds), *The Beginnings of Christianity* (Jerusalem: Yad Izhak Ben-Tzvi, 2005), pp. 205–17.
—— '"What Parting of the Ways?" Jews, Gentiles, and the Ancient Mediterranean City', in Adam H. Becker and Annette Yoshiko Reeds (eds), *The Ways that Never Parted. Jews and Christians in Late Antiquity and the Early Middle Ages* (Tübingen: Mohr Siebeck, 2003), pp. 35–64.
Freudenberger, R., 'Der Vorwurf ritueller Verbrechen', *ThZ* 23 (1967): 97–107.
Garnsey, P., *Famine and Food Supply in the Graeco-Roman World. Responses to Risk and Crisis* (Cambridge, New York: Cambridge University Press, 1988).
—— *Food and Society in Classical Antiquity* (Cambridge: Cambridge University Press, 1999).
—— 'Responses to Food Crises in the Ancient Mediterranean World', in Lucile F. Newman et al. (eds), *Hunger in History. Food Shortage, Poverty, and Deprivation* (Cambridge, MA: Basil Blackwell, 1990), pp. 126–46.
Gaster, T. H., *Purim and Hanukkah in Custom and Tradition* (New York: Schuman, 1950).
Gooch, P.D., *Dangerous Food: 1 Corinthians 8–10 in its Context* (Waterloo, ON: Wilfrid Laurier Press, 1993).
Goppelt, L., 'τρώγω', in G. Kittel (ed.), *Theologisches Wörterbuch zum Neuen Testament* (Stuttgart: Kohlhammer, 1949–73), Vol. 8: 236–7.
Graf, F. 'Mysterien', in M. Landfester, H. Cancik and H. Schneider (eds), *Der neue Pauly. Enzyklopädie der Antike,* Vol. 8 (16 vols; Stuttgart: J.B. Metzler, 1996–2003), pp. 615–26.
Grant, R. M., 'Charges of "Immorality" against Various Groups in Antiquity', in R. van Broek, M. J. Vermaseren and G. Quispeln (eds), *Studies in Gnosticism and Hellenistic Religions. Presented to Gilles Quispel on the Occasion of his 65th Birthday* (Leiden: Brill, 1981), pp. 161–70.
Grayson, A. K., *Assyrian Rulers of the Early First Millennium BC I (1114–859 BC)* (The Royal Inscriptions of Mesopotamia, 2; Toronto: University of Toronto Press, 1991).
Green, B., *A Study in Field and Seed Symbolism in the Biblical Story of Ruth* (unpublished doctoral dissertation, Graduate Theological Union, 1980).
Gsell, S. and J. Carcopino, 'La base de M. Sulpicius Felix et le décret des décurions de Sala', in *Mélanges d'archéologie et d'histoire*, Vol. 48 (Paris: Ecole française de Rome, 1931).
Guillaume, P., *Waiting for Josiah: The Judges* (JSOTSup, 385; London: T&T Clark International, 2004).
Gunkel, H., *Das Märchen im Alten Testament* (Tübingen: Mohr, 1921).
Hacham, A., *Da'at Ha-Miqra Megillat Ester* (Jerusalem: Mossad Ha-Rav Kook, 1973).
Hands, A. R., *Charities and Social Aid in Greece and Rome* (London: Thames and Hudson, 1968).
Hanslik-Andrée, J., 'Panamaros', *RE* 26 (1949): 450–5.

Harland, P., *Associations, Synagogues, and Congregations: Claiming a Place in Ancient Mediterranean Society* (Minneapolis: Fortress Press, 2003).

Harrill, J. A., 'Cannibalistic Language in the Fourth Gospel and Greco-Roman Polemics of Factionalism (John 6:52-66)', *JBL* 127 (2008): 133–58.

Harrison, J. E., *Prolegomena to the Study of Greek Religion* (Princeton: Princeton University Press, 1991).

Hauck, F., 'καθαρός', *Theologisches Wörterbuch zum Neuen Testament*, Vol. 3 (Stuttgart: Kohlhammer Verlag, 1990), pp. 416–21, 427–34.

Hayes, C., *Gentile Impurities and Jewish Identities: Intermarriage and Conversion from the Bible to the Talmud* (New York: Oxford University Press, 2002).

Hays, R. B., *Echoes of Scripture in the Letters of Paul* (New Haven: Yale University Press, 1989).

Heil, J. P., *The Meal Scenes in Luke-Acts. An Audience-Oriented Approach* (Atlanta: Society of Biblical Literature, 1999).

Heising, A., *Die Botschaft der Brotvermehrung. Zur Geschichte und Bedeutung eines Christusbekenntnisses im Neuen Testament* (SBS 15; Stuttgart: Kohlhammer Verlag, 1996).

Held, H. J., 'Matthäus als Interpret der Wundergeschichte', in Günther Bornkamm et al. (eds), *Überlieferung und Auslegung im Matthäusevangelium* (WMANT 1; Neukirchen-Vluyn: Neukirchener Verlag, 6th edn, 1970).

Henrichs, A., 'Greek Maenadism from Olympias to Messalina', *Harvard Studies in Classical Philology* 82 (1978): 121–60.

——'Pagan Ritual and the Alleged Crimes of the Early Christians. A Reconsideration', in P. Granfield, J. A. Jungmann and J.Quasten (eds), *Kyriakon. Festschrift Johannes Quasten* (Münster: Aschendorff, 1970), pp. 18–35.

Higger, M., *Seven Minor Treatises* (New York: Bloch, 1930).

Hodges, J. H., *Food as Synecdoche in John's Gospel and Gnostic Texts* (PhD thesis, University of California, 1996).

Hodot, R., 'Décret de Kymè en L'honneur du Prytane Kléanax', *The Getty Museum Journal* 10 (1982): 165–80.

Horbury, W. and D. Noy, *Jewish Inscriptions of Graeco-Roman Egypt* (Cambridge: Cambridge University Press, 1992).

Hossfeld, F.-L. and E. Zenger, *Psalmen 101–150* (HTKAT; Freiburg i.Br.: Herder, 2008).

Hutter, M., 'Iranische Elemente im Buch Esther', in H. D. Galter (ed.), *Kulturkontakte und ihre Bedeutung in Geschichte und Gegenwart des Orients* (Graz: Verlag für die Technische Universität Graz, 1986), pp. 51–66.

James, E., 'A Portion of a Field: Agrarianism and the Book of Ruth' (paper presented in the Old Testament Seminar, Princeton Theological Seminary, 23 January 2010).

Jaroš, K., *Das Neue Testament und seine Autoren: Eine Einführung* (Köln: Böhlau, Uni-Taschenbücher, 2008).

Jeanmaire, H., *Dionysos: Histoire du culte de Bacchus* (Paris: Payot, 1951).

Jervell, J., *Die Apostelgeschichte* (Göttingen: Vandenhoeck & Ruprecht, 1998).

Johnston, S. I., 'The Myth of Dionysos', in F. Graf and S. I. Johnston (eds), *Ritual Texts for the Afterlife. Orpheus and the Bacchic Gold Tablets* (London: Routledge, 2007), pp. 66–93.

Jüngling, H.-W., 'Der Bauplan des Buches Jesus Sirach', in H.-W. Jüngling, J. Hainz and R. Sebott (eds), *Den Armen eine Frohe Botschaft* (Festschrift F. Kamphaus; Frankfurt a. M.: Knecht, 1997), pp. 89–105.

Kahl, B., *Galatians Re-Imagined: Reading with the Eyes of the Vanquished* (Minneapolis: Fortress Press, 2010).

Kaiser, O., 'Athen und Jerusalem. Die Begegnung des spätbiblischen Judentums mit dem griechischen Geist, ihre Voraussetzungen und ihre Folgen', in M. Witte and S. Alkier (eds), *Die Griechen und der Vordere Orient. Beiträge zum Kultur- und Religionskontakt zwischen Griechenland und dem Vorderen Orient im 1. Jahrtausend v. Chr.* (OBO 191; Fribourg: Universitätsverlag et al., 2003), pp. 87–120.

—— *Weisheit für das Leben. Das Buch Jesus Sirach übersetzt und eingeleitet* (Stuttgart: Radius, 2005).

Kane, J. P., 'The Mithraic Cult Meal in its Greek and Roman Environment', in J. R. Hinnells (ed.), *Mithrais Studies II* (Manchester: University of Manchester Press, 1974), pp. 313–51.

Keener, C. S., *The Gospel of John: A Commentary* (Peabody: Hendrickson, 2003).

Kern, O., 'Dionysos', in G. Wissowa (ed.), *Paulys Realencyclopädie der classischen Altertumswissenschaft,* Vol. 5.1 (83 vols; München: Alfred Druckenmüller, 1893–1980), pp. 1008–46.

Kertelge, K., *Die Wunder Jesu im Markusevangelium* (München: Kösel Verlag, 1970).

Kieweler, H.-V., 'Benehmen bei Tisch', in Renate Egger-Wenzel and Ingrid Krammer (eds), *Der Einzelne und seine Gemeinschaft bei Ben Sira* (BZAW 270; Berlin: de Gruyter, 1998), pp. 191–215.

—— *Ben Sira zwischen Judentum und Hellenismus. Eine Auseinandersetzung mit Theophil Middendorp* (BEAT 30; Frankfurt a. M.: Lang, 1992).

Kim, C.-H., 'The Papyrus Invitation', *Journal of Biblical Literature* 94 (1975): 391–402.

Kircher, K., *Die sakrale Bedeutung des Weines im Altertum* (Giessen: Töpelmann, 1910).

Klauck, H.-J., *Herrenmahl und hellenistischer Kult: Eine religionsgeschichtliche Untersuchung zum ersten Korintherbrief* (Münster: Aschendorff, 1982).

Klawans, J., *Impurity and Sin in Ancient Judaism* (Oxford: Oxford University Press, 2000).

Klein, H., *Das Lukasevangelium (*KEK 3.1; Göttingen: Vandenhoeck & Ruprecht, 2006).

Klinghardt, M., *Gemeinschaftsmahl und Mahlgemeinschaft: Soziologie und Liturgie frühchristlicher Mahlfeiern* (Basel: Francke Verlag, 1996).

Klinghardt, M. and T. Staubli, 'Essen, gemeinsames', in F. Crüsemann, K. Hungar, C. Janssen and L. Schottroff (eds), *Sozialgeschichtliches Wörterbuch zur Bibel* (Gütersloh: Gütersloher Verlagshaus, 2009), pp. 116–22.

Kobel, E., *Dining with John. Communal Meals and Identity Formation in the Fourth Gospel and its Historical and Cultural Context* (Biblical Interpretation Series; Leiden: Brill, 2011).

Koch, D.-A., 'The God-fearers between facts and fiction: Two theosebeis-inscriptions from Aphrodisias and their bearings for the New Testament', in *Studia Theologica – NJT*, Vol. 60 (2006): 62–90.

Koester, C. R., 'John Six and the Lord's Supper', *LQ* 4 (1990): 419–37.

Köhlmoos, M., *Rut* (ATD, 9,3; Göttingen: Vandenhoek & Ruprecht, 2010).

Kollmann, B., *Ursprung und Gestalten der frühchristlichen Mahlfeier* (Göttingen: Vandenhoeck & Ruprecht, 1990).

Korpel, M.C.A., *The Structure of the Book of Ruth* (Pericope, 2; Assen: Van Gorcum, 2001).

Körtner, U., 'Das Fischmotif im *Speisungswunder*', *ZNW* 75 (1984): 24–35.

Kostermann, E., *Das Markusevangelium* (HNT 3; Tübingen: Mohr, 3rd edn, 1936).

Kratz, R. G., 'Die Gnade des täglichen Brots: Späte Psalmen auf dem Weg zum Vaterunser', *ZTK* 89 (1992): 1–40.

—— 'Das Schema des Psalters: Die Botschaft vom Reich Gottes nach Psalm 145', in *Gott und Mensch im Dialog* (Festschrift Otto Kaiser; BZAW, 345/II; Berlin: Walter de Gruyter, 2004), pp. 623–38.

Labahn, M., *Offenbarung in Zeichen und Wort* (WUNT II/17; Tübingen: Mohr, 2000).

Lanzillotta, L. R., 'The Early Christians and Human Sacrifice', in J. N. Bremmer (ed.), *The Strange World of Human Sacrifice* (Leuven: Peeters Press, 2007), pp. 81–102.

Lau, P. H. W., *Identity and Ethics in the Book of Ruth: a Social Identity Approach* (BZAW, 416; Berlin: de Gruyter, 2011).

Le Cornu, H. and J. Shulam, *A Commentary on the Jewish Roots of Acts*, Vol. 1 (Jerusalem: Academon, 2003).

Lehmeier, K., 'Verächtliche Mähler. Epikureische Gemeinschaftsmähler und Formen des Abendmahles im Vergleich', in J. Hartenstein, S. Petersen and A. Standhartinger (eds), *Eine gewöhnliche und harmlose Speise? Von den Entwicklungen frühchristlicher Abendmahlstraditionen* (Gütersloh: Gütersloher Verlagshaus, 2008), pp. 57–73.

Leonhard, C., 'Blessings over Wine and Bread in Judaism and Christian Eucharistic Prayers: Two Independent Traditions', in Albert Gerhards et al. (eds), *Jewish and Christian Liturgy and Worship. New Insights into its History and Interaction* (Jewish and Christian Perspectives series 15; Leiden: Brill, 2007), pp. 309–26.

Levenson, J. D., *Esther. A Commentary* (Louisville, KY: Westminster/John Knox Press, 1996).

Levine, L. I., *Judaism and Hellenism in Antiquity: Conflict or Confluence* (Seattle: University of Washington Press, 1998).

Levinskaya, I., *The Book of Acts in its Diaspora Setting* (Grand Rapids, MI: Eerdmans, 1996).

Liddell, H. G. and R. Scott, *A Greek-English Lexicon* (Oxford: Clarendon Press, 1996).

Lieu, J., *Image and Reality. The Jews in the World of the Christians in the Second Century* (Edinburgh: T&T Clark, 1996).

Lim, K.Y. *The Sufferings of Christ Are Abundant in Us: A Narrative Dynamics Investigation of Paul's Sufferings in 2 Corinthians* (London, New York: T&T Clark 2009)

Linafelt, T., *Ruth* (Berit Olam; Collegeville, MI.: Liturgical Press, 1999).

Lohfink, N., *Lobgesänge der Armen: Studien zum Magnifikat, den Hodajot von Qumran und einigen späten Psalmen* (SBS, 143; Stuttgart: Katholisches Bibelwerk, 1990).

Longenecker, B. W., *Remember the Poor: Paul, Poverty and the Graeco-Roman World* (Grand Rapids: Eerdmans, 2010).

Luckenbill, D. D., *Ancient Records of Assyria and Babylonia* (Chicago: The University of Chicago Press, 1926).

Lührmann, D., *Das Markusevangelium* (HNT 3/1; Tübingen: Mohr, 1987).

MacDonald, N., *Not Bread Alone: The Uses of Food in the Old Testament* (Oxford: Oxford University Press, 2008).

Malina, B. J. and J. J. Pilch, *Social-Science Commentary on the Book of Acts* (Minneapolis: Fortress Press, 2008).

Marböck, J., *Jesus Sirach 1–23* (HThK.AT; Freiburg et al.: Herder, 2010).

—— 'Structure and Redaction History in the Book of Ben Sira. Review and Prospects', in J. Marböck (ed.), *Weisheit und Frömmigkeit. Studien zur alttestamentlichen Literatur der Spätzeit* (ÖBS 29; Frankfurt a. M.: Peter Lang, 2006), pp. 31–45.

Marks, S., 'The Table and Early Judaism II', paper presented at the SBL Annual Meeting 2010, Atlanta, now available at: http://www.philipharland.com/meals/GrecoRomanMealsSeminar.htm.

Masuda, S., 'The Good News of the Miracle of Bread. The Tradition and its Markan Redaction', *NTS* 28 (1982): 191–219.

McGowan, A., 'Eating People. Accusations of Cannibalism against Christians in the Second Century', *JECS* 2 (1994): 413–24.

Meggitt, J., *Paul, Poverty and Survival* (Edinburgh: T&T Clark International, 1998).

Menken, M. J., 'John 6:51c-58: Eucharist or Christology', in R. Culpepper (ed.), *Critical Readings of John 6* (Leiden: Brill, 1987), pp. 183–204.

Merkelbauch, R., 'Ehrenbeschluss der Kymäer für den Prytanis Kleanax', *Epigraphia Anatolica* 1 (1983): 33–7.

De Moor, J. C., 'Seventy!', in Manfried Dietrich and Ingo Kottsieper (eds), *'Und Mose schrieb dieses Lied auf': Studien zum Alten Testament und zum alten Orient* (AOAT, 250; Münster: Ugarit-Verlag, 1998), pp. 199–203.

Mowinckel, S., *The Psalms in Israel's Worship* (2 vols; Oxford: Blackwell, 1962).

Mussner, F., *Apostelgeschichte* (Würzburg: Echter Verlag, 1984).

Nagel, P., 'LXX Esther. "More" God "Less" Theology', *Journal for Semitics* 17 (2008): 129–55.

Nanos, Mark D., 'Why the "Weak" in 1 Corinthians 8–10 Were Not Christ-Believers', in C. J. Belezos, S. Despotis and C. Karakolis (eds), *Saint Paul and Corinth: 1950 Years Since the Writing of the Epistles to the Corinthians: International Scholarly Conference Proceedings (Corinth, 23–25 September 2007)*, Vol. 2 (Athens, Greece: Psichogios Publications S.A., 2009), pp. 385–404.

Nielsen, K., *Ruth* (trans. E. Broadbridge; OTL; Louisville, KY: Westminster John Knox, 1997).

Nilsson, M. P., 'En Marge De La Grande Inscription Bacchique Du Metropolitan Museum', *Studi e materiali di storia delle religioni* 10 (1934): 1–18.

Noy, D., 'The Sixth Hour is the Mealtime for Scholars: Jewish Meals in the Roman World', in I. Nielsen and H. S. Nielsen (eds), *Meals in a Social Context: Aspects of the Communal Meal in the Hellenistic and Roman World* (Aarhus Studies in Mediterranean Antiquity, 1; Aarhus: Aarhus University Press, 1998), pp. 134–44.

Pagán, V. E., *Conspiracy Narratives in Roman History* (Austin, TX: University of Texas Press, 2004).

Parkin, A., '"You do him no service": An Exploration of Pagan Almsgiving', in M.Atkins and R. Osborne (eds), *Poverty in the Roman World* (Cambridge: University of Cambridge Press, 1996), pp. 60–82.

Paulsen, T., *Geschichte der griechischen Literatur* (Stuttgart: Philipp Reclam, 2004).

Perels, O., *Die Wunderüberlieferung in ihrem Verhältnis zur Wortüberlieferung* (Stuttgart: Kohlhammer Verlag, 1934).

Perry, J. M., 'The Evolution of the Johannine Eucharist', *NTS* 39 (1993): 22–23.

Pervo, R. I., 'Panta Kiona: The Feeding Stories in the Light of Economic Data and Social Practice', in Lukas Bormann et al. (eds), *Religious Propaganda and Missionary Competition in the New Testament World* (Leiden: Brill, 1994), pp. 163–94.

Pesch, R., *Die Apostelgeschichte. Evangelisch-katholischer Kommentar zum Neuen Testament* (Neukirchen-Vluyn: Neukirchener Verlag, 1986).

—— *Das Markusevangelium* (HThKNT 2, 1; Freiburg: Herder, 1976).

Peters, N., *Das Buch Jesus Sirach oder Ecclesiasticus* (EHAT, 25; Münster: Aschendorfsche Verlagsbuchhandlung, 1913).

Petersen, S., 'Jesus zum "Kauen"?: Das Johannesevangelium, das Abendmahl und die Mysterienkulte', in J. Hartenstein (ed.) *Eine gewöhnliche und harmlose Speise?': Von den Entwicklungen frühchristlicher Abendmahlstraditionen* (Gütersloh: Gütersloher Verlagshaus, 2008), pp. 105–30.

Phua, L. S. R., *Idolatry and Authority: A Study of 1 Corinthians 8.1–11.1 in Light of the Jewish Diaspora* (London, New York: T&T Clark, 2005).

Pitard, W. T. and M. S. Smith, *The Ugaritic Baal Cycle: Introduction with Text, Translation and Commentary of KTU/CAT 1.3–1.4* (VTSup, 114; Leiden: Brill, 2009).

Plass, P., *The Game of Death in Ancient Rome: Sport and Political Suicide* (Madison: University of Wisconsin Press, 1995).

Porter, S. 'The Use of the Old Testament in the New Testament', in C. Evans and J. Sanders (eds), *Early Christian Interpretation of the Scriptures of Israel. Investigations and Proposals* (Sheffield: Sheffield Academic Press, 1997).

Poser, R., '"Das Gericht geht durch den Magen" Die verschlungene Schriftrolle (Ez 2:8b-3:3) und andere Essensszenarien im Ezechielbuch', in Michaela Geiger et al. (eds), *Essen und Trinken in der Bibel. Ein literarisches Festmahl für Rainer Kessler zum 65. Geburtstag* (Gütersloh: Gütersloher Verlagshaus, 2009), pp. 116–30.

Prell, M., *Armut im antiken Rom* (Beiträge zur Wirtschafts- und Sozialgeschichte 77; Stuttgart: Steiner, 1997).

Purcell, N., 'Eating Fish. The Paradoxes of Seafood', in John Wilkins et al. (eds), *Food in Antiquity* (Exeter: University of Exeter Press, 1995), pp. 132–49

—— 'Rome and Its Development under Augustus and His Successors', in Alan K. Bowman et al. (eds), *The Cambridge Ancient History X: The Augustan Empire, 43 B.C.–A.D. 69* (Cambridge: Cambridge University Press, 2nd edn, 1996), pp. 800–11.

Rajak, T., 'Intertextuality and the Subject of Reading/Writing', in J. Clayton and E. Rothstein (eds), *Influence and Intertextuality in Literary History* (Madison: University of Wisconsin Press, 1991), pp. 61–74.

—— *The Jewish Dialogue with Greece and Rome: Studies in Cultural and Social Interaction* (Leiden: Brill, 2002).

—— *Jews and Christians as Groups in a Pagan World* (Boston, Leiden: Brill, 2002).

Rapp, U. and M. E. Aigner, 'Texte, um das Leben zu verstehen. Exegese und Bibliolog "im Inter" am Beispiel von Ester 1', in J. Kügler, E. Souga Onomo and S. Feder (eds), *Bibel und Praxis. Beiträge des internationalen Bibel-Symposiums 2009 in Bamberg*, bayreuther forum TRANSIT, Vol. 11 (Münster: Lit Verlag, 2011), pp.145–72.

Rosenblum, J. 'The Table and Early Judaism III', paper presented at the SBL Annual Meeting 2010, Atlanta, now available at: http://www.philipharland.com/meals/GrecoRomanMealsSeminar.htm.

Roussel, P., *Les Cultes Égyptiens à Délos du IIIe au Ier Siècle Av. J.-C* (Nancy: Berger-Levrault, 1916).

Rubenstein, J., 'Purim, Liminality and Communitas', *AJS Review* 17/2 (1992): 247–77, 249.

Russell, J. R., 'Zoroastrian Elements in the Book of Esther', in Shaul Shaked (ed.), *Irano-Judaica II* (Jerusalem: Ben-Zvi Institute for the Study of Jewish Communities in the East, 1990), pp. 33–40.

Ryssel, Victor, '"Die Sprüche Jesus", des Sohnes Sirachs', in E. Kautsch (ed.), *Die Apokryphen und Pseudepigraphen des Alten Testaments. I: Die Apokryphen des Alten Testaments* (Tübingen: Mohr Siebeck, 1900), pp. 230–475.

Şahin, C., *Die Inschriften von Stratonikeia I Panamara* (Inschriften Griechischer Städte aus Kleinasien 21; Bonn: Habelt, 1981).

Sakenfeld, K. D., *Ruth* (Interpretation; Louisville, KY: Westminster John Knox, 1999).

Sanchez, D. A., *From Patmos to the Barrio: Subverting Imperial Myths* (Minneapolis: Fortress Press, 2008).

Sauer, G., *Jesus Sirach (Ben Sira)* (JSHRZ III, 5; Gütersloh: Gütersloher Verlagshaus, 1981).

—— *Jesus Sirach / Ben Sira* (ATD.A 1; Göttingen: Vandenhoeck & Ruprecht 2000).

Schenke, L., *Die wunderbare Brotvermehrung. Die neutestamentlichen Erzählungen und ihre Bedeutung* (Würzburg: Echter Verlag, 1983).

Schille, O., *Die urchristliche Wundertradition. Ein Beitrag zur Frage nach dem irdischen Jesus* (Stuttgart: Calwer Verlag, 1967).

Schmitt Pantel, P., *La cité au banquet. Histoire des repas publics dans les cités grecques* (Rome: de Boccard, 1992).

—— 'Public Feast in the Hellenistic Greek City: Forms and Meanings', in *Conventional Values of the Hellenistic Greeks* (Aarhus: Aarhus University Press, 1997), pp. 29–47.

Schottroff, L., '"Gesetzfreies Heidenchristentum" – und die Frauen?', in Luise Schottroff and Marie-Theres Wacker (eds), *Von der Wurzel getragen. Christlich-feministische Exegese in Auseinandersetzung mit Antijudaismus* (Leiden: Brill, 1996), pp. 227–45.

Scott, J. C., *Domination and the Arts of Resistance* (New Haven: Yale University Press, 1992).

Seaford, R., *Dionysos* (London: Routledge, 2006).

Siquans, A., 'Foreignness and Poverty in the Book of Ruth: a Legal Way for a Poor Foreign Woman to be Integrated into Israel', *JBL* 128 (2009): 443–52.

Skehan, P. and A. A. Di Lella, *The Wisdom of Ben Sira* (AncB.A 39; Garden City, NY: Doubleday, 1987).

Smend, R., *Die Weisheit des Jesus Sirach* (Berlin: G. Reimer, 1906).

Smit, P.-B., *Fellowship and Food in the Kingdom. Eschatological Meals and Scenes of Utopian Abundance in the New Testament* (WUNT II/234; Tübingen: Mohr, 2008).

Smith, D. E., 'The Egyptian Cults at Corinth', *HTR* 70 (1977): 201–31.
—— *From Symposium to Eucharist: The Banquet in the Early Christian World* (Minneapolis: Fortress Press, 2003).
Smith, D. E., and H. Taussig, *Many Tables: The Eucharist in the New Testament and Liturgy Today* (London, Philadelphia: SCM Press, Trinity Press International, 1990).
Smith, J. Z., 'The Domestication of Sacrifice', in Robert G. Hamerton-Kelly (ed.), *Violent Origins: Walter Burkert, Rene Girard, and Jonathan Z. Smith on Ritual Killing and Cultural Formation* (Stanford, CA: Stanford University Press, 1987).
—— *Imagining Religion: From Babylon to Jonestown* (Chicago: University of Chicago Press, 1982).
—— *To Take Place: Toward Theory in Ritual* (Chicago: University of Chicago Press, 1987).
Smith, M., *God in Translation* (Tübingen: Mohr Siebeck, 2008).
Sokolowski, F., *Lois sacrées de l'Asie Mineure* (Paris: Boccard, 1955).
Speyer, W., 'Zu den Vorwürfen der Heiden gegen die Christen', *JAC* 6 (1963): 129–35.
Stambaugh, J. E., *Sarapis under the Early Ptolemies* (Leiden: Brill, 1972).
Standhartinger, A., 'Frauen in Mahlgemeinschaften. Diskurs und Wirklichkeit einer antiken, frühjüdischen und frühchristlichen Praxis', *lectio difficilior* 2 (2005).
—— '"Mit einer verheirateten Frau schmause nicht beim Wein" (*Sir* 9.9). Egalitäre Tischgemeinschaften im Kontext antiker, jüdischer und frühchristlicher Symposiumskultur', in M. Geiger, C. M. Maier und U. Schmidt (eds), *Essen und Trinken in der Bibel. Ein literarisches Festmahl für Rainer Kessler zum 65. Geburtstag* (Gütersloh: Gütersloher Verlagshaus, 2009), pp. 286–300, 298.
Staufer, E., 'Zum apokalyptischen Festmahl in Mk 6,34ff', *ZNW* 45 (1955): 264–6.
Stavrianopoulou, E., 'Die Bewirtung des Volkes: Öffentliche Speisungen in der römischen Kaiserzeit', in Olivier Hekster et al. (eds), *Ritual Dynamics and Religious Change in the Roman Empire* (Impact of Empire 9; Leiden: Brill, 2009), pp. 159–83.
Stephens, S. A. and J. J. Winkler, *Ancient Greek Novels: The Fragments* (Princeton: Princeton University Press, 1995).
Stone, T., 'Six Measures of Barley: Seed Images and Inner-Textual Interpretation in Ruth', paper presented at the SBL Annual Meeting 2010, Atlanta.
Strotmann, A., 'Die göttliche Weisheit als Nahrungsspenderin, Gastgeberin und sich selbst anbietende Speise', in J. Hartenstein (ed.), *'Eine gewöhnliche und harmlose Speise'? Von den Entwicklungen frühchristlicher Abendmahlstraditionen* (Gütersloh: Gütersloher Verlagshaus, 2008).
Sutter Rehmann, Luzia, 'Abgelehnte Tischgemeinschaft in Tobit, Daniel, Ester, Judit. Ein Plädoyer für Differenzierung', *lectio difficilior* (2008).
Taussig, H., 'Greco-Roman Meals and Performance of Identity: A Ritual Analysis', paper presented at the SBL Annual Meeting 2007, San Diego, now available at: http://www.philipharland.com/meals/GrecoRomanMealsSeminar.htm.
—— *In the Beginning was the Meal: Social Experimentation & Early Christian Identity* (Minneapolis: Fortress Press, 2009).
Terlibakou, Z., 'The Presence of Women in the Feeding Stories in the Synoptic Gospels', in Sabine Bieberstein et al. (eds), *Building Bridges in a Multifaceted Europe. Religious Origins, Traditions, Contexts, and Identities*, Journal of European

Society of Women in Theological Research 14, 2007 (Leuven: Peeters, 2007), pp. 175–84.

Theißen, G., *Urchristliche Wundergeschichten. Ein Beitrag zur formgeschichtlichen Erforschung der synoptischen Evangelien* (Gütersloh: Gütersloher Verlagshaus, 1987).

Thiselton, A. C., *The First Epistle to the Corinthians: A Commentary on the Greek Text* (Grand Rapids: Eerdmans, 2000).

Thyen, H., *Das Johannesevangelium* (Tübingen: Mohr Siebeck, 2005).

Tomson, P. J., 'The Wars Against Rome, the Rise of Rabbinic Judaism and of Apostolic Gentile Christianity, and the Judaeo-Christians: Elements for a Synthesis', in P. J. Thomson and D. Lambers-Petry (eds), *The Image of the Judaeo-Christians in Ancient Jewish and Christian Literature* (Tübingen: Mohr Siebeck, 2003), pp. 1–31.

Tomson, P., *Paul and the Jewish Law: Halakha in the Letters of the Apostle to the Gentiles* (Minneapolis: Fortress Press, 1990).

Totti, M., *Ausgewählte Texte der Isis- und Sarapis-Religion* (Hildesheim, Zürich, New York: Georg Olms, 1985).

Trible, P., *God and the Rhetoric of Sexuality* (OBT, 2; Philadelphia: Fortress, 1978).

De Troyer, K., *The End of the Alpha Text of Esther. Translation and Narrative Technique in MT 8.1-17, LXX 8.1-117 and AT 7.14-41*, Brian Doyle, transl. (Atlanta: Society of Biblical Literature, 2000).

—— *Die Septuaginta und die Endgestalt des Alten Testaments* (Göttingen: Vandenhoeck & Ruprecht, 2005).

Tucker, J. B., *'You Belong to Christ': Paul and the Formation of Social Identity in 1 Corinthians 1-4* (Eugene, OR: Wipf & Stock, 2010)

Turner, V. W., *The Forest of Symbols: Aspects of Ndembu Ritual* (Ithaca, NY: Cornell University Press, 1967).

—— *Revelation and Divination in Ndembu Society* (Ithaca, NY: Cornell University Press, 1985).

—— *Ritual Process: Structure and Anti-Structure* (Chicago: Aldine, 1969).

Vandoni, M., *Feste Pubbliche e Private nei Documenti Greci* (Milano, Varese, Cisalpino, 1st edn, 1964).

van Iersel, B., 'Die wunderbare Speisung und das Abendmahl in der synoptischen Tradition (Mk vi 35-44par., viii 1-10par)', *NT* 7 (1964): 167–94.

Vattioni, F., *Ecclesiastico. Testo ebraico con apparato critico e versioni greaca, latina e siriaca* (Publicazioni del Seminario di Semitistica 1; Napoli: Istituto orientale di Napoli, 1968).

Versnel, H. S., *Ter unus: Isis, Dionysos, Hermes* (Leiden: Brill, 1990), pp. 134–46.

Veyne, P., *Brot und Spiele. Gesellschaftliche Macht und politische Herrschaft in der Antike* (München: dtv, 1994).

Vidman, L., *Isis und Sarapis bei den Griechen und Römern: Epigraphische Studien zur Verbreitung und zu den Trägern des Ägyptischen Kultes* (Berlin: De Gruyter, 1970).

Vössing, K., *Mensa Regia. Das Bankett beim hellenistischen König und beim römischen Kaiser* (Beiträge zur Altertumskunde 193; München, Leipzig: Saur, 2004).

Wacker, M.-T., 'Das Ester-Buch in der Septuaginta', in K. Butting, G. Minaard and M.-T. Wacker (eds), *Ester* (Wittingen: Erev-Rav, 2005), pp. 73–7.

Walfish, B. D., 'Kosher Adultery? The Mordecai-Esther-Ahasuerus Triangle in Talmudic, Medieval and Sixteenth Century Exegesis', in S. White Crawford and L. J. Greenspoon (eds), *The Book of Esther in Modern Research* (London: T&T Clark International, 2003), pp. 111–36.

Waltzing, J. P., 'Le crime rituel reproché aux Chrétiens du IIe siècle', *Bulletins de la classe des lettres de l'Académie Royale Belge* (1925): 205–39.

West, M. L., *The Orphic Poems* (Oxford: Clarendon Press, 1983).

Westermann, C., *Genesis 1–11: A Commentary* (Minneapolis: Augsburg Press, 1984).

Wick, P., 'Jesus gegen Dionysos? Ein Beitrag zur Kontextualisierung des Johannesevangeliums', *Bib.* 85 (2004): 179–98.

Wiesel, E. at the Petra Conference, June 2008: http://www.eliewieselfoundation.org/petraconferences.aspx.

Williams, G., *The Spirit World in the Letters of Paul the Apostle: A Critical Examination of the Role of Spiritual Beings in the Authentic Pauline Letters* (Göttingen: Vandenhoeck & Ruprecht, 2009).

Williamson, H. G. M., *Ezra, Nehemiah* (WBC, 16; Waco, TX: Word Books, 1985).

Wilson, H. G., *The Editing of the Hebrew Psalter* (SBLDS, 76; Chico, CA: Scholars Press, 1985).

Winter, B., *Seek the Welfare of the City: Christians as Benefactors and Citizens* (Grand Rapids, MI: Eerdmans, 1994).

Witherington, B., *The Acts of the Apostles. A Socio-Rhetorical Commentary* (Grand Rapids, MI: Eerdmans, 1998).

Youtie, H. C., 'The Kline of Sarapis', *HThR* 41 (1948): 9–29.

Zapff, B., *Jesus Sirach* (NEB 39; Würzburg: Echter Verlag, 2010).

Zenger, E., *Einleitung in das Alte Testament* (Stuttgart: Kohlhammer Verlag, 7th edn, 2008).

Zuiderhoek, A., *The Politics of Munificence in the Roman Empire* (Cambridge: Cambridge University Press, 2009).

INDEX OF ANCIENT AUTHORS

Index of Modern Authors